The Best American
S

The Best American Spiritual Writing™ 2008

EDITED BY *Philip Zaleski*

INTRODUCTION BY *Jimmy Carter*

HOUGHTON MIFFLIN COMPANY
BOSTON · NEW YORK   2008

www.houghtonmifflinbooks.com

ISSN 1555-7820
ISBN 978-0-618-83374-0
ISBN 978-0-618-83375-7 (pbk.)

Printed in the United States of America

MP 10 9 8 7 6 5 4 3 2 1

Contents

Foreword

WELCOME TO THE tenth volume of *The Best American Spiritual Writing.* Ten years: to borrow from Pascal, nearly nothing in relation to infinity, nearly everything in relation to nothing. An eyeblink in geologic time; a good chunk of a human life; time enough for this editor to collect nearly three thousand pages of the best spiritual and religious prose and poetry around.

What will future historians of America and its spiritual life make of the past decade? We witnessed the nightmare of 9/11, which, as nightmares can do, led some to despair and others to faith. We mourned the deaths of two great figures — neither of them American, but both close to our country's heart — John Paul II and Mother Teresa, champions of the poor and oppressed. We endured a spate of atheist tracts, hastily composed and poorly argued, revealing in most cases the authors' misplaced anger and sorrow and to be received, in that light, with forbearance and compassion. We suffered through more than our share of spiritual fads — kabbalah in Hollywood, yoga in the suburbs — embarrassing dilutions of complex, valuable religious traditions. All these matters were written in darkness, but light entered as well. The Dalai Lama, benevolence incarnate in his orange robes, inspired many to a deeper inner life. Bono's social activism and confessional lyrics brought sophistication to rock-and-roll evangelism. The influence of the Inklings — C. S. Lewis, J.R.R. Tolkien, and their Christian circle — continued to mount, their writings exemplifying the marriage, in modern idiom, of art and spirituality. Above all, America remained deeply, enthusiastically, joyously religious, its vitality placing it closer to the vibrant spirituality of the Southern Hemisphere than to the lukewarm practice of much of Europe. Here lies hope — and perhaps the key to the future.

Through these years of dark and light, the aim of the Best American Spiritual Writing series has remained constant: to publish writing that both illuminates and delights. This combination is rarer than one might suspect, as rare as gold (or, as I believe on bad days, as golden eggs), and searching for it can occasion anxious days and sleepless nights. I've finished each annual collection with a sigh of relief — and more often than not, I'm happy to say, with real optimism for the well-being of the genre. So, many thanks to the writers that have enlivened this series over the past decade and to the journals, magazines, and newspapers from which their work has been culled.

I'd like to affirm, in this tenth-anniversary edition, one or two ideas that have informed the Best American Spiritual Writing series from the start. Above all, this: that by spiritual writing, I mean writing that sheds light upon the life of the soul, that reveals the manifold ways in which human beings respond to truth, beauty, and goodness, and the depth and mystery and suffering and glory of our relationship to God. As this (rather long) definition suggests, spiritual writing is about more than psyche or emotions or the body. It incorporates and transcends these realms; it is, in its own lowly way, analogous — although not by any means identical — to sacrament; a medium for contemplating, via the things of the flesh, the things of the spirit.

With this in mind, I thought it might be interesting to consider a question often posed these days, one that speaks volumes about the temperament of our times and that, I suspect, will be eyed with amusement by those future historians mentioned above. The question usually goes: is it possible to be spiritual without being religious? Adapting this to the purposes of this series, I'd like to ask: is it possible to be a spiritual writer without being a religious writer? The answer is: yes, but it's not easy. The reason is that spiritual openness — a willingness to stand in front of the great questions of the universe, especially the ur-question, Why is there something rather than nothing? — leads, as if in conformity to cosmic law, to awe, and awe to devotion, and devotion to worship. Coleridge put it nicely: "In wonder all philosophy began, in wonder it ends . . . but the first wonder is the offspring of ignorance; the last is the parent of adoration." We see the same pattern in every culture, every era: the soul, facing mystery, opens to the transcendent, turning for expression to prayer, ritual, and sacrifice. This is why almost all great spiritual writers, from Augustine to Rumi to Basho, work within traditional religious structures, using the rich and supple vocabulary and grammar of these structures to record the twists and turns of the inner life.

Reversing terms, we can also ask whether it's possible to be a religious writer without being a spiritual writer. The answer remains the same: yes, but it's not easy. Everyone recognizes the figure of the religious hypocrite, mouthing prayers or offering devotions with no attention to inner meaning. But how many such people are there, really? The truth is that religious activity has an ineluctable effect upon the soul; unless actively resisted — and sometimes even then — it tends to reshape those who engage in it. The theme receives definitive treatment in the delightful 1951 Edgar G. Ulmer B-movie classic *St. Benny the Dip*, about a gang of swindlers who pose as priests and discover that praying and feeding the poor melt even the coldest hearts. Go into a church, synagogue, mosque, or ashram and take a random sample: you'll find that the average schlep in the pews, ignorant of theology and innocent of mysticism, praying with half his mind on his girlfriend or his golf game, has nonetheless amassed, week by week and year by year, a bank of wisdom that's born of common sense, goodwill, and regular practice. He may pray inadequately, but who is adequate to eternal truths? What is true of Everyman is true also of writers, who, at least insofar as they care for their art, attend to every idea, image, and word that they produce — and who reap, often in ways beyond conscious perception, the rewards of this sometimes bitter discipline.

The spiritual writer, then, acts in service to something higher, purer, truer than himself. In a sense, of course, everyone does; Eliade correctly observed that "even beneath its radically desacralized forms, Western culture camouflages magico-religious meanings that our contemporaries, with the exception of a few poets and artists, do not suspect." Don Juan chasing skirts, eccentric collectors chasing Lepidoptera, nuclear physicists chasing the quark: all are chasing God. This is true also of those of us who chase reality through the artistic manipulation of words. Every mystery novel points toward the mystery of existence; every erotic tale, the divine lover; every poem, the language of paradise. In spiritual writing, however, the implicit becomes explicit, eschatology lifts its veil, and — following Coleridge — ignorance gives birth, after a mighty labor, to adoration. Spiritual writing, whether storytelling, confession, exposition, memoir, manifesto, argument, scholarship, poetry, or any of its other myriad modes, becomes the literary equivalent of *puja,* of self-effacing devotion and service. This shared sense of service binds together the writings in this and every volume of the series. How could it be otherwise? In a thousand years, all the words we write will be dust; only the good they may have done will continue to bear fruit.

As always, submissions are welcome for future volumes of this series. Only essays and poems previously published in an American periodical are eligible. Please send manuscripts (with a self-addressed, stamped envelope) to Philip Zaleski, 138 Elm Street, Smith College, Northampton MA 01063. The best way for a magazine or journal to ensure that its contents will be read and considered for future volumes is to add the Best American Spiritual Writing series, at the above address, to its subscription list.

I would like to thank all who contributed to this year's volume, including President Jimmy Carter; all the good people at Houghton Mifflin; Kim Witherspoon and David Forrer of Inkwell Management; and, as always, Carol, John, and Andy, who light my way.

PHILIP ZALESKI

Introduction

WHEN ASKED TO name my favorite poet, I usually answer, "Dylan Thomas." The reasons are many — his love of nature, his sense of awe at the mystery of existence, and, as much as anything, the sheer beauty of his verse. Thomas was in love with words, fascinated by their music as well as their meaning. Perhaps I like him so much because for much of my life I too have experienced the importance of words. As a young child, I listened to the advice of my father and mother. I also learned to pray and to read and memorize passages from the Bible, marveling at the wisdom contained in Holy Scripture. In high school, I absorbed the good words of my beloved teacher Miss Julia Coleman, including one saying that stuck with me so thoroughly that I quoted it during my presidential inauguration address: "We must adjust to changing times but hold still to unchanging principles." This saying, which has been one of the guiding lights of my life, exemplifies the great power and beauty of words when thoughtfully chosen and effectively expressed.

Every public official knows the value of words. I've tried to bear this in mind through the many responsibilities I've had as a naval officer, businessman, governor of Georgia, president of the United States, and worker for peace and human rights. In every speech I've given, from my first political campaign through my Nobel Peace Prize lecture, word selection and conveyance has been critical. In my private life too, as a son, brother, husband, and father, I've tried to remember the power of language, knowing how easily a word can hurt or heal. As the proverb says, "The words of a man's mouth are deep waters, the fountain of wisdom is a gushing stream" (Proverbs 18:4).

Above all, words count in the life of faith. As a Christian, I believe that Jesus Christ is the Word made flesh, the incarnation of God, the eternal logos. The Gospel of John (1:3) declares that "all things were made through him" — including the words that each of us uses every day, no matter what language he or she may speak. If we employ words in a benevolent way, whether through prayer, giving thanks, confessing our sins, or forgiving others, we are helping to do the work of Christ.

The most potent expression of Christ the Word is found in the Bible. For many years now, I've enjoyed teaching Sunday-school classes, fascinated by the colorful, helpful, often surprising stories and lessons contained in the Old and New Testaments. It's stimulating and rewarding to discuss this material with other people, who often have very different perspectives on the origin, purpose, and meaning of scripture. I've found, too, that reading theologians can shed light on what the Bible is trying to say, and I've benefited greatly from studying the words of Dietrich Bonhoeffer, Karl Barth, Martin Buber, Reinhold Niebuhr, Paul Tillich, and others. Scripture, as I've come to see and as most of these thinkers affirm, can be our most precious guide to daily living. When I was president, I began each day by reciting a verse from Psalm 19, "Let the words of my mouth and the meditation of my heart be acceptable in thy sight, O Lord, my strength and my redeemer." After all, as president, I knew that I was speaking for the American people and making some of the most important, life-changing decisions in the world; praying that my words and thoughts would be acceptable to God gave me strength and courage. To this day Rosalynn and I read aloud a portion of the Bible every night, drawing confidence and strength from its wisdom.

It is fascinating to see what Jesus himself said about words, going so far as to state that "by your words you will be justified, and by your words you will be condemned" (Matthew 12:37). Jesus didn't write books or letters, as far as we know, but he loved to tell stories in the form of parables, which provide wonderful advice in dealing with the many problems we all face in life. His words have lasted two thousand years, and today they probably are read, repeated, meditated upon, and prayed over by more people than at any time in history. Jesus knew and respected the power of language, using it to bless, rebuke, give thanks, praise, and worship, in keeping with his teaching that "blessed are they that hear the word of God, and keep it" (Luke 11:28).

I have also been aware of the spiritual power of words through my work as a poet. I began to write poetry as a young man, during long stretches of solitude on submarines. I would write love poems to Rosalynn and poems about life on the submarine. Much later, I decided to approach poetry in a more systematic way, learning the craft from two very talented poets, Miller Williams and James Whitehead. In 1995 I published a collection of poems, *Always a Reckoning*. The book doesn't include any explicitly religious verse, but I believe that every poem I write reflects to some degree my religious faith. The discipline of poetry has allowed me to explore my soul and to express my feelings freely, without the constraints that I faced as a public official. Poetry is, in a way, a kind of spiritual practice.

You hold in your hands the tenth-anniversary edition of *The Best American Spiritual Writing,* a series that approaches the writing of both poetry and prose as a spiritual discipline, a way to explore the mysteries of the soul and the soul's relationship to God. Congratulations to the writers in this year's volume for their outstanding literary work, which makes a real contribution to the spiritual life of our nation, and to Philip Zaleski for the work he has done during the last ten years in bringing this important and beautiful literature before the eyes of the public.

JIMMY CARTER

The Best American
Spiritual Writing 2008

STEPHEN M. BARR

Faith and Quantum Theory

FROM *First Things*

QUANTUM THEORY IS UNSETTLING. Nobel laureate Richard Feynman admitted that it "appears peculiar and mysterious to everyone — both to the novice and to the experienced physicist." Niels Bohr, one of its founders, told a young colleague, "If it does not boggle your mind, you understand nothing." Physicists have been quarreling over its interpretation since the legendary arguments between Bohr and Einstein in the 1920s. So have philosophers, who agree that it has profound implications but cannot agree on what they are. Even the man on the street has heard strange rumors about the Heisenberg Uncertainty Principle, of reality changing when we try to observe it, and of paradoxes where cats are neither alive nor dead till someone looks at them.

Quantum strangeness, as it is sometimes called, has been a boon to New Age quackery. Books such as *The Tao of Physics* (1975) and *The Dancing Wu Li Masters* (1979) popularized the idea that quantum theory has something to do with Eastern mysticism. These books seem almost sober today when we hear of "quantum telepathy," "quantum ESP," and, more recently, "quantum healing," a fad spawned by Deepak Chopra's 1989 book of that name. There is a flood of such quantum flapdoodle (as the physicist Murray Gell-Mann called it). What, if anything, does it all mean? Amid all the flapdoodle, what are the serious philosophical ideas? And what of the many authors who claim that quantum theory has implications favorable to religious belief? Are they on to something, or have they been taken in by fuzzy thinking and New Age nonsense?

It all began with a puzzle called wave-particle duality. This puzzle first appeared in the study of light. Light was understood by the end of the nineteenth century to consist of waves in the electromagnetic field that fills all of space. The idea of fields goes back to Michael Faraday, who thought of magnetic and electrical forces as being caused by invisible "lines of force" stretching between objects. He envisioned space as being permeated by such force fields. In 1864, James Clerk Maxwell wrote down the complete set of equations that govern electromagnetic fields and showed that waves propagate in them, just as sound waves propagate in air.

This understanding of light is correct, but it turned out there was more to the story. Strange things began to turn up. In 1900, Max Planck found that a certain theoretical conundrum could be resolved only by assuming that the energy in light waves comes in discrete, indivisible chunks, which he called quanta. In other words, light acts in some ways like it is made up of little particles. Planck's idea seemed absurd, for a wave is something spread out and continuous, while a particle is something pointlike and discrete. How can something be both one and the other?

And yet, in 1905, Einstein found that Planck's idea was needed to explain another puzzling behavior of light, called the photoelectric effect. These developments led Louis de Broglie to make an inspired guess: if waves (such as light) can act like particles, then perhaps particles (such as electrons) can act like waves. And, indeed, this proved to be the case. It took a generation of brilliant physicists (including Bohr, Heisenberg, Schrödinger, Born, Dirac, and Pauli) to develop a mathematically consistent and coherent theory that described and made some sense out of wave-particle duality. Their quantum theory has been spectacularly successful. It has been applied to a vast range of phenomena, and hundreds of thousands of its predictions about all sorts of physical systems have been confirmed with astonishing accuracy.

Great theoretical advances in physics typically result in profound unifications of our understanding of nature. Newton's theories gave a unified account of celestial and terrestrial phenomena; Maxwell's equations unified electricity, magnetism, and optics; and the theory of relativity unified space and time. Among the many beautiful things quantum theory has given us is a unification of particles and forces. Faraday saw that forces arise from fields, and Maxwell saw that fields give rise to waves. Thus, when quantum theory showed that waves are particles (and particles waves), a deep unity of nature came into view: the forces by which matter interacts and the particles of which it is composed are both manifestations of a single kind of thing — "quantum fields."

The puzzle of how the same thing can be both a wave and a particle remains, however. Feynman called it "the only real mystery" in science. And he noted that, while we "can tell how it works," we "cannot make the mystery go away by 'explaining' how it works." Quantum theory has a precise mathematical formalism, one on which everyone agrees and that tells how to calculate right answers to the questions physicists ask. But what really is going on remains obscure — which is why quantum theory has engendered unending debates over the nature of physical reality for the past eighty years.

The problem is this: at first glance, wave-particle duality is not only mysterious but inconsistent in a blatant way. The inconsistency can be understood with a thought experiment. Imagine a burst of light from which a light wave ripples out through an ever-widening sphere in space. As the wave travels, it gets more attenuated, since the energy in it is getting spread over a wider and wider area. (That is why the farther you are from a light bulb, the fainter it appears.) Now, suppose a light-collecting device is set up, a box with a shutter — essentially, a camera. The farther away it is placed from the light burst, the less light it will collect. Suppose the light-collecting box is set up at a distance where it will collect exactly a thousandth of the light emitted in the burst. The inconsistency arises if the original burst contained, say, fifty particles of light. For then it appears that the light-collector must have collected 0.05 particles (a thousandth of fifty), which is impossible, since particles of light are indivisible. A wave, being continuous, can be infinitely attenuated or subdivided, whereas a particle cannot.

Quantum theory resolves this by saying that the light-collector, rather than collecting 0.05 particles, has a 0.05 *probability* of collecting *one* particle. More precisely, the *average* number of particles it will collect, if the same experiment is repeated many times, is 0.05. Wave-particle duality, which gave rise to quantum theory in the first place, forces us to accept that quantum physics is inherently probabilistic. Roughly speaking, in pre-quantum, classical physics, one calculated what actually happened, while in quantum physics, one calculates the relative probabilities of various things happening.

This hardly resolves the mystery. The probabilistic nature of quantum theory leads to many strange conclusions. A famous example comes from varying the experiment a little. Suppose an opaque wall with two windows is placed between the light-collector and the initial burst of light. Some of the light wave will crash into the wall, and some will pass through the windows, blending together and impinging on the light-collector. If the light-collector collects a particle of light, one might imagine that the particle had to have come through either one window or the other. The rules of the quantum probability calculus, however, compel the weird conclusion that in some unimaginable way the single particle came through both windows at once. Waves, being spread out, can go through two windows at once, and so the wave-particle duality ends up implying that individual particles can also.

Things get even stranger, and it is clear why some people pine for the good old days when waves were waves and particles were particles. One of those people was Albert Einstein. He detested the idea that a fundamental theory should yield only probabilities. "God does not play dice!" he insisted. In Einstein's view, the need for probabilities simply showed that the theory was incomplete. History supported his claim, for in classical physics the use of probabilities always stemmed from incomplete information. For example, if one says that there is a 60 percent chance of a baseball hitting a glass window, it is only because one doesn't know the ball's direction and speed well enough. If one knew them better (and also knew the wind velocity and all other relevant variables), one could definitely say whether the ball would hit the window. For Einstein, the probabilities in quantum theory meant only that there were as-yet-unknown variables: hidden variables, as they are called. If these were known, then in principle everything could be predicted exactly, as in classical physics.

Many years have gone by, and there is still no hint from any experiment of hidden variables that would eliminate the need for probabilities. In fact, the famed Heisenberg Uncertainty Principle says that probabilities are ineradicable from physics. The thought experiment of the light burst and light-collector showed why: if one and the same entity is to behave as both a wave and a particle, then an understanding in terms of probabilities is absolutely required. (For, again, 0.05 of a particle makes no sense, whereas a

0.05 *chance* of a particle does.) The Uncertainty Principle, the bedrock of quantum theory, implies that even if one has all the information there is to be had about a physical system, its future behavior cannot be predicted exactly, only probabilistically.

This last statement, if true, is of tremendous philosophical and theological importance. It would spell the doom of determinism, which for so long had appeared to spell the doom of free will. Classical physics was strictly deterministic, so that (as Laplace famously said) if the state of the physical world were completely specified at one instant, its whole future development would be exactly and uniquely determined. Whether a man lifts his arm or nods his head *now* would (in a world governed by classical physical laws) be an inevitable consequence of the state of the world a billion years ago.

But the death of determinism is not the only deep conclusion that follows from the probabilistic nature of quantum theory. An even deeper conclusion that some have drawn is that materialism, as applied to the human mind, is wrong. Eugene Wigner, a Nobel laureate, argued in a famous essay that philosophical materialism is not "logically consistent with present quantum mechanics." And Sir Rudolf Peierls, another leading physicist, maintained that "the premise that you can describe in terms of physics the whole function of a human being . . . including its knowledge, and its consciousness, is untenable."

These are startling claims. Why should a mere theory of matter imply anything about the mind? The train of logic that leads to this conclusion is rather straightforward, if a bit subtle, and can be grasped without knowing any abstruse mathematics or physics.

It starts with the fact that for *any* physical system, however simple or complex, there is a master equation — called the Schrödinger equation — that describes its behavior. And the crucial point on which everything hinges is that the Schrödinger equation yields only probabilities. (Only in special cases are these exactly 0, or 100 percent.) But this immediately leads to a difficulty: there cannot always remain *just* probabilities; eventually there must be definite outcomes, for probabilities must be the probabilities *of* definite outcomes. To say, for example, there is a 60 percent chance that Jane will pass the French exam is meaningless unless at some point there is going to be a French exam on which Jane will receive a definite grade. Any mere probability must eventually stop being a mere probability and become a certainty or it has no meaning even as a probability. In quantum theory, the point at which this happens, the moment of truth, so to speak, is traditionally called the collapse of the wave function.

The big question is when this occurs. Consider the thought experiment again, where there was a 5 percent chance of the box collecting one particle and a 95 percent chance of it collecting none. When does the definite outcome occur in this case? One can imagine putting a mechanism in the box that registers when a particle of light has been collected by making, say, a red indicator light to go on. The answer would then seem plain: the definite outcome happens when the red light goes on (or fails to do so). But this does *not* really produce a definite outcome, for a simple reason: any mechanism one puts into the light-collecting box is just itself a physical system and is therefore described by a Schrödinger equation. And that equation *yields only probabilities*. In particular, it would say there is a 5 percent chance that the box collected a particle and that the red indicator light is on, and a 95 percent chance that it did not collect a particle and that the indicator light is off. No definite outcome has occurred. Both possibilities remain in play.

This is a deep dilemma. A probability must eventually get resolved into a definite outcome if it is to have any meaning at all, and yet the equations of quantum theory when applied to any physical system yield only probabilities and not definite outcomes.

Of course, it seems that when a *person* looks at the red light and comes to the knowledge that it is on or off, the probabilities do give way to a definite outcome, for the person knows the truth of the matter and can affirm it with certainty. And this leads to the remarkable conclusion of this long train of logic: as long as only physical structures and mechanisms are involved, however complex, their behavior is described by equations that yield only probabilities — and once a mind is involved that can make a rational judgment of fact, and thus come to knowledge, there is certainty. Therefore, such a mind cannot be just a physical structure or mechanism completely describable by the equations of physics.

Has there been a sleight-of-hand? How did mind suddenly get into the picture? It goes back to probabilities. A probability is a measure of someone's state of knowledge or lack of it. Since quantum theory is probabilistic, it makes essential reference to someone's state of knowledge. That someone is traditionally called the observer. As Peierls explained, "The quantum mechanical description is in terms of knowledge, and knowledge requires *somebody* who knows."

I have been explaining some of the implications (as Wigner, Peierls, and others saw them) of what is usually called the traditional, Copenhagen, or standard interpretation of quantum theory. The term "Copenhagen interpretation" is unfortunate, since it carries with it the baggage of Niels Bohr's philosophical views, which were at best vague and at worst incoherent. One can accept the essential outlines of the traditional interpretation (first clearly delineated by the great mathematician John von Neumann) without endorsing every opinion of Bohr.

There are many people who do not take seriously the traditional interpretation of quantum theory — precisely because it gives too great an importance to the mind of the human observer. Many arguments have been advanced to show its absurdity, the most famous being the Schrödinger Cat Paradox. In this paradox one imagines that the mechanism in the light-collecting box kills a cat rather than merely making a red light go on. If, as the traditional view has it, there is not a definite outcome until the human observer knows the result, then it would seem that the cat remains in some kind of limbo, not alive or dead, but 95 percent alive and 5 percent dead, until the observer opens the box and looks at the cat — which is absurd. It would mean that our minds create reality or that reality is perhaps only in our minds. Many philosophers attack the traditional interpretation of quantum theory as denying objective reality. Others attack it because they don't like the idea that minds have something special about them not describable by physics.

The traditional interpretation certainly leads to thorny philosophical questions, but many of the common arguments against it are based on a caricature. Most of its seeming absurdities evaporate if it is recognized that what is calculated in quantum theory's wave function is not to be identified simply with what is happening, has happened, or will happen but rather with *what someone is in a position to assert* about what is happening, has happened, or will happen. Again, it is about someone's (the observer's) *knowledge*. Before the observer opens the box and looks at the cat, he is not in a position to assert definitely whether the cat is alive or dead; afterward, he is — but the traditional interpretation does *not* imply that the cat is in some weird limbo until the observer looks. On the contrary, when the observer checks the cat's condition, his observation can include all the tests of forensic pathology that would allow him to pin down the time of the cat's death and say, for instance, that it occurred thirty minutes before he opened the box. This is entirely consistent with the traditional interpretation of quantum theory. Another observer who checked the cat at a different time would have a different "moment of truth" (so the wave function that expresses *his* state of knowledge would collapse when *he* looked), but he would deduce the same time of death for the cat. There is nothing subjective here about the cat's death or when it occurred.

The traditional interpretation implies that just knowing A, B, and C, and applying the laws of quantum theory, does not always answer (except probabilistically) whether D is true. Finding out definitely about D may require another observation. The supposedly absurd role of the observer is really just a concomitant of the failure of determinism.

The trend of opinion among physicists and philosophers who think about such things is away from the old Copenhagen interpretation, which held the field for four decades. There are, however, only a few coherent alternatives. An increasingly popular one is the many-worlds interpretation, based on Hugh Everett's 1957 paper, which takes the equations of physics as the whole story. If the Schrödinger equation never gives definite and unique outcomes, but leaves all the possibilities in play, then we ought to accept this, rather than invoking mysterious observers with their minds' moments of truth.

So, for example, if the equations assign the number 0.05 to the situation where a particle has been collected and the red light is on, and the number 0.95 to the situation where no particle has been collected and the red light is off, then we ought to say that *both situations are parts of reality* (though one part is in some sense larger than the other by the ratio 0.95 to 0.05). And if an observer looks at the red light, then, since he is just part of the physical system and subject to the same equations, there will be a part of reality (0.05 of it) in which he sees the red light on and another part of reality (0.95 of it) in which he sees the red light off. So physical reality splits up into many versions or branches, and each human observer splits up with it. In some branches a man will see that the light is on, in some he will see that the light is off, in others he will be dead, in yet others he will never have been born. According to the many-worlds interpretation, there are an infinite number of branches of reality in which objects (whether particles, cats, or people) have endlessly ramifying alternative histories, all equally real.

Not surprisingly, the many-worlds interpretation is just as controversial as the old Copenhagen interpretation. In the view of some thinkers, the Copenhagen and many-worlds interpretation both make the same fundamental mistake. The whole idea of wave-particle duality was a wrong turn, they say. Probabilities are needed in quantum theory because in no other way can one make sense of *the same entity* being both a wave and a particle. But there is an alternative, going back to de Broglie, which says they are *not* the same entity. Waves are waves and particles are particles. The wave guides, or "pilots," the particles and tells them where to go. The particles surf the wave, so to speak. Consequently, there is no contradiction in saying both that a tiny fraction of the wave enters the light-collector and that a whole number of particles enters — or in saying that the wave went through two windows at once and each particle went through just one.

De Broglie's pilot-wave idea was developed much further by David Bohm in the 1950s, but it has only recently attracted a significant following. "Bohmian theory" is not just a different interpretation of quantum theory; it is a different theory. Nevertheless, Bohm and his followers have been able to show that many of the successful predictions of quantum theory can be reproduced in theirs. (It is questionable whether all of them can be.) Bohm's theory can be seen as a realization of Einstein's idea of hidden variables, and its advocates see it as a vindication of Einstein's well-known rejection of standard quantum theory. As Einstein would have wanted, Bohmian theory is completely deterministic. Indeed, it is an extremely clever way of turning quantum theory back into a classical and essentially Newtonian theory.

The advocates of this idea believe that it solves all of the quantum riddles and is the only way to preserve philosophical sanity. However, most physicists, though impressed by its cleverness, regard it as highly artificial. In my view, the most serious objection to it is that it undoes one of the great theoretical triumphs in the history of physics: the unification of particles and forces. It gets rid of the mysteriousness of quantum theory by sacrificing much of its beauty.

What, then, are the philosophical and theological implications of quantum theory? The answer depends on which school of thought — Copenhagen, many-worlds, or Bohmian — one accepts. Each has its strong points, but each also has features that many experts find implausible or even repugnant.

One can find religious scientists in every camp. Peter E. Hodgson, a well-known nuclear physicist who is Catholic, insists that Bohmian theory is the only metaphysically sound alternative. He is unfazed that it brings back Newtonian determinism and mechanism. Don Page, a well-known theoretical cosmologist who is an evangelical Christian, prefers the many-worlds interpretation. He isn't bothered by the consequence that each of us has an infinite number of alter egos.

My own opinion is that the traditional Copenhagen interpretation of quantum theory still makes the most sense. In two respects it seems quite congenial to the worldview of the biblical religions: it abolishes physical determinism, and it gives a special ontological status to the mind of the human observer. By the same token, it seems quite uncongenial to Eastern mysticism. As the physicist Heinz Pagels noted in his book *The Cosmic Code:* "Buddhism, with its emphasis on the view that the mind-world distinction is an illusion, is really closer to classical, Newtonian physics and not to quantum theory [as traditionally interpreted], for which the observer-observed distinction is crucial."

If anything is clear, it is that quantum theory is as mysterious as ever. Whether the future will bring more compelling interpretations of, or even modifications to, the mathematics of the theory itself, we cannot know. Still, as Eugene Wigner rightly observed, "It will remain remarkable, in whatever way our future concepts develop, that the very study of the external world led to the conclusion that the content of the consciousness is an ultimate reality." This conclusion is not popular among those who would reduce the human mind to a mere epiphenomenon of matter. And yet matter itself seems to be telling us that its connection to mind is more subtle than is dreamt of in their philosophy.

WENDELL BERRY

Sabbaths 2005

FROM *Shenandoah*

I.

I know that I have life
only insofar as I have love.

I have no love
except it come from Thee.

Help me, please, to carry
this candle against the wind.

II.

They gather like an ancestry
in the centuries behind us:
the killed by violence, the dead
in war, the "acceptable losses" —
killed by custom in self-defense,
by way of correction, as revenge,
for love of God, for the glory
of the world, for peace; killed
for pride, lust, envy, anger,
covetousness, gluttony, sloth,
and fun. The strewn carcasses
cease to feed even the flies,
the stench passes from them,

the earth folds in the bones
like salt in a batter.

And we have learned
nothing. "Love your enemies,
bless them that curse you,
do good to them that hate you" —
it goes on regardless, reasonably:
the always uncompleted
symmetry of just reprisal,
the angry word, the boast
of superior righteousness,
hate in Christ's name,
scorn for the dead, lies
for the honor of the nation,
centuries bloodied and dismembered
for ideas, for ideals,
for the love of God!

III.

"Are you back to normal?" asks
my old friend, ill himself, after I,
who have been ill, am well. "Yes,
the gradient of normality now
being downward." For when I walk
now from rock to rock in the tumble
of Camp Branch, under the trees,
the singing stream, the stream
of light that all my life
has drawn me as it has drawn
the ever-renewing waters, I clamber
where I used to leap, where once I could
have been a ghost for all the care
I paid to flesh and bone until
some hunger turned me home.

IV.

We were standing by the road,
seven of us and a small boy.

We had just rescued a yellow swallowtail
disabled on the pavement when a car
approached too fast. I turned to make sure
of the boy, and my old border collie
Nell, too slow coming across,
was hit, broken all to pieces, and died
at once, while the car sped on.
And I cried, not thinking what
I meant, "God damn!" And I did wish
all automobiles in Hell,
where perhaps they already are.

V.

Nell's small grave, opening
at the garden's edge to receive her
out of this world's sight forever,
reopens many graves. Digging,
the old man grieves for his old dog
with all the grief he knows,
which seems again to be approaching
enough, though he knows there is more.

VI.

How simple to be dead! — the only
simplification there is, in fact, Thoreau
to the contrary notwithstanding.
Nell lay in her grave utterly still
under the falling earth, the world
all astir above, a million leaves
alive in the wind, and what do we know?

VII.

I know I am getting old and I say so,
but I don't think of myself as an old man.
I think of myself as a young man
with unforeseen debilities. Time is neither
young nor old, but simply new, always

counting, the only apocalypse. And the clouds
 — no mere measure or geometry, no cubism,
can account for clouds or, satisfactorily, for bodies.
There is no science for this, or art either.
Even the old body is new — who has known it
before? — and no sooner new than gone, to be
replaced by a body yet older and again new.
The clouds are rarely absent from our sky
over this humid valley, and there is a sycamore
that I watch as, growing on the river bank,
it forecloses the horizon, like the years
of an old man. And you, who are as old
almost as I am, I love as I loved you
young, except that, old, I am astonished
at such a possibility, and am duly grateful.

VIII.

I tremble with gratitude
for my children and their children
who take pleasure in one another.

At our dinners together, the dead
enter and pass among us
in living love and in memory.

And so the young are taught.

IX.

Here in the woods near
the road where the public lives
the birds are at their daily work,
singing, feeding, feeding
the young, as if the road
does not exist.
Here
by the loud road, populous
and vacant, there is quiet

where birds are singing.
The birds
are waiting to sing in the trees
that will grow in the quiet
that will come when the last
of the dire machines has passed,
burning the world, and the burning
has ceased.
And so am I.

x.

Mowing the hillside pasture — where
the flowers of Queen Anne's lace

float above the grass, the milkweeds
flare and bee balm, cut, spices

the air, the butterflies light and fly
from bloom to bloom, the hot

sun dazes the sky, the wood thrushes
sound their flutes from the deep shade

of the woods nearby — these iron teeth
chattering along the slope astound

the vole in her low run and bring down
the field sparrow's nest cunningly hung

between two stems, the young long flown.
The mower moves between the beauty

of the half-wild growth and the beauty
of growth reduced, smooth as a lawn,

revealing again the slope shaped of old
by the wearing of water and, later, the wear

of human will, hoof and share and wheel
hastening the rain's work, so that the shape

revealed is the shape of wounds healed,
covered with grass and clover and the blessèd

flowers. The mower's work too is beautiful,
granting rest and health to his mind.

He drives the long traverses of the healed
and healing slant. He sweats and gives thanks.

XI.

My young grandson rides with me
as I mow the day's first swath
of the hillside pasture,
and then he rambles the woods beyond
the field's edge, emerging
from the trees to wave, and I wave back,

remembering that I too once
played at a field's edge and waved
to an old workman who went mowing by,
waving back to me as he passed.

XII.

If we have become a people incapable
of thought, then the brute-thought
of mere power and mere greed
will think for us.

If we have become incapable
of denying ourselves anything,
then all that we have
will be taken from us.

If we have no compassion,
we will suffer alone, we will suffer
alone the destruction of ourselves.

These are merely the laws of this world
as known to Shakespeare:

When we cease from human thought,
a low and effective cunning
stirs in the most inhuman minds.

XIII.

Eternity is not infinity.
It is not a long time.
It does not begin at the end of time.
It does not run parallel to time.
In its entirety it always was.
In its entirety it will always be.
It is entirely present always.

XIV.

God, how I hate the names
of the body's chemicals and anatomy,
the frore and glum department
of its parts, each alone in the scattering
of the experts of Babel.

The body
is a single creature, whole,
its life is one, never less than one, or more,
so is its world, and so
are two bodies in their love for one another
one. In ignorance of this
we are talking ourselves to death.

XV.

The painter Harlan Hubbard said
That he was painting Heaven when
The places he painted merely were
The Campbell or the Trimble County
Banks of the Ohio, or farms
And hills where he had worked or roamed:
A house's gable and roofline
Rising from a fold in the hills,
Trees bearing snow, two shanty boats
At dawn, immortal light upon

The flowing river in its bends.
And these were Heavenly because
He never saw them clear enough
To satisfy his love, his need
To see them all again, again.

XVI.

I am hardly an ornithologist,
nevertheless I live among the birds
and on the best days my mind
is with them, partaking of their nature
which is earthly and airy.

I live with the heavenly swallows
who fly for joy (to live, yes, but also for joy)
as they pass again and again over
the river, feeding, drinking, bathing
joyfully as they fly.

Sometimes my thoughts are up there
with the yellow-throated warbler, high
among the white branches and gray-green
foliage of the sycamores, singing
as he feeds among the lights and shadows.

A ringing in my ears from hearing
too many of the wrong things
surrounds my head some days
like a helmet, and yet I hear the birds
singing: the song sparrow by the water,
the mockingbird, the ecstasy of whose song
flings him into the air.

Song comes from a source unseen
as if from a stirring leaf, but I know
the note before I see the bird.
It is a Carolina wren whose goodcheer
never falters all year long.

Into the heat, into the smells
of horse sweat, man sweat, wilting

foliage, stirred earth,
the song of the wood thrush flows
cool from the deep shade.

I hear the sounds of wings.
What man can abide the rule
of "the market" when he hears,
in his waking, in his sleep,
the sound of wings?

In the night I hear the owls
trilling near and far;
it is my dream that calls,
my dream that answers.

Sometimes as I sit quiet
on my porch above the river
a warbler will present himself,
parula or yellow-throated or prothonotary,
perfect beauty in finest detail,
seemingly as unaware
of me as I am aware of him.

Or, one never knows quite when,
the waxwings suddenly appear,
numerous and quiet, not there
it seems until one looks,
as though called forth, like angels,
by one's willingness for them to be.

Or it has come to be September
and the blackbirds are flocking.
They pass through the riverbank trees
in one direction erratically
like leaves in the wind.

Or it is June. The martins are nesting.
The he-bird has the fiercest
countenance I have ever seen. He drops
out of the sky as a stone falls
and then he breaks his fall and alights
light on the housetop
as though gravity were not.

Think of it! To fly
by mere gift, without the clamor
and stain of our inert metal,
in perfect trust.

It is the Sabbath of the birds
that so moves me. They belong
in their ever-returning song, in their flight,
in their faith in the upholding air,
to the Original World. They are above us
and yet of us, for those who fly
fall, like those who walk.

In all the millennia of their flight
from which every one finally
has fallen, not one has complained.

XVII.

Hardly escaping the limitless machines
that balk his thoughts and torment his dreams,
the old man goes to his own
small place of peace, a patch of trees
he has lived from many years,
its gifts of a few fence posts and boards,
firewood for winter, some stillness
in which to know and wait. Used
and yet whole this dear place is, whole
by its own nature and by his need.
While he lives it will be whole,
and after him, God willing, another
will follow in that membership
that craves the wholeness of the world
despite all human loss and blame.

In the lengthening shadow he has climbed
again to the ridgetop and across
to the westward slope to see the ripe
light of autumn in the turning trees,
the twilight he must go by now

that only grace could give. Thus far
he keeps the old sectarian piety:
By grace we live. But he can go
no further. Having known the grace
that for so long has kept this world,
haggard as it is, as we have made it,
we cannot rest, we must be stirring
to keep that gift dwelling among us,
eternally alive in time. This
is the great work, no other, none harder,
none nearer rest or more beautiful.

XVIII.

A hawk in flight
The clearing sky
A young man's thought
An old man's cry

XIX.

Born by our birth
Here on the earth
Our flesh to wear
Our death to bear

BEN BIRNBAUM

Jerusalem Manor

FROM *Image*

> God did not create religion; he created the world.
> — Franz Rosenzweig

I WALKED IN on my mother once during her crisis of faith. She
was lounging in my father's recliner in what we called "the front
room." It was a room generally reserved for television and for special company. Here on Sunday evenings we watched *Davy Crockett*
and then the *Jackie Gleason Show*. And my father, gazing between his
stockinged feet at the June Taylor Dancers arrayed on their backs
on the stage floor like a dozen long flower petals, their heads making one blond and brunette pistil, their bare legs swishing like syn-
chronized wiper blades — my father breathed, "Amazing. Can you
believe that?" Here we saw visitors to our house who required a
more respectful — or distancing — welcome than was afforded by
a place on our old living room sofa: salesmen, contractors, teachers
on home visits, our shul's rabbi, people my father did business
with, and the bearded solicitors of charity for orphans, rabbinical
seminaries, and girls without dowries in America and "Palestine"
(though it had been a state called Israel for more than a decade).
And here, too, though not to my father's pleasure, we received
Mr. Friedman, a neighborhood madman who made visits unan-
nounced on lazy Sabbath afternoons, who wore eyeglasses with
lenses so thick that his eyeballs bulged and deflated as he turned
his head, and whose waxen shins gleamed between his fallen silk
socks and the cuffs of his trousers as he worked his way through
bowls of grapes and plates of cookies and mused on Uriel Acosta —

the seventeenth-century heretic from rabbinic Judaism who, trumping Spinoza, was *twice* excommunicated by the Jewish community of Amsterdam and who, after offering a final apology to his coreligionists, shot himself in the head. It was Mr. Friedman's belief that he harbored Acosta's transmigrated soul, and nobody held that nuttiness against him because first of all, it could have been true, and second, he'd been a brilliant medical student until an anti-Semitic professor scheduled an exam for the Sabbath, and Mr. Friedman would not write on the Sabbath and was dismissed from medical school and suffered his breakdown. Such was the story.

I didn't expect to see my mother in my father's chair when I walked into the front room, but there she was, as relaxed as though it were her chair, gazing out the window at our street, which was lined, like many of the streets in our Brooklyn neighborhood, with mature London plane trees, which had been an inexplicable favorite of the city's Depression-era parks department. "Did you know," my mother said to me, "that leaves have tiny holes on the bottom for drinking water?" I did know, as it happened, but the question was clearly an introduction. "And when it's about to rain," she continued, "they know it and they turn themselves over. How can anybody believe there is no God?"

The oldest of the six children my mother bore before she was thirty-five, I was by this time, at age twelve or so, her household confidant and keenly attuned to the flailings of her wounded and childish heart. And while abysmally educated in many ways, I was well schooled theologically, already on the road to what everyone in the neighborhood predicted would be an important life as a rabbinical scholar — "a sage of our generation," God willing. And so I understood that my mother no longer believed in God, and that she would never again believe: not in the revelation at Sinai or the laws that preserved the sanctity of the Sabbath or kashrut or fasting or prayer or those that kept her faithful to my father and to her children and to the community of Orthodox Jews at the far end of Brooklyn to which we belonged utterly. I felt terrified, hollowed out — as though I had caught a glimpse of a bomb a moment before it exploded, casting everything I knew into orbits I could not then imagine.

Forty or so years later, my mother was visiting me and my sister and our families in Boston, where I worked as a writer, editor,

and senior administrative adviser at Boston College, a significant
Jesuit university, and my sister was a public-school teacher married to a tender and smart Methodist-raised engineer. Of the other
four children, one brother was a policeman in California, divorced
from his first wife and living with a divorcée and her children, while
three brothers lived as Orthodox Jews in Israel, as did my father,
with his second wife, a tractable and pleasant woman, by all accounts, and with whom he'd had a large second family. And there
was a seventh child, our youngest brother, who was half a dozen
years from being born on the day I walked in on my mother in the
front room. He was now a postdoctoral fellow in molecular biology
in Colorado, and carrying the surname of a man — another tender and smart Methodist — with whom my mother had an affair
while still married to my father. My mother married her lover a few
years later (after his wife died). They moved to his summer home,
fifteen acres of homespun in the woods of Vermont, where she developed an unreliable local accent, a gardening habit, and a patri-
cian bearing much admired in town. Then the tender and smart
husband took sick and was sick a very long and hard time and died.

It was not long after his death, while on that visit to Boston, that
my mother took a walk with my sister and set her foot wrong and
fell over onto someone's lawn and broke a hip. Following emer-
gency surgery, she began a program of physical therapy in a nurs-
ing home that my sister had located equidistant from our two
homes and close to my university. It was a place with a decent rep-
utation and a dining room that smelled agreeably of thorough
cooking and that looked, also agreeably, as though it had been air-
lifted, chandelier and papered walls and burnished sconces, from a
Borscht-Belt resort with pretensions to upper-class elegance — the
kind of place that in 1955 would have called itself something like
Jerusalem Manor. But it was not a happy place for my mother, given
that the staff were not careful or generous or well trained or, in
many cases, English-speaking, that the cries and honks of the de-
mented sounded day and night, and that the place was for most of
its residents a life sentence: a catered, sedated, chandelier-lit, lin-
ens-supplied journey to the tomb.

With the help of her friends in Vermont, we began to plan my
mother's transfer to a rehabilitation center near her home, but her
surgeon didn't want her traveling yet, and in any case no vacancy

would become available in Vermont for three weeks. I visited her often at Jerusalem Manor, sometimes bringing one of my children, and a few times my wife (it was charity on her part, for my mother had developed a bad habit of being slyly unkind to her). But mostly I went alone, usually on my lunch hour and then again on the way home from work, to sit by my mother's bed and discourse on such subjects as the number of steps she'd been able to take that morning and how tired but good she'd felt afterward, and how the nice young physical therapist and his wife were expecting their first baby and were so nervous about being parents, and my mother was able to say: "Don't worry; no parent can be perfect. It'll be fine, believe me. If you only knew *my* story." (And then she probably told the young man whatever version of her story it pleased her to tell that day.)

We talked as well about my children and my sister's children, and about my mother's friends in Vermont — the members of her Unitarian church and her choirs and political action groups. We talked about my distant brothers in Israel and their children (only a few of whom I'd met, and many of whom my mother was only allowed to see if she disguised herself as a Torah-observant *bubbeh* in a kerchief, long skirt, and long-sleeved blouse). We even talked about Mr. Friedman, who many years earlier was stabbed to death one night in a graveyard in Brooklyn where he believed he was standing at the tomb of Uriel Acosta's lost fiancée (the wedding was called off by the young woman's family). "Did you know he was in love with me?" my mother asked. "Everyone knew," I said. My mother was stunningly beautiful once. When she was seventeen, the story is told, during the Great Depression, a neighborhood doctor, a man of middle age, came to her parents and offered money in return for my mother as his bride. My grandparents were willing — there were two younger daughters to feed, clothe, and educate — but my mother refused. Instead she soon took up with my father, whom her parents did not like and whom she did not like — and for sound reasons, each of them. "It used to really bother your father when Mr. Friedman would show up," my mother said. *And it would please you then and still does,* I thought but did not say. And of course we talked about the way you trip on a piece of broken sidewalk and your life changes, bang, like that. Occasionally my mother tried to coax me into saying what I thought about the course of our en-

twined century of life. But it had been a long time since I trusted
her. She probed: "Do you remember when . . . ?"

One day, telling me about the panic that sometimes seized her
when she woke in her room during the night, she asked what I did
when I felt afraid. After some hesitation, I told her that for such occasions I kept an old Soncino edition of the Psalms close at hand.
Ah, she sighed. The Soncino edition of the Psalms was familiar to
both of us from old Brooklyn, where the Soncino Press's English
translations — whether of Scripture, Mishnah, or Talmud — were
among the few accepted as legitimate by the rabbis to whose severe
views we attended. And they were lovely books. The Soncino Baby-
lonian Talmud, published in thirty hardcover maroon volumes,
was printed on a tough semitransparent paper that endowed the
pages with the same kind of runic beauty one found in a Talmudic
line of argument about the various settlements owed if one man's
ram impregnated another man's ewe after breaking through a
fence that had been damaged by a third party. (Was he aware that
he'd done the damage, or was he not? Did the owner intend to
breed the ewe or butcher it?) The volume of Psalms itself was
girded in a dust cover the color of sun-bleached yellow brick, and
the type was arranged on the pages according to a severe and perfectly realized geometry: the Hebrew making up a dense column
on the right, with the English translation in a crisper font (English
is a profligate tongue) on the left, and both supported below by a
dense, wide plinth of scholarly notes. And while my mother and I
would have read the Hebrew when we read, the English was also
satisfying, the work of an opaque American group known as the
Jewish Publication Society, whose members had here joined rabbinic pedantry with King James flourish and made it seem a viable
marriage.

My mother said that she, too, still found Psalms comforting to
read. "It's silly, but what can you do?" she said, laughing at herself, a
woman from Vermont, with an Irish surname, real oil paintings on
her walls, commitments to Central American villages and nature
preserves, and a role in the First Unitarian Church's Christmas
pageant. I laughed as well. What, indeed, could you do? On this
matter, my mother and I were agreed.

The next day, I went to a bookstore that served Boston's Orthodox Jewish community and bought a copy of the Soncino Psalms. I

mean "copy" two ways, in that it was a copy of the book, yes, but also a facsimile — no longer draped in a jacket the color of desert, and no longer pressed, but photocopied from the original printed pages. Still, words serve, and my mother was happy with the gift I brought, and she wanted to talk more about what those sticky verses meant to me and to her, in old times and now. I wasn't inclined to talk, but I had made her happy.

I don't need to be instructed by anyone as to the appalling outgrowths of religious belief, whether in Holy Writ, history, today's *Times,* or in the hotel room in which my mother disguised herself so as to be fit to be seen by her grandchildren. The world's a broken place. (It cracked at the moment God withdrew himself in order to give creation room to be, say the kabbalists.) And it remains broken in spite of religion, in spite of atheism, in spite of bourbon, penicillin, *King Lear,* and everything else we've fashioned to bind it whole again.

"In the beginning God created," said Rav Menachem Mendel of Kotzk (1787–1859), the great dark light of the Hasidic movement in its decline. "From that point onwards, it was up to man to build himself and his world."

Unlike some faith systems — socialism, Las Vegas, and Andrew Weil, MD, come to mind — religious faith (at least the faiths I know something about, which are Judaism and Christianity) expects of us that we will continue to fashion, bind, and build with (not despite) the certain knowledge that the work will not be completed, cannot be completed — not here and not by the likes of you and me.

"There is abundant hope, but there is none for us," Kafka put it, and I tend to believe that the Catholic existentialist theologian Gabriel Marcel, who drank from the other end of the same rotten century as did Kafka, meant the sane thing when he said that hope is not a denial of the facts of life but an expression of them. Yet another remarkable sage is reported to have instructed: "The day is short, the task is great," and then concluded: "While you are not required to complete [the work], neither are you free to desist from it." He was Rav Tarfon, and he lived around the turn of the second century (not a terrific hundred years either), and if I had become the rabbi I was once meant to be, I would have stood at the front of the study hall and looked out at my students and glossed his oft-cited contribution to *Ethics of the Fathers* this way: What Rav Tarfon tells us is that we are blessed to be in a world in which we are free to work continually on becoming free. Now pick up your books and continue studying.

Once upon a time, I was certain that civil life was unsustainable without religion as its foundation. Then I was certain that civil life was unsustainable on a foundation of religion. I also used to be certain about God — even feeling his presence once in a high meadow behind a hotel to which my parents had brought us for a few weeks of country summer. I was six years old, and I told no one. And I've been certain about no-God, too, and told no one as well, until one day I had to speak, because I was a student in a rabbinical seminary, and I had to get away before my cracked self came apart. The rabbi to whom I confessed was one of the deans, a Shoah refugee, a short, bearded, broad-shouldered, and homely man in a black frock coat (he resembled Henri de Toulouse-Lautrec, I would discover when I discovered Toulouse-Lautrec). He absorbed the news that I was an atheist, and he nodded and said, "But you still pray three times a day, right?"

JOSEPH BOTTUM

The End of Advent

FROM *First Things*

CHRISTMAS HAS DEVOURED ADVENT, gobbled it up with the turkey giblets and the goblets of seasonal ale. Every secularized holiday, of course, tends to lose the context it had in the liturgical year. Across the nation, even in many churches, Easter has hopped across Lent, Halloween has frightened away All Saints', and New Year's has drunk up Epiphany.

Still, the disappearance of Advent seems especially disturbing — for it's injured even the secular Christmas season: opening a hole, from Thanksgiving on, that can be filled only with fiercer, madder, and wilder attempts to anticipate Christmas.

More Christmas trees. More Christmas lights. More tinsel, more tassels, more glitter, more glee — until the glut of candies and carols, ornaments and trimmings, has left almost nothing for Christmas Day. For much of America, Christmas itself arrives nearly as an afterthought: not the fulfillment, but only the end, of the long Yule season that has burned without stop since the stores began their Christmas sales.

Of course, even in the liturgical calendar, the season points ahead to Christmas. Advent genuinely is *adventual* — a *time before,* a *looking forward* — and it lacks meaning without Christmas. But maybe Christmas, in turn, lacks meaning without Advent. All those daily readings from Isaiah, filled with visions of things yet to be, a constant barrage of the future tense: *And it shall come to pass . . . And there shall come forth . . .* A kind of longing pervades the Old Testament selections read in church over the weeks before Christmas — an anxious, almost sorrowful litany of hope only in what has not yet come. Zephaniah. Judges. Malachi. Numbers. *I shall see him, but not now: I shall behold him, but not nigh: There shall come a star out of Jacob, and a scepter shall rise out of Israel.*

What Advent is, really, is a *discipline:* a way of forming anticipation and channeling it toward its goal. There's a flicker of rose on the third Sunday — *Gaudete!* that day's Mass begins: *Rejoice!* — but then it's back to the dark purple that is the mark of the season in liturgical churches. And what those somber vestments symbolize is the deeply penitential design of Advent. Nothing we can do earns us the gift of Christmas, any more than Lent earns us Easter. But a season of contrition and sacrifice prepares us to understand and feel something about just how great the gift is when at last the day itself arrives.

More than any other holiday, Christmas seems to need its setting in the church year, for without it we have a diminishment of language, a diminishment of culture, and a diminishment of imagination. The Jesse trees and the Advent calendars, St. Martin's Fast and St. Nicholas's Feast, Gaudete Sunday, the childless crèches, the candle wreaths, the vigil of Christmas Eve: they give a shape to the anticipation of the season. They discipline the ideas and emotions that otherwise would shake themselves to pieces, like a flywheel wobbling wilder and wilder till it finally snaps off its axle.

Maybe that's what has happened to Christmas. The ideas and the emotions have all broken free and smashed their way across the fields. From Henry Wadsworth Longfellow's *I heard the bells on Christmas Day / Their old, familiar carols play* to Irving Berlin's *I'm dreaming of a white Christmas / Just like the ones I used to know,* there has been for a long time now something oddly backward-looking about Christmas music — some nostalgia that insists on substituting its melancholy for the somber contrition and sorrow of forward-looking Advent.

For a similar reason, the memoir of childhood has become the dominant form of Christmas writing. Often beautiful — from Dylan Thomas's "A Child's Christmas in Wales" to Lillian Smith's *Memory of a Large Christmas* — those stories nonetheless deploy their golden-hued Christmassy emotions only toward the past: a kind of contrite feeling without the structure of Advent's contrition, all the regret and sense of absence cast back to what has been and never will be again.

*

On the other hand, there are plenty of Christmas elements that remain forward-looking. In many ways, the season has become little except anticipation — anticipation run amuck, like children so sick with expectation that the reality, when at last it arrives, can never be satisfying. This, too, is something broken off from the liturgical year: another group of adventual feelings without the Advent that gave them form, another set of Christmas ideas set loose to run themselves mad.

Back in the early 1890s, William Dean Howells published a funny little fable called "Christmas Every Day" in one of the most popular venues of the time, *St. Nicholas Magazine for Boys and Girls*. Once upon a time, the narrator explains as the story begins, "there was a little girl who liked Christmas so much that she wanted it to be Christmas every day in the year." What's more, she found a fairy to grant her wish, and she was delighted when Christmas came again on December 26, and December 27, and December 28.

Of course, "after it had gone on about three or four months, the little girl, whenever she came into the room in the morning and saw those great ugly, lumpy stockings dangling at the fireplace, and the disgusting presents around everywhere, used to sit down and burst out crying. In six months she was perfectly exhausted, she couldn't even cry anymore." By October, "people didn't carry presents around nicely anymore. They flung them over the fence or through the window, and, instead of taking great pains to write 'To dear Papa,' or 'Mama,' or 'Brother,' or 'Sister,' they used to write, 'Take it, you horrid old thing!' and then go and bang it against the front door."

These days, by the time Christmas actually rolls around, it feels as though this is very nearly what we've had: Christmas every day, at least since Thanksgiving. Often it starts even earlier. This year the glossy catalogs of Christmas clothing and seasonal bric-a-brac started arriving in September, and there were Christmas-shopping ads on the highway billboard signs before Halloween. The anticipatory elements reach a crescendo by early December, and their constant scream makes the sudden quiet of Christmas Day almost a relief from the Christmas season.

I don't remember this opposition of Christmas and the Christmas season when I was young. When I was little — ah, the nostalgia of the childhood memoir — I always felt that the days right before

Christmas were a time somehow out of time. Christmas Eve, especially, and the arrival of Christmas itself at midnight: the hours moved in ways different from their passage in ordinary time, and the sense of impending completion was somehow like a flavor even to the air we breathed.

I've noticed in recent years, however, that the feeling comes over me more rarely than it used to, and for shorter bits of time. I have to pursue the sense of wonder, the taste in the air, and cling to it self-consciously. Even for me, the endless roar of untethered Christmas anticipation is close to drowning out the disciplined anticipation of Advent. And when Christmas itself arrives, it has begun to seem a day not all that different from any other. Oh, yes, church and home to a big dinner. Presents for the children. A set of decorations. But nothing special, really.

It is this that Advent, rightly kept, would prevent — the thing, in fact, it is designed to halt. Through all the preparatory readings, through all the genealogical Jesse trees, the somber candles on the wreaths, the vigils, and the hymns, Advent keeps Christmas on Christmas Day: a fulfillment, a perfection, of what had gone before. *I shall see him, but not now: I shall behold him, but not nigh.*

JOHN COATS

Who Am I?

FROM *Portland*

I'VE HAD A NUMBER of them, actually, all unexpected. There was, for example, the moment I came face to face with van Gogh's self-portrait in Paris, the one in which he is without a hat, in which his craziness seems, literally, to radiate off him like rays from the sun. All that mad beauty left me wide open, on the edge of something glorious and transcendent. And there've been other moments of magnitude. But the big one for me came in 1958, a few months after my twelfth birthday, less than a mile from my home, and in a place as foreign to my experience as Pluto.

I'd grown up a Southern Baptist, with its Low-Church Protestantism, its plain architecture, and minimalist sanctuaries. I'd never seen anything like the beauty and vibrancy of the silken, embroidered cloth on St. Paul's altar that day, nor the golden candelabra, nor the statuary, especially Mary, nor what impressed me then as the rather miserable-looking Jesus on the cross above the altar — a far cry from the tepid portraits of Jesus on the walls of our Sunday-school rooms. And there was a faint fragrance in the air, something of the place itself, spicy, old, remnant-like, haunting, and mysterious.

My family and I were at St. Paul's for a Nuptial Mass. I'd been angry when we'd arrived; it was, after all, the first cold Saturday of autumn, a day for playing football with my buddies, not sitting in church. But all the beauty had surprised me, and I was calmer now, even peaceful. Then the music swelled. People stood, some half-turning toward the back, straining their necks to see, like people waiting for a parade. Curious, I turned, and through the adults, saw a boy holding what appeared to be a brass cross mounted atop a varnished broomstick, and in front of that was a fellow about my age swinging a smoking pot. As they passed, a bit of the smoke wafted toward me, and it was the same scent.

It was like a scene from an old movie when someone remembers the past and the picture dissolves into wavy lines, but this was only in one spot, sort of oval-shaped, and just above and in front of the cross. Then, as if that spot marked a door between here and somewhere else, it seemed to open and close in a blink, like a camera's shutter. I had the sensation of something hitting me in the belly, but not hard. With that, it — whatever it was — was over.

I was aware of a heaviness that had not been there, a numb heartache of the sort I'd felt when my dog died or when a dear friend moved away. As for the rest of the service, I have a dreamy memory of the priest's murmurings in Latin, the bride and groom, more of the incense, and the presence of something I could not name.

I went to bed early that night. I wanted to fall asleep, then wake up with the usual dread of another three hours of Sunday school and church service; and I wanted that sad ache to go away, or at least to know the source of it. Closing my eyes, I drifted toward sleep. Then, as though having fallen through some cosmic hole, I had the sensation of tumbling backward in slow motion, and into some other place where I was surrounded by stars. The physical sensation of it was like the best part of being dizzy, as when my friends and I would twirl round and round, finally falling to the grass and watching the world spin.

Then: *Who am I?*

The voice was soft, intimate. But where had it come from? Was it my voice? That *presence* I'd sensed? Was the question about me? About *it?* I was more curious than frightened. The tumbling continued, and the question repeated every ten or fifteen seconds until I fell asleep.

Our after-church meal on that or any Sunday was pot roast, mashed potatoes, a canned green vegetable, pull-apart rolls browned in the oven, a lettuce and tomato salad with French dressing, and a world-class dessert — pecan or apple pie, or chocolate cake with ice cream, or brownies. I'd not eaten breakfast, and was still not hungry, but ate to satisfy my mother. My buddies wanted me to come out, but I begged off, claiming too much homework, then closed myself in my room, lay down, and shut my eyes. The tumbling started, then the question, then sleep.

Sunday night was always leftovers followed by *Bonanza*. As soon as the lights were out and my eyes closed, the tumbling and the question returned. Then, after a few minutes: *Who am I asking the question? Who am I?*

The next few months were a time for baffled wonder. Something was different about me, but what? Moreover, what was the point? I was a twelve-year-old boy awash in the cultural zeitgeist of southeast Texas in the late 1950s, where boys were supposed to play football, learn to shoot things, and grow up to be like their daddies, where Low-Church Protestantism reigned supreme and it was not unusual to hear absurdist whisperings such as *Catholics don't even believe in Jesus; they think the pope is God.* So, exactly what was I supposed to do with a peculiar experience I'd had in, of all places, a Roman Catholic church, one that wouldn't go away, and, depending on the day, was making me a little crazy? I wanted to talk to someone, but to whom? Almost certainly my nonreligious father would've half-listened, rolled his eyes, and said, *Go talk to your mother.* Who'd have listened, then dragged me down the street to the pastor's house; or called together church members for a full-throttle gang-save; or phoned my grandfather, who might well have boarded the next train with the intention of saving me from eternity in hell.

I was pretty much on my own, with two boys inside my skin, one who wanted it all to go away, another who couldn't wait to turn out the lights, who hadn't a clue what was happening, but trusted it more than the other boy had ever trusted anything.

Besides, there *did* seem to be a certain logic in what was happening. Given that its genesis was in a church, it followed that I was having a "religious" experience, and that my attitude toward church would shift — certainly a result that would thrill my mother and grandparents. It shifted all right — to a track that would end in a sort of ontological train wreck. Sunday school, worship services, and other church activities soon became like visits to an asylum in which nothing made sense. There were times when being there was so intolerable that I feared I might lose control and start screaming, though at what, or about what, I didn't know.

The tumbling and the questions repeated each night for months, then several times a week for the next few years. The questions were never intrusive, but more like koans, satisfied to *be* rather than demanding answers — a relief, since I had none. Finally, it all stopped. Then, almost ten years after it had started, it happened again — or seemed to — this time in an Episcopal church during the Nuptial Mass for my college roommate. Whether it was a repeat of the same event, anamnesis, or simple déjà vu, the tumbling and the questions returned, as did the sadness, which, finally, I recognized as hunger and longing.

Though it was a single moment, a split second in my sixty years, the man I've become, all that I've done in my professional life — parish priest (Episcopal), speaker and trainer for an international foundation, management consultant, writer — can be traced to it. And yet it remains a mystery. I've tried saying it was "of God," but the name arrives like a king and his court; there is simply too much baggage and too many extras for my small house. Other names present the same. I've come to prefer the mystery, the illogicalness in the fact that I understand it far better when I don't try to understand it.

Understanding has its own timetable and comes when I'm not looking for it. While still a teenager, the word "milieu" came as a welcome guest because that was the sense of it for me that Saturday afternoon — an immersion, a *surrounding* too vast ever to say, "It's here, but not there" or "Under this roof, but not that one." Later I would stumble across the Latin *mysterium tremendum* and know its meaning without asking, and the vast experience to which it pointed. Some years back, I came across the German mystic Meister Eckhart, who centuries ago wrote, "That which one says is God, he is not; that which one does not say, he is more truly that than that which one says he is." Except for the "G" word and the gendering, it fit for me, sort of. I've loved the image inherent there, of the definition of the *infinite* existing only in the spaces between the words, whether written or spoken. There has been no form, no pillar of fire or burning bush. Moreover, there's been nothing to *believe* in. In fact, I've come to think that trying to believe in what happened that day is the worst idea of all.

DAVID JAMES DUNCAN

Lost River

FROM *Portland*

I DREAMED THE PEOPLE who fished the river never knew want, seldom knew confusion, and with the salmon's self-sacrifice to guide us we could always find love. I dreamed I obeyed the river so gratefully the name of every rapid, fall & riffle engraved itself on my tongue, & the salmon came back to us again & again, & I never once doubted they would bless my family's table forever.

I dreamed Big & Little Dalles & Methow & Priest Rapids & Lodgepole & Entiat Rapids. I dreamed Coulee Bend & Kettle Falls & beautiful Celilo. I dreamed Chalwash Chilni & Picture Rocks Bay & Spanish Castle & Victoria & Beacon Rocks. I dreamed Black Canyon & Deschutes & Klickitat Canyons & Rocky Reach and Ribbon Cliff. I dreamed I fished by the peach groves of the place called Penawawa, drunk on the river's sweetness within the fruit.

I dreamed I fell asleep to the sound of water, & when I woke a cloud had enveloped the minds of the ruling pharaohs, & they had attacked the river as if its song & flow were curses. I dreamed 227 dams clogged the river & all that I knew was submerged.

I dreamed the salmon young lost strength & direction in the slackwaters, couldn't reach the sea, & when they no longer brought the ocean back to us we grew as lost as they. I dreamed my people stood shoulder to shoulder in casinos the way we'd once stood by the river, our fists full of quarters, our minds full of broken hope & smoke.

I dreamed I asked why the salmon had to die & the pharaohs told me, "So wheat can ride the slackwater in barges." I dreamed I tried to reason, telling them of wheat shipped by railroad, & they laughed and marched off to conduct business hard to distinguish from war.

I dreamed I led the last salmon people out into the wheat fields, & in a golden light we launched our dories, & we went fishing in the stubble. I dreamed I cast the Spey of a Nez Perce named Levi, & the beauty of hidden salmon gleamed in the field and sky, & our fishing became prayer. But still the pharaohs ruled the water. I dreamed the one who reads even lost rivers then said it is finished, & the last salmon floated by as a cloud above us.

I dream I am an old man, & Levi and the farmer whose fields we sailed sit with me at Penawawa beside a river finally freed. I dream we hold rods in one hand, sweet peaches in the other, & our lines run true as prayer into the shine. But whether the salmon come, whether they bring the lost ocean back to us, my dreams, like the river, refuse to stay.

PAUL ELIE

A Man for All Reasons

FROM *The Atlantic Monthly*

THE VITAL CENTER was not holding. Arthur Schlesinger Jr., bow-tied eminence of American liberalism, stepped in. The "war on terror" was sputtering into its fifth year, and there was no end in sight; Schlesinger was eighty-seven, and the hour was getting late. He tapped out an essay for the *New York Times,* confident that the men down in Washington could be set straight if only they had the right guide. Where, he asked, was the wisdom of his old friend Reinhold Niebuhr when the country needed it? "Why, in an age of religiosity, has Niebuhr, the supreme American theologian of the twentieth century, dropped out of twenty-first-century religious discourse?"

Schlesinger was evidently unaware that the Niebuhr revival he called for was already under way. In think tanks, on op-ed pages, and on divinity-school quadrangles, Niebuhr's ideas are more prominent than at any time since his death, in 1971. The seminary professor who was anointed the national conscience during the atomic era is once more a figure whose very name suggests a principled, hardheaded approach to war and peace.

In his lifetime, Niebuhr was a restless and paradoxical figure: an evangelical preacher and the author of the Serenity Prayer, a foe of U.S. isolationism in the 1930s and of U.S. intervention in Vietnam in the 1960s. After his death, "Niebuhrian" became a synonym for American political realism — the school of thought that places national self-interest above idealistic schemes for social reform. But the war on terror has brought Niebuhr's broader vision into focus: not only the struggle between realism and idealism in our foreign affairs, but the ongoing debate over the place of religion in America's sense of itself. The fresh interest in his work, then, ought to be invigorating — a source of clarity and perspective.

It hasn't been. On the contrary, the Niebuhr revival has been perplexing, even bizarre, as people with profoundly divergent views of the war have all claimed Niebuhr as their precursor: bellicose neoconservatives, chastened "liberal hawks," and the stalwarts of the antiwar left. Inevitably, politicians have taken note, and by now a well-turned Niebuhr reference is the speechwriter's equivalent of a photo op with Bono. In recent months alone, John McCain (in a book) celebrated Niebuhr as a paragon of clarity about the costs of a good war; New York governor Eliot Spitzer (at the Chautauqua Institution) invoked Niebuhr as a model of the humility lacking in the White House; and Barack Obama (leaving the Senate floor) called Niebuhr "one of [his] favorite philosophers" for his account of "the compelling idea that there's serious evil in the world."

Who's right about Niebuhr, and why does it matter? It matters especially because Niebuhr, better than any contemporary thinker, got to the roots of the conflict between American ideals and their unintended consequences, like those the United States now faces in Iraq. The story of the uses and misuses of his work during the war so far is the story of how the war went wrong; and yet a look at the partial, partisan Niebuhrs that have emerged produces something like a rounded portrait, a view of a man who really does have something essential to tell us about the world and our place in it.

In 1967, with the country in the midst of what he called "the two main collective moral issues of our day — the civil-rights movement that seeks democratic improvements for our black minority, and opposition to the terrible and mistaken war in Vietnam," Niebuhr looked back at his career in an essay written "from the sidelines," where he had found himself since suffering a stroke in 1952, when he was fifty-nine. He recalled his

> rather too-hectic activities as a member of the Union Theological Seminary faculty; as a weekly circuit rider preaching every Sunday in the colleges of the east; and as a rather polemical journalist who undertook to convert liberal Protestantism from its perfectionist illusions in the interventionist political debates at a time when Hitler threatened the whole of Western culture.

It's a telling piece of self-portraiture, for it suggests that the divergent views of Niebuhr today have their basis in his life — a whirlwind of preaching, speaking, writing, and organizing. Born in 1892, one of four children of a minister in the Deutsche Evangelische Synode von Nord-Amerika, Niebuhr trained for the ministry from age fifteen, and at twenty took over the pulpit of his boyhood church, in Lincoln, Illinois, after his father died suddenly. He went east to the School of Religion at Yale, then accepted the pastorate of the Bethel Evangelical Church in Detroit. There he began writing polemical articles "in profusion," the biographer Richard Wightman Fox reports, in part to support his mother, who lived with him, and a spendthrift older brother. He "ended up doing a million things at once — he talked to student groups and YMCA meetings, he threw himself into community betterment projects, he became a pamphleteer," his daughter Elisabeth Sifton explained in a 2003 memoir. He became an editorialist for the *Christian Century,* which led to a job offer from Union Theological Seminary in New York; by then, his advocacy on behalf of ill-paid autoworkers in Detroit had thrust him into public life — an agitator in a gray flannel suit, bald and bright-eyed, voluble and inexhaustible.

At Union, Niebuhr taught what he called "applied Christianity," and insisted that he was not a theologian (perhaps in deference to his younger brother, Helmut Richard, who was). His preoccupation with the workings of society more than with God or the individual put him closer to Max Weber than to Jonathan Edwards. Yet he was suspicious of the abstractions of sociology and politics alike. In one early piece (published in the *Atlantic Monthly* in 1916) he called war "The *Nation*'s Crime Against the Individual," because it asked a young man to give "a life of eternal significance for ends that have no eternal value." After a trip to Germany, where he saw the aftermath of the Great War firsthand, he became a pacifist.

He then became a socialist, too, even running for the New York state senate in 1930 on the Socialist ticket, but by the mid-1930s, he counted himself a liberal. *Moral Man and Immoral Society,* published in 1932, records both his disillusionment with radicalism and his abiding sense of liberalism's shortcomings. The book is a quick, deep thrust against the liberal accommodation with evil through naïveté, inaction, and confidence in "reform" rather than the use of force. It's a devastating critique of the yearning for purity and the radical forms that this yearning takes, whether the Christian wish to purify society of sin or the "rationalist" wish to purify society of religion and other superstitions. Against these he set a Christian realism rooted in his sense of human sinfulness. The human person, in Niebuhr's account, is self-interested in the extreme. While the individual "moral man" can check his natural selfishness through conscience, self-discipline, and love, social groups — tribes, movements, nations — look out for their own and strive to dominate other groups. Everybody's motives are always mixed. Order in society is achieved through the threat of force, so "society is in a perpetual state of war." Peace among nations "is gained by force and is always an uneasy and an unjust one." "Conflict is inevitable, and . . . power must be challenged by power."

When it was published, *Moral Man and Immoral Society* seemed to describe the conflict between liberalism and radicalism at home; but in the years to follow, it seemed to describe the conflict between civilization and totalitarianism abroad, because Niebuhr, better and earlier than anybody else, had foreseen both the mass hysteria of Nazism and the liberal appeasement of Chamberlain and Roosevelt. But the book's power is finally a literary power. There's no grasping for precursors, no revisiting of the debates of the era just past. The allusions are to Augustine, Kant, and the prophets of Israel. Written in the white heat of the Depression, labor strife, Stalinist fervor, and the Weimar meltdown, it has the granite objectivity of the great chronicles of the vanity of human wishes.

Niebuhr's long perspective — the sense of history being understood from a distance even as it's happening — was the source of his authority, and he spent the rest of his career spelling out his sense of history in ever-greater depth. "This drama of human history is indeed partly our construct," he wrote in 1960, "but it stands under a sovereignty much greater than ours . . . a mysterious sovereignty which the prophets are always warning that we must not spell out too much." Today, his biblical sense of history — of what he calls "the limits of all human striving" — is what makes his account of American strivings still ring true. For him, history isn't a record of past events but the story of human injustice and divine mercy — the ongoing, little-changing story of "the curious compounds of good and evil in which the actions of the best men and nations abound."

The biblical sense of history can make Niebuhr seem something other than a liberal. In the '60s, his religiosity made him suspect on the New Left, and in the years after his death, his work resonated with the thinkers who were turning against that era's liberal reforms. It was no great surprise when they claimed him posthumously as the "first neoconservative," in their account of the recovery from the '60s revels, and then as a precursor to the "theocons," who emphasized the new conservatism's roots in religious truths rather than in free trade or small government.

It was no great surprise, either, that in 2001, the theocons enlisted him to support the war on terror, using his work to vault over Vietnam to an earlier age when the United States had fought a noble war abroad in the defense of freedom at home.

They saw the terrorist attacks (and the swiftness with which some secular liberals said we'd had it coming) as dramatic proof that the United States was embroiled in a religious war, with Christians and Jews on one side and secular liberals and Muslims on the other. It seemed not to matter that the Bush team's plan to remake the political culture of the Middle East was idealist rather than realist. For the theocons, the "preemptive" wars in Afghanistan and Iraq were a Niebuhrian test of America's willingness to rejoin the struggle of good and evil — to set aside "accommodation" and oppose force with force once more.

Six months after 9/11, the historian Wilfred McClay set out the argument with special vigor in a talk to the Family Research Council, in Washington, D.C. McClay is a theocon yeoman with a chair at the University of Tennessee. After learning of the attacks, he told his audience, he'd turned to Niebuhr's *The Irony of American History,* whose themes he synopsized in such a way that they converged neatly with the preemptive-war and global-responsibility themes coming out of the White House. McClay wholly supported the war on terror ("When the president says, 'Let's roll,' I'm ready"), and he was sure that Niebuhr would have, too. "What might we learn from Niebuhr about our current challenges, which are so different from those presented by the Cold War?" he asked rhetorically.

"First and foremost, that it is right and just for Christians to support this war. Indeed, they have an obligation to do so." He went on to say that he suspected "Niebuhr might well approve of President Bush's remarkably skillful and sensitive handling of the events of the past few months."

Published in *First Things*, the house organ of the theocons, Mc-Clay's talk caught the eye of the commentator David Brooks. In the *Weekly Standard* shortly after the attacks, Brooks had called for a new, Niebuhr-style "humble hawkishness" in the prosecution of the war on terror; in the *Atlantic* ten months later, he put out the call for a "modern-day Reinhold Niebuhr," a philosopher of power in an age of conflict. Where McClay's Niebuhr was a muscular Christian in a Humvee, ready to roll, Brooks's Niebuhr was "a Man on a Gray Horse" — a sage of ambiguity who liked to "argue the middle against both ends." Niebuhr, in what became a famous formulation, had written:

> Our idealists are divided between those who would renounce the responsibilities of power for the sake of preserving the purity of our soul and those who are ready to cover every ambiguity of good and evil in our actions by the frantic insistence that any measure taken in a good cause must be unequivocally virtuous.

Now Brooks, echoing Niebuhr, set realism against two extreme forms of idealism — "the idealism of noninterventionists, who are embarrassed by power, and the idealism of imperialists, who disguise power as virtue." These were the extremes of Chomsky and Cheney, of Huffington and Halliburton. The effect was to make Brooks's unmistakable support for the war appear the moderate — the Niebuhrian — position.

Brooks concluded that what America needed was a new, Niebuhrian "hawkish left . . . a left suspicious of power but willing to use it to defend freedom." He got his wish. But the speed date between liberal pundits and massive military force came with unintended consequences.

"Our age is involved in irony because so many dreams of our nation have been so cruelly refuted by history," Niebuhr wrote in 1951. By then he had the American people as his congregation. He had given the prestigious Gifford Lectures (later published as *The Na-*

ture and Destiny of Man). He had been featured in a *Time* cover story as America's "No. 1 Theologian," the man who had "restored to Protestantism a Christian virility." He had joined Arthur Schlesinger, Eleanor Roosevelt, Walter Reuther, and others in founding Americans for Democratic Action, which sought to claim "the vital center" by cutting ties with the "doughface" sympathizers with communism. He had advised the State Department on the cultural reconstruction of Europe and had even been touted for president. Yet *This Nation Under God,* as he called it, would be his last major book; retitled *The Irony of American History,* it went to press in early 1952, shortly before the stroke from which he never fully recovered.

The irony of American history, as Niebuhr explained it, is that our virtues and our vices are inextricably joined. From the beginning, our national purpose has been "to make a new beginning in a corrupt world." Our prosperity leads us to believe "that our society is so essentially virtuous that only malice could prompt criticism of any of our actions." Yet our counterparts abroad see us as at once naive and crudely imperialistic, and our power, ironically, has undermined our virtue, for "the same technical efficiency which provided our comforts has also placed us at the center of the tragic developments in world events," bringing about a "historic situation in which the paradise of our domestic security is suspended in a hell of global insecurity."

What should America do about the Soviet threat? The Cold Warrior answered coolly but surely, with Sunday-morning lyricism: in foreign affairs, we should proceed vigorously but cautiously. We should take "morally hazardous actions," risking our purity in the course of "defending freedom against tyranny." Yet we should also recognize that all human motives are mixed and that weapons like the atomic bomb, which grant the United States unprecedented power, also raise the prospect that "we shall cover ourselves with a terrible guilt." So we should "establish community with many nations," be mindful of the unintended consequences of our actions, beware of the pretensions of "our contemporary wise men" to manage history, and let humility guide our actions abroad.

Those are words that Peter Beinart now knows well. As the White House framed the war on terror, he was among the most promi-

nent of the liberal hawks who saw their support for the war as an ex-
orcism of all the evil spirits of American liberalism's recent past.
During the long run-up to the war in Iraq, the liberal hawks ran-
sacked modern history, seeking analogies in every U.S. war of the
previous hundred years. Then, as it turned out to be a war all its
own, they sought an exit strategy in Niebuhr's ironic view of history, for they found themselves covered with guilt.

A graduate of Yale, Beinart went from his Rhodes Scholarship at
Oxford to the *New Republic,* and was made editor at age twenty-
eight. Under his direction, the magazine editorialized early and often in support of the wars in Afghanistan and Iraq. A September
2002 editorial, for example, took a "realist" approach, basing its arguments in the supposedly clear threat posed by Saddam Hussein's
weapons of mass destruction. But the magazine's arguments were
plainly idealistic salvos in the culture wars in the United States and
the Middle East. A February 2003 editorial bemoaned "the intellectual incoherence of the liberal war critics" and argued that recent events had exposed the "moderate antiwar position . . . for the
abject pacifism it truly is." In the *Washington Post,* Beinart proudly
likened the arguments to the arguments the magazine had made
in support of the Nicaraguan contras two decades earlier.

This self-righteousness dissipated quickly. As it became clear that
no weapons of mass destruction would be found and no exemplary
democracy would flower, liberal hawks from Paul Berman to Jacob
Weisberg to Christopher Hitchens stepped back from the brink of
certainty and into the world of paradox and ambiguity. The *New Republic* caught the changing mood. "Were We Wrong?" it asked in
June 2004, in a full issue devoted to the war. The responses varied,
but the theme was one of Niebuhrian "ironic refutations" — the
war just hadn't gone the way the liberal hawks thought it would.
Beinart confessed that he had been "too bipartisan," claiming he
overzealously supported the war in an effort to put his sense of
the national interest ahead of his dislike of the Republicans. But
when President Bush defeated John Kerry, Beinart changed his
tack again. The problem for the Democrats wasn't that they had
supported the war in Iraq too eagerly; it was that they hadn't supported the larger war on terror eagerly enough. In a strident post-
mortem cover story that December, Beinart called on the party to
adopt "A Fighting Faith" that would put the struggle against Islamic terrorism at the top of the agenda. To do this, he explained,

the party would have to purge itself of the forces on its far left, represented by the filmmaker and author Michael Moore and the Web activist organization MoveOn.org. Beinart's supporting argument was simple: it had worked before. In 1947, he explained, Reinhold Niebuhr and his friends "met at Washington's Willard Hotel to save American liberalism." With the founding of Americans for Democratic Action, they courageously separated themselves from Communists and fellow travelers, bringing on two decades of Democratic clarity of purpose.

Early in 2005, Beinart was offered six hundred thousand dollars to expand the article into a book. He left the *New Republic* for the Brookings Institution, but not before propagating the Niebuhr revival in *TNR*'s ninetieth-anniversary issue. It was a group-therapy effort with a "whither liberalism?" theme, and Niebuhr loomed as a messiah whose return was longed for. E. J. Dionne Jr. argued that what liberalism needed, if it was to recover itself, was a Niebuhrian blend of activist religion and activist politics; a few pages away, Martin Peretz asked: "So who has replaced Niebuhr, the once-commanding tribune to both town and gown? It's as if no one even tries to fill the vacuum."

Beinart tried. By the time the book, called *The Good Fight*, was published, he was a full-on Niebuhrian. "The hero of the book in a way," he would tell an interviewer, "is the theologian Reinhold Niebuhr." There was Niebuhr in the *New York Times Magazine*, exhibit A in Beinart's call for "The Rehabilitation of the Cold-War Liberal"; there was *The Irony of American History* on an Amazon list of "Peter Beinart's 10 Books to Read on Liberalism." (The irony was that *The Irony* was out of print.)

The aim in telling the story of the Cold War liberals was to equate "our fight" against Islamic terrorism with "their fight" against totalitarianism, giving liberals a "usable past" to match the conservative one of a Reagan-era restoration. What made Niebuhr the hero of the story was his sense of limits — of "the danger of unrestrained, unreflective power." For Beinart, the policy implications of this "old theme" were clear:

> America must recognize its capacity for evil and build the restraints that hold it in check. But it must still act to prevent greater evil. It cannot take refuge in the moral innocence that comes from no meaningful action at all.

So far, so good, but that's not very far. For as it developed, the argument showed the liberal blind spots that Niebuhr had pointed out in *Moral Man and Immoral Society*. No fighting faith, Beinart's usable past is as secular as the glass-box office complexes on K Street, and his Niebuhr is not a teacher of Christian ethics but a "tall, unaffected Midwesterner" who drafts position papers and attends briefings at the State Department. His sense of the need for limits in foreign policy is rooted not (as Niebuhr's was) in human nature and history and religious faith — with all that those tell us about the limitations of people and nations — but in utility: we should observe limits because they're useful to our national interests.

Truly, this was Niebuhrian realism turned on its head. An idealistic transformation of American domestic politics had been made a precondition for a supposedly realist foreign policy. A vision of the political transformation of Iraq had been replaced by a vision of the political transformation of Washington.

Rhodes Scholar + *New Republic* + "Were We Wrong?" + $600,000 = big target, and when *The Good Fight* was published, the supposedly conflict-averse American left piled on. Michael Tomasky of the *American Prospect* was especially aggressive. He was all for a recovery of the "Niebuhrian doctrine of self-restraint." But would Niebuhr have seen a parallel between the Cold War and the Iraq War? The answer, Tomasky was sure, was "a reverberating, ear-splitting 'no.'" Explaining why in an exchange with Beinart on *Slate*, he predicted that the war in Iraq "renders the grand visions for liberal internationalism that you and I share useless nullities, for a generation, maybe more."

The exchange had the sense of history that *The Good Fight* lacked, but it showed the perils of finding one's antecedents in the recent American past rather than in the much longer, broader history that Niebuhr claimed as his and ours. And its retrospective tone suggested how fully the left had already left the war behind.

Now the antiwar voice was one of experience, the voice for military power one of credulity and naïveté. The Niebuhr who called for the triumph of force over inaction was being supplanted by the Niebuhr who ruefully described "the triumph of experience over dogma." Enter Andrew Bacevich: retired army colonel, Roman Catholic, contributor to the *American Conservative*. With his crew-neck sweaters and helmet of white hair, Bacevich is a right-of-center Howard Dean — an establishment figure who's made his mark by opposing established positions. In a review of *The Good Fight* for the *Nation,* he accused Beinart of casting "hawkish liberals as heroes, doves as fools and conservatives as knaves" in a "largely spurious" allegory — and of "channeling" Niebuhr in a way that amounted to "ritual abuse." "He uses Niebuhr," Bacevich wrote, "much as Jerry Falwell uses Jesus Christ, and just as shamelessly: citing him as an unimpeachable authority and claiming his endorsement, thereby preempting any further discussion.

"The real Niebuhr," Bacevich confidently went on, didn't worry "about Americans demonstrating their moral superiority"; he worried that they would succumb to temptation and do the wrong thing:

> The real Niebuhr did not conceive of history as a narrative of national greatness. Rather than bend the past to suit a particular agenda, liberal or otherwise, he viewed it as beyond our understanding and fraught with paradox.

Bacevich, who teaches at Boston University, characterized Niebuhr as a man like himself: a thinker beyond category who "would likely align himself with those dissidents on the left and the right . . . who view as profoundly dangerous the claims of both neoliberals and neoconservatives to understand history's purposes and destination." The emergence of such a figure as a hero in the unequivocally left-of-center, antiwar *Nation* seemed itself paradoxical. But a graver paradox was yet to come. In May, Bacevich's son, Andrew Jr., serving as a first lieutenant in Iraq, was killed by a suicide bomber while on patrol. "I Lost My Son to a War I Oppose," the elder Bacevich wrote in the *Washington Post* over Memorial Day weekend; but the headline went on to say, "We Were Both Doing Our Duty" — at once refuting the arguments of the people who claimed his opposition to the war had helped the enemy kill his son and acknowledging that for every family with a member in Iraq, death in battle is the cruelest of unintended consequences.

"The beginning of wisdom," Niebuhr wrote, "lies in recognizing that history cannot be coerced." But history can be changed by the force of righteousness; of this Niebuhr was sure, and of this Martin Luther King Jr. is modern proof. When King read *Moral Man and*

Immoral Society in divinity school in 1950, he was struck both by Niebuhr's frank appraisal of the role of power in society and by his application of it to race relations in the South. Having rejected pacifism, Niebuhr made his case for Christian participation in war by distinguishing between "nonresistance" and "nonviolent resistance." He argued that because Jesus counseled nonresistance (urging his followers to turn the other cheek), nonviolent resistance was no more faithful to the Gospel than violence — after all, it *did* resist. Nor was it practical, for it ceded all force to people who would use it without scruple. But Niebuhr, with characteristic subtlety, saw some merit in nonviolence even so. In peacetime, he allowed, nonviolent resistance could be an effective way to close the gap between the powerful and the powerless — as Gandhi had recently shown with his campaign of strikes and boycotts against the British in India. He added:

> The emancipation of the Negro race in America probably waits upon the adequate development of this kind of social and political strategy . . . The white race in America will not admit the Negro to equal rights if it is not forced to do so. Upon that point one may speak with a dogmatism which all history justifies.

In jail in Birmingham, Alabama, in 1963, King drew on the passage from memory in his open letter to eight of the city's white clergymen, recalling:

> As Reinhold Niebuhr has reminded us, groups tend to be more immoral than individuals. We know through painful experience that freedom is never voluntarily given by the oppressor; it must be demanded by the oppressed.

In a striking paradox, King had identified the philosopher of armed conflict with the cause of nonviolence.

When Stanley Hauerwas found himself "silenced" during the war on terror, he too sat down and wrote an open letter, and he too had Niebuhr in mind. Hauerwas, who teaches in the divinity school at Duke University, is the most prominent voice for Christian pacifism in America. A September 2001 issue of *Time* declared him "America's Best Theologian." Then the terrorists struck. A *First Things* editorial, "In a Time of War," set out the journal's stance. The target was recognizably Hauerwas, a member of the

First Things editorial board, and the rhetoric was recognizably that of the editor in chief, Richard John Neuhaus, a Catholic priest who is to theoconservatism what Hauerwas is to pacifism. Support for the war, Neuhaus proposed, was not a matter of debate "between idealism and realism, nor between moral purity and moral compromise"; it was a matter of duty. Anyone with a "decent respect for mankind" would join the war effort. As for the "fraudulent" pacifists who promoted "nonviolent resistance," they were living in "an unreal world of utopian fantasy that has no basis in Christian faith." As opponents of military force, they should have no say "in the discussion about how military force should be used."

"I have been silenced," Hauerwas responded in a letter to the editors. He found it "almost beyond belief" that *First Things* had resorted to "the Niebuhrian distinction between nonviolent resistance and nonresistance in order to silence the pacifist voice." As he saw it, that distinction affected more than pacifists; it forced all Christians to "leave Jesus behind when they come to the political realm" and reconcile themselves to "the order of disguised violence" — the world of legislatures and politics that leads, inevitably, to the order of undisguised violence that is war. His point made, he resigned from the editorial board.

Niebuhr's "hold on Neuhaus' soul seems permanent," Hauerwas later wrote, and so it is on Hauerwas's. It was from Niebuhr, he says, that he learned "that if you desire justice you had better be ready to kill someone along the way." But an encounter with the work of the Mennonite theologian John Howard Yoder convinced him that "if there is anything to this Christian 'stuff' it must surely involve the conviction that the Son [of God] would rather die on the cross than have the world to be redeemed by violence."

Since then, Hauerwas has been what might be called a Niebuhrian inside-out, laying the problems of American Protestantism at Niebuhr's feet. In his view — set out in his Gifford Lectures, given in 2000 and 2001, sixty years after Niebuhr's — the Christian Church must bring the power of the Gospels to the world rather than seek accommodation with worldly power, and Niebuhr, in an attempt to make faith relevant to the age and acceptable to the cultured despisers of religion, became "the theologian of a domesticated god capable of doing no more than providing comfort to the anxious conscience of the bourgeoisie."

Published in a book shortly after the terrorist attacks, Hauerwas's challenge to Niebuhr could be seen as a critique of the Bush administration and of the close ties between Christianity and patriotism. Six years into the war, Hauerwas is firmer than ever in his conviction that Niebuhrian realism is not realistic. As he sees it, the war on terrorism is not only not winnable; it isn't even a war, for it has no clear enemy, purpose, or end. As in all wars, however, violence and the threat of violence are everywhere, from Baghdad to Abu Ghraib to Guantánamo. The ubiquity of violence, he insists, shows the emptiness of Niebuhrian realism, for all Niebuhr's further arguments lead to the crude conclusion that "the nations with the largest armies get to determine what counts for 'justice'"; and the diversity of Niebuhrian opinions shows that Niebuhr has no clear answers to give us.

In 1943, with the Axis powers still strong in Europe and the Pacific, Niebuhr began to plan for the postwar situation, sketching out a peacetime alliance that would represent a mean between the extremes of anarchy and world government. As the military intervention he'd sought was becoming a fact on the ground, making American predominance in world affairs felt as never before, he was looking ahead to a time when the United States would need to "establish community with many nations."

It was at this time that he wrote the Serenity Prayer, the thirty-three words now uttered countless times each day in twelve-step recovery programs worldwide: "God, give us grace to accept with serenity the things that cannot be changed, courage to change the things that should be changed, and the wisdom to distinguish the one from the other."

More than a prayer, this was Niebuhr's prescription for action in the new era waiting on the far side of the war. He foresaw that the American struggle in the postwar years would be a struggle with our addiction to power, and that our national story would be a story of our efforts to distinguish between the courageous and the foolish uses of that power — a story of our reluctant recognition that power can bring about necessary change, but that it can also have brutal unintended consequences. Moreover, he saw that distinguishing the one from the other would call for wisdom, a quality born of "the triumph of experience over dogma."

Such wisdom is needed now more than at any time since 1945. The war in Iraq is far from over, no matter what any politician says. The forces of globalization and terrorism have made the United States at once more powerful and more vulnerable than ever before, bringing the "hell of global insecurity" to our office towers and mailboxes. With the so-called American Century safely behind us, we can once more begin to see that we are just one nation among many, for better and for worse.

Where, in such a situation, is the wisdom Niebuhr called for to be found? All the recent ritual invocation of his thought suggests that the place to look is not in his aphorisms and pronouncements, not in the particular petitions he signed or the committees he founded, but in his sense of history and our role in it.

Niebuhr was what Flannery O'Connor called a "realist of distances," and the distance that gave his realism its clarity and explanatory power was gained through a grasp of what was known in his time as sacred history. In his view, the youth and optimism of the American experience was offset by the Founders' conviction that we are a biblical people, enacting in the New World an older history. For Niebuhr, the aspirations that shaped our common life predated the republic: they were the visions of the promised land held by the patriarchs and the apostles, described in the history of Israel's origins and destiny, which, in our early settlers' account, became the story of our origins and destiny as well. This history tells of a people confident of its special role yet thwarted again and again on account of its pride, and growing in wisdom through a sense of the frailty of human nature and the limits of earthly powers. This history records that nations rage and peoples rise up together — that war sets brother against brother, despoils the land, and rends the social fabric; it counsels that you go to war with a heavy heart, for the truly good war has never been fought. This history acts as a restraint on national pride, not a stimulant to it, for it is not merely history, but in some sense our history, a story that cannot but be a cautionary tale, for it tells us who we are and what we are prone to do.

The war in Iraq, and the debates about the war, suggest that this history is now lost to us. On the surface, our society is thick with religion, but it is religion whose history is merely decorative, like the fiberglass pillars and aluminum gaslights of a McMansion in the suburbs. The Christianity that has a voice in official Washington has as its patriarchs Reagan and Falwell, not Abraham, Isaac, and Jacob; and yet it has managed to make the nation's longer biblical history repulsive to the liberals who once acknowledged it as a basic fact of our heritage. Lacking this history, liberals have a mainly ahistorical, secular political culture — one that assumes liberalism began with the New Deal or in 1948 and that would stand apart from religion altogether at a time when an understanding of the religious outlook is crucial to our grasp of the challenges of a globalized world.

In such circumstances, it's no surprise that we fail to hear the voices of prophets like those who, during all the U.S. wars of the past century, called the ruling powers to account. To an astonishing degree, churches have underwritten the war in Iraq, recasting the biblical tradition in accord with the policies of the White House. They've replaced two millennia of thinking about war and peace with grade-school tutorials on Islam and facile comparisons between Iraq and Vietnam, attempting to make a usable past out of events that are hardly even past.

Niebuhr would say that a biblical perspective, once lost, is not easily recovered — cultural regeneration being an abstract enterprise doomed to failure, like most human projects. Yet it's worth recalling his conviction that history isn't a true measure of things, that posterity is only a proximate judgment. "There is no way of transmuting the Christian gospel into a system of historical optimism," he observed. "The final victory over man's disorder is God's and not ours."

Even so, Niebuhr insisted, "we do have a responsibility for proximate victories" — "for the health of our communities, our nations, and our cultures." What might this mean for the war in Iraq? It would mean frankly acknowledging, first of all, that the war as fought — in the misbegotten hope that Iraq, with its fractious history, could be remade in our image — has been lost. And second, that a full American withdrawal from the country is no more possible than a swift and easy victory was. Americans and Iraqis are bound together for the foreseeable future, regardless of the terms on which U.S. forces are drawn down — even if we are driven out of their country by rival factions in a civil war. "To love our enemies cannot mean that we must connive with their injustice," Niebuhr wrote in 1942. "It does mean that beyond all moral distinctions of history we must know ourselves one with our enemies not only in the bonds of common humanity but also in the bonds of common guilt by which that humanity has become corrupted."

As it was in Western Europe, so it is in Iraq. Its history now has an American chapter — and the other way around — and this shared history brings a shared responsibility, whether we like it or not. The recognition of this fact would be not only realistic, but the beginning of wisdom — the first step in the recognition of the limits of our power.

PETER EVERWINE

Aubade in Autumn

FROM *The New Yorker*

This morning, from under the floorboards
of the room in which I write,
Lawrence the handyman is singing the blues
in a soft falsetto as he works, the words
unclear, though surely one of them is *love*,
lugging its shadow of sadness into song.
I don't want to think about sadness;
there's never a lack of it.
I want to sit quietly for a while
and listen to my father making
a joyful sound unto his mirror
as he shaves — slap of razor
against the strop, the familiar rasp of his voice
singing his favorite hymn, but faint now,
coming from so far back in time:
Oh, come to the church in the wildwood . . .
my father, who had no faith, but loved
how the long, ascending syllable of *wild*
echoed from the walls in celebration
as the morning opened around him . . .
as now it opens around me, the light shifting
in the leaf-fall of the pear tree and across
the bedraggled back-yard roses
that I have been careless of
but brighten the air, nevertheless.
Who am I, if not one who listens

for words to stir from the silences they keep?
Love is the ground note; we cannot do
without it or the sorrow of its changes.
Come to the wildwood, love,
Oh, to the wiiildwood as the morning deepens,
and from a branch in the cedar tree a small bird
quickens his song into the blue reaches of heaven —
hey sweetie sweetie hey.

KATE FARRELL

Lullaby

FROM *Harvard Divinity Bulletin*

For my mother

When they got out on land, they saw a charcoal fire there,
with fish on it, and bread. — John 21:9

I think I was dreaming of   the atmosphere of dreams,
or is it only certain dreams: low clouds almost
hide the water; you slip outside,   untie the boat, take
it out beyond the harbor; a world   that knows you
pulls you into just the knowing   it's composed of;
Then heading home, you wake   up dreaming
of the atmosphere in which   you still half-float

or think of the kind of   lullaby where a child
sets sail for a distant   kingdom; the singer sings
as if the boat will   return, as if sleeper and singer
meet in the dream;   the singer watches from
the dock; the boat,   the farthest dot on the sea;
I think I was sailing   to that kind of meeting

or take a lit room above   a dark city where
the composer slow-dances   with the soprano
past boats and bridges, stars   and rivers; only
love, says the song, is never   blind; any
two have a link unlike any   other; with eyes
closed, you would find   one another, past
sleep and death and   unbelief; he goes

to the kitchen; she   opens a book; I guess
we were moving   through levels of ourselves,
ways of thinking,   degrees of being; from love
to love, purposeless   surface to surfaceless purpose
into the dream behind   the dream: where
the pulse unties; the boat   pulls free; she steers

it out from the inlet to open   water, shifts the net to
the other side, sees a figure   onshore, jumps into
the water, swims toward   land like a young
apostle; I think I was   dreaming of finding the way
across the night to   the room through the door
where the one we   sailed away from
is making breakfast   on the shore.

NOAH FELDMAN

Orthodox Paradox

FROM *The New York Times Magazine*

A NUMBER OF YEARS AGO, I went to my tenth high-school reunion, in the backyard of the one classmate whose parents had a
pool. Lots of my classmates were there. Almost all were married,
and many already had kids. This was not as unusual as it might
seem, since I went to a yeshiva day school, and nearly everyone remained Orthodox. I brought my girlfriend. At the end, we all
crowded into a big group photo, shot by the school photographer,
who had taken our pictures from first grade through graduation.
When the alumni newsletter came around a few months later, I
happened to notice the photo. I looked, then looked again. My
girlfriend and I were nowhere to be found.

I didn't want to seem paranoid, especially in front of my girlfriend, to whom I was by that time engaged. So I called my oldest
school friend, who appeared in the photo, and asked for her explanation. "You're kidding, right?" she said. My fiancée was Korean
American. Her presence implied the prospect of something that
from the standpoint of Orthodox Jewish law could not be recognized: marriage to someone who was not Jewish. That hint was reason enough to keep us out.

Not long after, I bumped into the photographer, in synagogue,
on Yom Kippur. When I walked over to him, his pained expression
told me what I already knew. "It wasn't me," he said. I believed him.

Since then I have occasionally been in contact with the school's
alumni director, who has known me since I was a child. I say "in
contact," but that implies mutuality where none exists. What I really mean is that in the nine years since the reunion I have sent him
several updates about my life, for inclusion in the "Mazal Tov" sec-

tion of the newsletter. I sent him news of my marriage. When our son was born, I asked him to report that happy event. The most recent news was the birth of our daughter this winter. Nothing doing. None of my reports made it into print.

It would be more dramatic if I had been excommunicated like Baruch Spinoza, in a ceremony complete with black candles and a ban on all social contact, a rite whose solemnity reflected the seriousness of its consequences. But in the modern world, the formal communal ban is an anachronism. Many of my closest relationships are still with people who remain in the Orthodox fold. As best I know, no one, not even the rabbis at my old school who disapprove of my most important life decisions, would go so far as to refuse to shake my hand. What remains of the old technique of excommunication is simply nonrecognition in the school's formal publications, where my classmates' growing families and considerable accomplishments are joyfully celebrated.

The yeshiva where I studied considers itself modern Orthodox, not ultra-Orthodox. We followed a rigorous secular curriculum alongside traditional Talmud and Bible study. Our advanced Talmud and Hebrew classes were interspersed with advanced-placement courses in French literature and European political history, all skillfully coordinated to prime us for the Ivy League. To try to be at once a Lithuanian yeshiva and a New England prep school: that was the unspoken motto of the Maimonides School of Brookline, Massachusetts, where I studied for twelve years.

That aspiration is not without its difficulties. My own personal lesson in nonrecognition is just one small symptom of the challenge of reconciling the vastly disparate values of tradition and modernity — of Slobodka and St. Paul's. In premodern Europe, where the state gave the Jewish community the power to enforce its own rules of membership through coercive force, excommunication literally divested its victim of his legal personality, of his rights and standing in the community. The modern liberal state, though, neither polices nor delegates the power to police religious membership; that is now a social matter, not a legal one. Today a religious community that seeks to preserve its traditional structure must maintain its boundaries using whatever independent means it can muster — right down to the selective editing of alumni newsletters.

Despite my intimate understanding of the mindset that requires

such careful attention to who is in and who is out, I am still somehow taken by surprise each time I am confronted with my old
school's inability to treat me like any other graduate. I have tried in
my own imperfect way to live up to values that the school taught
me, expressing my respect and love for the wisdom of the tradition
while trying to reconcile Jewish faith with scholarship and engagement in the public sphere. As a result, I have not felt myself to have
rejected my upbringing, even when some others imagine me to
have done so by virtue of my marriage.

Some part of me still expects — against the judgment of experience — that the individual human beings who make up the institution and community where I spent so many years of my life will put
our long-standing friendships ahead of the imperative to define
boundaries. The school did educate me and influence me deeply.
What I learned there informs every part of my inner life. In the
sense of shared history and formation, I remain of the community
even while no longer fully in the community.

If this is dissonance, it is at least dissonance that the modern Orthodox should be able to understand: the desire to inhabit
multiple worlds simultaneously and to defy contradiction with coexistence. After all, the school's attempt to bring the ideals of
Orthodox Judaism into dialogue with a certain slice of late-twen-
tieth-century American life was in many ways fantastically rich and
productive. For those of us willing to accept a bit of both worlds, I
would say, it almost worked.

Since the birth of modern Orthodox Judaism in nineteenth-century Germany, a central goal of the movement has been to normalize the observance of traditional Jewish law — to make it possible
to follow all 613 biblical commandments assiduously while still par-
ticipating in the reality of the modern world. You must strive to be,
as a poet of the time put it, "a Jew in the home and a man in the
street." Even as we students of the Maimonides School spent half
of every school day immersed in what was unabashedly a medieval curriculum, our aim was to seem to outsiders — and to ourselves — like reasonable, mainstream people, not fanatics or cult
members.

This ambition is best exemplified today by Senator Joe Lieberman. His run for the vice presidency in 2000 put the "modern" in
modern Orthodox, demonstrating that an Orthodox Jewish candi-

date could be accepted by America at large as essentially a regular guy. (Some of this, of course, was simply the result of ignorance. As John Breaux, then a senator from Louisiana, so memorably put it with regard to Lieberman during the 2000 campaign, "I don't think American voters care where a man goes to church on Sunday.") Whatever concerns Lieberman's Jewish identity may have raised in the heartland seem to have been moderated, rather than stoked, by the fact that his chosen Jewish denomination was Orthodox — that he seemed to really and truly believe in something. His Orthodoxy elicited none of the half-whispered attacks that Mitt Romney's Mormonism prompted in the recent electoral cycle, none of the dark hints that it was, in some basic sense, weird.

Lieberman's overt normalcy really is remarkable. Though modern Orthodox Jews do not typically wear the long beards, side curls, and black, nostalgic Old-World garments favored by the ultra-Orthodox, the men do wear beneath their clothes a small fringed prayer shawl every bit as outré as the sacred undergarments worn by Mormons. Morning prayers are accompanied by the daily donning of phylacteries, which, though painless, resemble in their leather-strappy way the cinched cilice worn by the initiates of Opus Dei and so lasciviously depicted in *The Da Vinci Code*. Food restrictions are tight: a committed modern Orthodox observer would not drink wine with non-Jews and would have trouble finding anything to eat in a nonkosher restaurant other than undressed cold greens (assuming, of course, that the salad was prepared with a kosher knife).

The dietary laws of kashrut are designed to differentiate and distance the observant person from the rest of the world. When followed precisely, as I learned growing up, they accomplish exactly that. Every bite requires categorization into permitted and prohibited, milk or meat. To follow these laws, to analyze each ingredient in each food that comes into your purview, is to construct the world in terms of the rules borne by those who keep kosher. The category of the unkosher comes unconsciously to apply not only to foods that fall outside the rules but also to the people who eat that food — which is to say, almost everyone in the world, whether Jewish or not. You cannot easily break bread with them, but that is not all. You cannot, in a deeper sense, participate with them in the common human activity of restoring the body through food.

And yet the Maimonides School, by juxtaposing traditional and secular curricula, gave me a feeling of being connected to the broader world. Line by line we burrowed into the old texts in their original Hebrew and Aramaic. The poetry of the prophets sang in our ears. After years of this, I found I could recite the better part of the Hebrew Bible from memory. Among other things, this meant that when I encountered the writings of the Puritans who founded the Massachusetts Bay Colony, I felt immediate kinship. They read those same exact texts again and again — often in Hebrew — searching for clues about their own errand into the American wilderness.

In our literature classes we would glimpse Homer's wine-dark sea, then move to a different classroom and dive headlong into the sea of the Talmud. Here the pleasure of legal-intellectual argument had no stopping place, no end. A problem in Talmud study is never answered, it is only deepened. The Bible prohibits work on the Sabbath. But what is work? The rabbis began with thirty-nine categories, each of which called for its own classification into as many as thirty-nine further subcategories. Then came the problem of intention: what state of mind is required for "work" to have occurred? You might perform an act of work absent-mindedly, having forgotten that it was the Sabbath, or ignorantly, not knowing that action constituted work. You might perform an action with the goal of achieving some permissible outcome — but that result might inevitably entail some prohibited work's taking place. Learning this sort of reasoning as a child prepared me well, as it has countless others, for the ways of American law.

Beyond the complementarities of Jewish learning and secular knowledge, our remarkable teachers also offered access to a wider world. Even among the rabbis there was a smattering of PhDs and near-doctorates to give us a taste of a critical-academic approach to knowledge, not just a religious one. And the teachers of the secular subjects were fantastic. One of the best taught me eighth-grade English when he was barely out of college himself, before he became a poet, a professor, and an important queer theorist. Given Orthodoxy's condemnation of homosexuality, he must have made it onto the faculty through the sheer cluelessness of the administration. Lord only knows what teachers like him, visitors from the real world, made of our quirky ways. (In the book of poems about his teaching years, we students are decorously transformed into Italian Americans.)

In allowing us, intentionally or not, to see the world and the Torah as profoundly interconnected, the school was faithful to the doctrines of its eponym, the great medieval Jewish legalist and philosopher Moses Maimonides. Easily the most extraordinary figure in postbiblical Jewish history, Maimonides taught that accurate knowledge of the world — physical and metaphysical — was, alongside studying, obeying, and understanding the commandments, the one route to the ultimate *summum bonum* of knowing God. A life lived by these precepts can be both noble and beautiful, and I believe the best and wisest of my classmates and teachers come very close indeed to achieving it.

For many of us, the consilience of faith and modernity that sometimes appears within the reach of modern Orthodoxy is a tantalizing prospect. But it can be undermined by the fragile fault lines between the moral substructures of the two worldviews, which can widen into deep ruptures on important matters of life and love.

One time at Maimonides a local physician — a well-known figure in the community who later died tragically young — addressed a school assembly on the topic of the challenges that a modern Orthodox professional may face. The doctor addressed the Talmudic dictum that the saving of a life trumps the Sabbath. He explained that in its purest form, this principle applies only to the life of a Jew. The rabbis of the Talmud, however, were unprepared to allow the life of a non-Jew to be extinguished because of the no-work commandment, and so they ruled that the Sabbath could be violated to save the life of a non-Jew out of concern for maintaining peaceful relations between the Jewish and non-Jewish communities.

Depending on how you look at it, this ruling is either an example of outrageously particularist religious thinking, because in principle it values Jewish life more than non-Jewish life, or an instance of laudable universalism, because in practice it treats all lives equally. The physician quite reasonably opted for the latter explanation. And he added that he himself would never distinguish Jewish from non-Jewish patients: a human being was a human being.

This appealing sentiment did not go unchallenged. One of my teachers rose to suggest that the doctor's attitude was putting him in danger of violating the Torah. The teacher reported that he had himself heard from his own rabbi, a leading modern Orthodox Talmudist associated with Yeshiva University, that in violating the Sabbath to treat a non-Jew, intention was absolutely crucial. If you intended to save the patient's life so as to facilitate good relations between Jews and non-Jews, your actions were permissible. But if, to the contrary, you intended to save the patient out of universal morality, then you were in fact guilty of violating the Sabbath, because the motive for acting was not the motive on the basis of which the rabbis allowed the Sabbath violation to occur.

Later, in class, the teacher apologized to us students for what he said to the doctor. His comments, he said, were inappropriate — not because they were wrong-headed, but because non-Jews were present in the audience when he made them. The double standard of Jews and non-Jews, in other words, was for him truly irreducible: it was not just about noting that only Jewish lives merited violation of the Sabbath, but also about keeping the secret of why non-Jewish lives might be saved. To accept this version of the tradition would be to accept that the modern Orthodox project of engagement with the world could not proceed in good faith.

Nothing in the subculture of modern Orthodoxy, however, brought out the tensions between tradition and modernity more vividly for a young man than the question of our relationship to sex. Modernity, and maybe the state-mandated curriculum (I have never checked), called for a day of sex ed in seventh grade. I have the feeling that the content of our sex-ed class was the same as in those held in public schools in Massachusetts around the same time, with the notable exception that none of us would have occasion to deploy even the most minimal elements of the lesson plan in the foreseeable future. After the scientific bits of the lesson were over, the rabbi who was head of the school came in to the classroom to follow up with some indication of the Jewish-law perspective on these questions. It amounted to a blanket prohibition on the activities to which we had just been introduced. After marriage, some rather limited subset of them might become permissible — but only in the two weeks of the month that followed the two weeks of ritual abstinence occasioned by menstruation.

After that memorable disquisition, the question of relations between the sexes went essentially unmentioned again in our formal education. We were periodically admonished that boys and girls must not touch one another, even accidentally. Several of the most attractive girls were singled out for uncomfortable closed-door sessions in which they were instructed that their manner of dress, which already met the school's standards for modesty, must be made more modest still so as not to distract the males around them.

Whatever their disjuncture with American culture of the 1980s, the erotics of prohibition were real to us. Once, I was called on the carpet after an anonymous informant told the administration that I had been seen holding a girl's hand somewhere in Brookline one Sunday afternoon. The rabbi insinuated that if the girl and I were holding hands today, premarital sex must surely be right around the corner.

My Talmud teacher — the one who took the physician to task — handed me four tightly packed columns of closely reasoned rabbinic Hebrew, a *responsum* by the preeminent Orthodox decisor Rabbi Moshe Feinstein "in the matter of a young man whose heart lures him to enter into bonds of affection with a young woman not for purposes of marriage." Rabbi Feinstein's legal judgment with respect to romantic love among persons too young to marry was definitive. He prohibited it absolutely, in part on the ground that it would inevitably lead to nonprocreative seminal emissions, whether intentional or unintentional.

What Feinstein lacked in romantic imagination was more than made up for by Moses Maimonides, who understood the soul pretty well. He once characterized the true love of God as all-consuming — "as though one had contracted the sickness of love." Feinstein's opinion directed my attention to a passage in Maimonides' legal writings prohibiting various sorts of contact with women. The most evocative bit runs as follows: "Even to smell the perfume upon her is prohibited." I have never been able to escape the feeling that this is a covert love poem enmeshed in the fourteen-volume web of dos and don'ts that is Maimonides' Code of Law. Perfume has not smelled the same to me since.

I have spent much of my own professional life focusing on the predicament of faith communities that strive to be modern while simultaneously cleaving to tradition. Consider the situation of those Christian evangelicals who want to participate actively in mainstream politics yet are committed to a biblical literalism that leads them to oppose stem-cell research and advocate intelligent design in the classroom. To some secularists, the evangelicals' predicament seems absurd and their political movement dangerously anti-intellectual. As it happens, I favor financing stem-cell research and oppose the teaching of intelligent design or creationism as a scientific doctrine in public schools. Yet I nonetheless feel some sympathy for the evangelicals' sure-to-fail attempts to stand in the way of the progress of science, and not just because I respect their concern that we consider the ethical implications of our technological prowess.

Perhaps I feel sympathy because I can recall the agonies suffered by my head of school when he stopped by our biology class to discuss the problem of creation. Following the best modern Orthodox doctrine, he pointed out that Genesis could be understood allegorically, and that the length of a day might be numbered in billions of years considering that the sun, by which our time is reckoned, was not created until the fourth such "day." Not for him the embarrassing claim, heard sometimes among the ultra-Orthodox, that dinosaur fossils were embedded by God within the earth at the moment of creation in order to test our faith in biblical inerrancy. Natural selection was for him a scientific fact to be respected like the laws of physics — guided by God but effectuated through the workings of the natural order. Yet even he could not leave the classroom without a final caveat. "The truth is," he said, "despite what I have just told you, I still have a hard time believing that man could be descended from monkeys."

This same grappling with tension — and the same failure to resolve it perfectly — can be found among the many Muslims who embrace both basic liberal democratic values and orthodox Islamic faith. The literature of democratic Islam, like that of modern Orthodox Judaism, may be read as an embodiment of dialectical struggle, the unwillingness to ignore contemporary reality in constant interplay with the weight of tradition taken by them as authentic and divinely inspired. The imams I have met over the years seem, on the whole, no less sincere than the rabbis who taught me. Their commitment to their faith and to the legal tradition that comes with it seems just as heartfelt. Liberal Muslims may even have their own Joe Lieberman in the Minnesota congressman Keith Ellison, the first Muslim elected to the U.S. Congress.

The themes of difference and reconciliation that have preoccupied so much of my own thinking are nowhere more stark than in trying to make sense of the problem of marriage — which is also, for me, the most personal aspect of coming to terms with modern Orthodoxy. Although Jews of many denominations are uncomfortable with marriage between Jews and people of other religions, modern Orthodox condemnation is especially definitive.

The reason for the resistance to such marriages derives from Jewish law but also from the challenge of defining the borders of the modern Orthodox community in the liberal modern state. Ultra-Orthodox Judaism addresses the boundary problem with methods like exclusionary group living and deciding business disputes through privately constituted Jewish-law tribunals. For modern Orthodox Jews, who embrace citizenship and participate in the larger political community, the relationship to the liberal state is more ambivalent. The solution adopted has been to insist on the coherence of the religious community as a social community, not a political community. It is defined not so much by what people believe or say they believe (it is much safer not to ask) as by what they do.

Marriage is the most obvious public practice about which information is readily available. When combined with the traditional Jewish concern for continuity and self-preservation — itself only intensified by the memory of the Holocaust — marriage becomes the sine qua non of social membership in the modern Orthodox community. Marrying a Jewish but actively nonobservant spouse would in most cases make continued belonging difficult. Gay Orthodox Jews find themselves marginalized not only because of their forbidden sexual orientation but also because within the tradition they cannot marry the partners whom they might otherwise choose. For those who choose to marry spouses of another faith, maintaining membership would become all but impossible.

In a few cases, modern Orthodoxy's line-drawing has been implicated in some truly horrifying events. Yigal Amir, the assassin of Yitzhak Rabin, was a modern Orthodox Jew who believed that Rabin's peace efforts put him into the Talmudic category of one who may be freely executed because he is in the act of killing Jews. In 1994, Dr. Baruch Goldstein massacred twenty-nine worshipers in the mosque atop the Tomb of the Patriarchs in Hebron. An American-born physician, Goldstein attended a prominent mod-

ern Orthodox Jewish day school in Brooklyn. (In a classic modern
Orthodox twist, the same distinguished school has also produced
two Nobel Prize winners.)

Because of the proximity of Goldstein's background and mine,
the details of his reasoning have haunted me. Goldstein committed
his terrorist act on Purim, the holiday commemorating the victory
of the Jews over Haman, traditionally said to be a descendant of the
Amalekites. The previous Sabbath, he sat in synagogue and heard
the special additional Torah portion for the day, which includes
the famous injunction in the Book of Deuteronomy to remember
what the Amalekites did to the Israelites on their way out of Egypt
and to erase the memory of Amalek from beneath the heavens.

This commandment was followed by a further reading from the
Book of Samuel. It details the first intentional and explicit genocide depicted in the Western canon: God's directive to King Saul to
kill every living Amalekite — man, woman, and child, and even the
sheep and cattle. Saul fell short. He left the Amalekite king alive
and spared the sheep. As a punishment for the incompleteness of
the slaughter, God took the kingdom from him and his heirs and
gave it to David. I can remember this portion verbatim. That Saturday, like Goldstein, I was in synagogue, too.

Of course, as a matter of Jewish law, the literal force of the biblical command of genocide does not apply today. The rabbis of the
Talmud, in another of their universalizing legal rulings, held that
because of the Assyrian king Sennacherib's policy of population
movement at the time of the First Temple, it was no longer possible
to ascertain who was by descent an Amalekite. But as a schoolboy I
was taught that the story of Amalek was about not just historical oc-
currence but cyclical recurrence: "In every generation, they rise up
against us to destroy us, but the Holy One, blessed be He, saves us
from their hands." The Jews' enemies today are the Amalekites
of old. The inquisitors, the Cossacks — Amalekites. Hitler was an
Amalekite, too.

To Goldstein, the Palestinians were Amalekites. Like a Puritan
seeking the contemporary type of the biblical archetype, he applied Deuteronomy and Samuel to the world before him. Commanded to settle the land, he settled it. Commanded to slaughter
the Amalekites without mercy or compassion, he slew them. Goldstein could see difference as well as similarity. According to one

newspaper account, when he was serving in the Israeli military, he refused to treat non-Jewish patients. And his actions were not met by universal condemnation: his gravestone describes him as a saint and a martyr of the Jewish people, "Clean of hands and pure of heart."

It would be a mistake to blame messianic modern Orthodoxy for ultranationalist terror. But when the evil comes from within your own midst, the soul-searching needs to be especially intense. After the Hebron massacre, my own teacher, the late Israeli scholar and poet Ezra Fleischer — himself a paragon of modern Orthodox commitment — said that the innocent blood of the Palestinian worshipers dripped through the stones and formed tears in the eyes of the patriarchs buried below.

Recently I saw my oldest school friend again and, recalling the tale of the reunion photograph, we shared a laugh over my continuing status as persona non grata. She remarked that she had never even considered sending in her news to our alumni newsletter. "But why not?" I asked. Her answer was illuminating. As someone who never took steps that would have led to her public exclusion, she felt that the school and the community of which it was a part always sought to claim her — a situation that had its own costs for her sense of autonomy.

For me, having exercised my choices differently, there is no such risk. With no danger of feeling owned, I haven't lost the wish to be treated like any other old member. From the standpoint of the religious community, of course, the preservation of collective mores requires sanctioning someone who chooses a different way of living. But I still have my own inward sense of unalienated connection to my past. In synagogue on Purim with my children reading the Book of Esther, the beloved ancient phrases give me a sense of joy that not even Baruch Goldstein can completely take away.

It is more than a little strange, feeling fully engaged with a way of seeing the world but also, at the same time, feeling so far from it. I was discussing it just the other day with my best friend — who, naturally, went to Maimonides, too. The topic was whether we would be the same people, in essence, had we remained completely within the bosom of modern Orthodoxy. He didn't think so. Our life choices are constitutive of who we are, and so different life choices would have made us into different people — not unrecognizably different, but palpably, measurably so.

I accepted his point as true — but for some reason I resisted the conclusion. Couldn't the contradictory world from which we sprang be just as rich and productive as the contradictory life we actually live? Would it really, truly, have made all that much difference? Isn't everyone's life a mass of contradictions? My best friend just laughed.

NATALIE GOLDBERG

Meeting the Chinese in St. Paul

FROM *Shambhala Sun*

As a soto zen student I had successfully steered clear of
koans for almost my full twenty-five years of practice. They were
considered more a part of the fierce Rinzai Zen training and
seemed enigmatic and scary. How would I know what the sound of
one hand clapping was, as one famous koan asked. Koans were
meant to be illogical and stump the student, to kick her into another way of thinking — or not thinking — so that she could have
insight into the nature of the universe.

My old Soto teacher said, "Soto is more like the not-so-bright,
kindly elder uncle." He admired Rinzai and indicated it was for
sharper types.

Despite my reservations, in 1998 I moved up to St. Paul, Minnesota, for two months to dive into koans. I would study of *The Book of
Serenity,* an ancient Chinese Zen text of one hundred koans (or
cases) depicting situations and dialogues between teacher and student, teacher and teacher, student and student.

Driving in the car through Colorado, Nebraska, Iowa, crossing
one state border after another, I repeated to myself, "Yes, I can
do it."

My old friend Phil Willkie and I were going to trade homes for
this mid-October through mid-December period. We didn't know
who was getting the better deal. I would live in his three-bedroom,
fourth-floor walkup flat on MacKuben in St. Paul, and he would inhabit my solar beer-can-and-tire house on the mesa six miles outside of Taos.

Phil's apartment was replete with photos of his family, including one of his grandfather Wendell Willkie, the 1940 contender for the presidency against FDR, and another of an aunt sitting in the back seat of a convertible with Dwight Eisenhower. Best of all, a former boyfriend of Phil's lived in the back bedroom. He too was studying Zen at the time. At night we'd often share a simple dinner of steamed broccoli and rice. He was a modest fellow, saving all the plastic yogurt containers and calling them his fine Tupperware collection. We had known each other years before, when he and Phil visited me in the Southwest.

During the day, I had little to do but wrestle with these Chinese ancestors who embodied the koans. I wanted to understand what was meant by their interchanges.

Luoshan runs into Yantou and asks: "When arising and vanishing go on unceasingly, what then?"

A perfectly good question, if you were thinking about the nature of the universe. We often ask, "What should I do with my life?" Usually it's asked in despair: I'm lost. Help me. We want a concrete answer: become a dentist and everything will be all right. But there is a deeper cry in the question. How should I live knowing the world is a confusing place?

First, Luoshan asked Shishuang his question: "When arising and vanishing go on unceasingly, what then?"

Shishuang replied: "You must be cold ashes, a dead tree, one thought for ten thousand years, box and lid joining, pure and spotlessly clear."

Luoshan didn't get it. Too complicated an answer. He only became more confused trying to figure it out. He went seeking Yantou and asked his question again: "When arising and vanishing go on unceasingly, what then?"

Yantou shouted and said, "Whose arising and vanishing is it?"

Maybe the shout would have been enough. Imagine that you're an earnest student going from teacher to teacher, saying, "Please clarify this," and one of the renowned, respected ones screams in your face. Maybe then you'd step back and see yourself. But Yantou offers more than his shout. He asks, Exactly who are you that is experiencing this coming and going? This time Luoshan is enfolded into his own question. Engulfed in radical nonseparation, he wakes up.

I understood what was happening to Luoshan. But my under-standing wasn't good enough. The koan wouldn't come alive until I demonstrated that understanding. There is an old adage in writ-ing: don't tell, but show. I could tell you what happened in the koan, but to show it, I had to become Luoshan and exhibit his — and my — insight. That's how I would pay true homage to the lin-eage of old Chinese practitioners I'd come to love, by making their work and effort alive and vital in me right now. To stay Natalie Goldberg from Brooklyn, with her usual collection of needs and desires, pains and complaints, wouldn't work. Becoming some idea of Chinese — or Japanese — wouldn't work either. These koans might have come through a particular culture but what they are aiming at is the core of human nature. Who are we really? What is this life about? I had to learn to become a fool, a barbarian, the moon, a lamppost, a fallen leaf — any angle necessary to answer the questions posed by these ancient fellows. But I couldn't get stuck, not even as a single, perfect plum blossom. My mind had to become greased in its skull, a pearl rolling in a silver bowl. No set-tling; no abiding; no fixed residence. The koan mind does not dwell; instead it is alive — and empty — like a dust mote in a ray of sun. In other words, I had to let go and to see fresh, like a blind donkey. Tell me, how can something sightless see?

I paced St. Paul's streets, past Scott Fitzgerald's old home on Sum-mit, the vast houses on Crocus Hill, the River Gallery, and the Har-vest Bread Bakery. I crossed the bridge on the mighty Mississippi, reveling in the long, slow display of burned leaves that marked the coming of the dark season. I wanted to know who these Chinese brothers — and the occasional Chinese sister, such as Iron-Grinder Lui, the woman of Taishan, and the teacake seller — were. I was used to studying Western literature, full of elaborate stories, sub-plots, metaphor, and flashbacks. These Chinese tales were so di-gested that only a few lines were enough.

As we were leaning over our supper plates one evening, Phil's old boyfriend from the backroom beseeched me, "So, Aunt Na-talie, tell me a bedtime koan before we drop off." It was his second year of practice, and his early enthusiasm met my old determina-tion.

I lunged into the koan about Luoshan. I described the rough

road, the jagged mountain where I imagined the interchange had taken place. I fleshed out the two men's ragged dress, their recent meal — "For sure, it was not hot dogs on a bun." I wanted to plant a deep impression in my faux nephew's mind so he would never forget these crazy, wild ancestors. I made faces, with lips turned out, eyes raised to the ceiling; I howled, groaned, drooled, clawed at Yantou. I demanded a response to rising and vanishing. We both went to bed tired and giddy that night to wake at 4:30 A.M. and drive the mile and a half to the zendo.

Later that morning I unfolded on my bedroom floor a glossy map of the whole Zen lineage from A.D. 532 to 1260 and knelt over it, running my finger from Matsu to Pai-Chang to Kuei-shan. These were all characters in *The Book of Serenity.* I relished the link between teacher and student and how the student of the next generation became the teacher in the next. Below all the dates and Chinese names was a drawing of an immense fork-tongued dragon sprouting out of the clouds. He was a feral force in the orderly map of connections.

The original *Book of Serenity* was lost after it was first compiled by Wansong in northern China, but it was reconstructed by Wansong at the urging of one of his disciples, Yelu Chucai, who was a statesman. He was one of a group of Chinese desperate to save their provinces from destruction by the ravaging army of Genghis Khan, and they wanted to study the text as a way to illuminate their minds and come up with a fresh solution. Through their work they eventually softened the harshness of the Mongol ruler.

Studying these cases brings one more fully and deeply into the structures that underlie conventional life. The cases were not created to help people disappear into a mist high on a mountain. The terrible truth, which is rarely mentioned, is that meditation doesn't directly lead us to some vaporous, glazed-eyed peace. It drops us right into the personal meat of human suffering. No distant, abstract idea of distress; instead we get to taste the bitter pain between our own twin eyes. With practice we settle right down into the barbed-wire nest, and this changes us. Working with koans creates a bigger heart, a tender, closer existence, a deeper seeing.

Near the end of November, I turned to page 108, case number 25. "Rhinoceros Fan" was the title. My mind froze. That's my usual tactic: when anything new comes along, I brake, clutch, and stop dead. What do I know about a rhinoceros? Aren't they African? I later found out that China did have rhinos, and that their horns were carved into fans.

What stumped me more was the juxtaposition of these two words: "rhinoceros," that huge, forceful animal, probably as close to a dinosaur as we are going to find now on earth, placed beside the word "fan," something light, used to create a breeze, a stirring of wind to refresh court ladies or southern belles.

I moved on from the title to the actual case:

One day Yanguan called to his attendant, "Bring me the rhinoceros fan."
The attendant said, "The fan is broken."
Yanguan said, "If the fan is broken, then bring me back the rhinoceros!"
The attendant had no reply.
Zifu drew a circle and wrote the word "rhino" inside it.

Yanguan was an illustrious disciple of Matsu. After his teacher's death, he had wandered until he became the abbot of Fayao Temple. This was a monastery situation. The attendant was not paid staff but was Yanguan's student. As an attendant, the student had the great opportunity of extra time with his teacher. In this particular story, the student is anonymous. All the better; he could be any of us — John or Sue or Sally, you or me.

I was not sure who Zifu was who appears at the end. I would look him up later. But for now I'd stay with the teacher-and-student interaction.

More than likely, their interchange takes place in a quiet moment when Yanguan has a little time to put his attention on this monk. He's going to test him, poke him: are you there? Yanguan and the attendant are in kinship. They had both probably lived in the monastery for many years, but Yanguan couldn't turn around to the attendant and say something simple like "Do you love me?" or "Are you happy here?" Instead, there is decorum. One person is made the attendant, the other the Zen master. Of course, one has been practicing longer than the other. Out of time we create hierarchy, levels, positions. In the large space of this true book, we eventually let go of these criteria, but we also play along.

So Yanguan asks for a fan. The fan is the excuse for an exchange, though it could also have been one of those unbearable hot summer days. Bring me some relief. Where's the fan?

The attendant replies that the fan is broken.

He can't find another one? I'm thinking. What was going on here?

That evening after I read this case I couldn't sleep. I tossed and turned.

The night became a deep and endless thing. My mind wandered over much terrain: a particular apple orchard, a young boy who died. I remembered an old friendship I once had. This line ran through my head: the relationship is broken.

Broken! I sat up in bed. That is the word the attendant used. I jumped up, ran to the shelf, and opened the book. I took a leap: the attendant was saying he himself was broken, even if he referred to a fan. He was the fan.

But that doesn't stop Yanguan, his teacher. Hell, if the fan — the product — was shattered, then bring back the whole rhinoceros. What a stunning concept! If the paper is torn, bring the enormous tree into the living room.

Yanguan was asking this of his student (and of us): take a tremendous step — not forward but backward — into your essential nature. Manifest your original face. Don't get stuck on something broken — a heart, a wish. Become the rhinoceros — reveal your full self, go to the source, nothing hidden.

And this is what I loved the most: "The attendant had no reply." What do we do when a rhino is charging us, when a bear of a teacher is storming us? We run for our lives. In no other case that I had studied so far was there such an abrupt stop. No action, nothing. The attendant had already given his all when he said the fan was broken, when he revealed he was not whole.

It's a naked thing to show we are fractured, that we do not have it all together. Broken all the way through to the bottom. What freedom that is, to be what we are in the moment, even if it's unacceptable. Then we are already the rhinoceros.

Think about it: we are always doing a dance — I'm good, I'm bad, I'm this, I'm that. Rather than the truth: I don't know who I am. Instead, we scurry to figure it out. We write another book, buy another blouse, exhaust ourselves. Imagine the freedom to let it be, this not knowing. How vulnerable. This is why I love the attendant. He said who he was — a broken man, a shattered fan derived from the concentrated point of a fierce beast. When his teacher asked for more, the monk didn't do a jig to win him over. There was no more. Usually we will do anything to cover up a reality so naked.

I know the relief, and ensuing shame or terror, of making that kind of simple statement. When I was in the middle of a divorce, I visited my parents in Florida. My father was on the first day of a new diet. He was looking forward to dinner. We were going out to a steak house for the early-bird special. My father made fun of my huarache sandals when I stepped out of the bedroom, ready to go.

"What are those, horse hooves?"

I was touchy and tired of his putdowns. I twirled around and marched back into the bedroom. "I'm leaving," I screamed. I threw clothes into a suitcase and charged out the front door and onto the nearby turnpike. I was walking on the divider line, headed for the airport fifteen miles away. A car pulled up beside me and drove the speed of my walking pace. I looked straight ahead.

"Nat." My father rolled down his window.

I burst out crying.

"Wait, stay here. I'll go get your mother. Do you promise not to move?"

I nodded, leaning against the guardrail.

Moments later my parents pulled up together. My mother ran out of the car. "Natli, what's the matter?"

I uttered three words: "I am lost." I had no energy for a cover-up. Those words came from my core.

Everything halted. My mother stood with her hands at her sides. My father looked straight ahead, his face frozen, his arm hanging over the door of the car.

Nothing was to be done. It was a huge, unbearable opening between us. My parents became embarrassed. So did I. We'd never been so naked with each other.

After a long, excruciating time my father's head turned. "Now can we go eat? I'm starving."

The monk did not have this distraction. No restaurant for him. My experience was that the monk stood his ground for all time. He did not reply after he showed his naked face. But like the rabbis making commentary on the Torah, later Zen teachers responded to koans, and in this case disagreed over the monk's state of mind. Maybe the attendant in his silence had emptied his depths, so that the rhinoceros, the source, stood there radiantly, painfully alive in his no reply. Or maybe he was just dumbfounded and petrified, thinking, *What should I do now in front of my teacher?*

In the next sentence, in steps Zifu. He draws a circle and writes the word "rhino" inside it. I imagine that he picked up a nearby stick and drew the circle in the dirt or in the air and then wrote the Chinese character boldly in the center.

I found out that Zifu was a Zen master who lived at least a hundred years after the interchange between Yanguan and the monk. These stories, passed on generation to generation, were kept splendidly alive. Sitting in his monastery, Zifu hears the situation and plunges in. Zifu's dust circle is a stamp of approval. His response radiates back through a century and screams forward to us now.

Attendant, I see you, Zifu calls out.

Yes, Zifu is saying, this exchange between student and teacher is complete. Nothing is left out. Even if the attendant was immobilized rather than inexpressively present, Zifu catches the whole thing and brings it to completion, enlightening the attendant, the rhino, the teacher, folding us all into the great circle.

I spent the autumn of my fiftieth year roaming through these Chinese minds. I began to see everything as a koan. The news announced that bread burned in someone's kitchen in Blue Earth and the house went down in flames. Everything now was related. The house, the bread, the town in southern Minnesota presented a koan. How could I step into those flames and burn too? Life became a revolving story. No matter from what age or country, it met me where I was.

I watched my friend Wendy, an old practitioner and the gardener for twenty years at Green Gulch, a Zen farm outside of San Francisco, answer questions after a reading from her forthcoming book, *Gardening at the Dragon's Gate.*

"How big is your garden?" one of my students queried.

Wendy was struck silent for a full minute. The audience fidgeted in their seats. I realized what was happening.

"Wendy." I leaned over. "This is not a koan — she's not challenging your whole being. She just wants to know in feet the area you garden."

Wendy snapped back. "Many feet are cultivated." Then she went on to speak of once putting a dead deer in the compost heap and a month later nothing was left but hooves and bones.

In *The Book of Serenity*, Guishan asks Yangshan where he comes from, and Yangshan replies, The fields. There are many fields to come from — playing fields, plowing fields, the upper or lower field, or the dharma field spread out before us.

Soon after I returned home to Taos, I had a week of teaching with my good friend Rob Wilder. He is sharp and has a generous heart. Little goes by him. We sat together at dinner the second night of the workshop. I was eager to share where I had been. I told him about koans, then I told him about the last one I worked on. I laid out the case, how I entered it, what I understood. He was listening intently, the way only a writer can from years of developing an attunement to story and sound. He nodded often. I felt encouraged.

I went to bed that night happy. I had been afraid, coming home from St. Paul, that no one would understand where I had been.

The next morning was a silent breakfast. Almost everyone had already cleared out of the dining room when Rob sidled up next to me. "Nat," he said in a low voice, "I was thinking how amazing it is. We can know each other so well. We can be such good friends, and I had no idea what you were talking about last night."

My head snapped back. What's going on here? The fan of our communication was fractured?

A student walked in and we shut up.

I gulped down some water to swallow the ball of cornflakes that sat in my mouth. I felt almost lonely, walked to the brink of isolation. Rob was on one side of the old adobe dining room and I on another. Suddenly something in front of my eyes shattered. The rhino emerged glistening. I abruptly started to laugh, big eruptions through my entire body. This was one whole world. Rob Wilder was my relation. We had plunged right into the lineage together. No one left out. The water glass, the spoon, the flowers in the vase, all glimmered and shook. Who was laughing? Hours melted in my hand. The walls of the building dissolved. Everyone and no one lifted the spoon to take the next bite of cereal.

DAVID BRENDAN HOPES

Carol of the Infuriated Hour

FROM *Image*

The stab to the heart that is such music,
the light beyond brightness that is such sight —
For the sake of this season in the stories
I will cease my wars with God tonight.

I will choose, with open eye, the talking beasts,
the white-in-the-snowdrift Christmas rose,
the legends of wandering a bitter way,
high hill and desert, for what? — God knows.

Someone turned the rose-tree to a cross
and the angels' thunder into penitential song:
such is the ancient sorrow: they who stole
the stories have the stories wrong.

What saved the old ones in the tangled land,
amid assorted enemies, is what saves still:
to see the white stag in the tangled wood,
the Cross and the Rose on the same snow hill

We are saved in our infuriated hour —
by cunning blackened, by omnipotence beguiled —
by the newborn cosmos crooked upon our arm,
motherly murmuring to him, *child, my child.*

WALTER ISAACSON

Einstein & Faith

FROM *Time*

HE WAS SLOW IN learning how to talk. "My parents were so worried," he later recalled, "that they consulted a doctor." Even after he had begun using words, sometime after the age of two, he developed a quirk that prompted the family maid to dub him "*der Depperte*," the dopey one. Whenever he had something to say, he would try it out on himself, whispering it softly until it sounded good enough to pronounce aloud. "Every sentence he uttered," his worshipful younger sister recalled, "no matter how routine, he repeated to himself softly, moving his lips." It was all very worrying, she said. "He had such difficulty with language that those around him feared he would never learn."

His slow development was combined with a cheeky rebelliousness toward authority, which led one schoolmaster to send him packing and another to declare that he would never amount to much. These traits made Albert Einstein the patron saint of distracted school kids everywhere. But they also helped make him, or so he later surmised, the most creative scientific genius of modern times.

His cocky contempt for authority led him to question received wisdom in ways that well-trained acolytes in the academy never contemplated. And as for his slow verbal development, he thought that it allowed him to observe with wonder the everyday phenomena that others took for granted. Instead of puzzling over mysterious things, he puzzled over the commonplace. "When I ask myself how it happened that I in particular discovered the relativity theory, it seemed to lie in the following circumstance," Einstein once explained. "The ordinary adult never bothers his head about the problems of space and time. These are things he has thought of as a child. But I developed so slowly that I began to wonder about space and time only when I was already grown up. Consequently, I probed more deeply into the problem than an ordinary child would have."

It may seem logical, in retrospect, that a combination of awe and rebellion made Einstein exceptional as a scientist. But what is less well known is that those two traits also combined to shape his spiritual journey and determine the nature of his faith. The rebellion part comes in at the beginning of his life: he rejected at first his parents' secularism and later the concepts of religious ritual and of a personal God who intercedes in the daily workings of the world. But the awe part comes in his fifties when he settled into a deism based on what he called the "spirit manifest in the laws of the universe" and a sincere belief in a "God who reveals Himself in the harmony of all that exists."

Einstein was descended, on both parents' sides, from Jewish tradesmen and peddlers who had, for at least two centuries, made modest livings in the rural villages of Swabia in southwestern Germany. With each generation they had become increasingly assimilated into the German culture they loved — or so they thought. Although Jewish by cultural designation and kindred instinct, they had little interest in the religion itself.

In his later years, Einstein would tell an old joke about an agnostic uncle who was the only member of his family who went to synagogue. When asked why he did so, the uncle would respond, "Ah, but you never know." Einstein's parents, on the other hand, were "entirely irreligious." They did not keep kosher or attend synagogue, and his father, Hermann, referred to Jewish rituals as "ancient superstitions," according to a relative.

Consequently, when Albert turned six and had to go to school, his parents did not care that there was no Jewish one near their home. Instead he went to the large Catholic school in their neighborhood. As the only Jew among the seventy students in his class, he took the standard course in Catholic religion and ended up enjoying it immensely.

Despite his parents' secularism, or perhaps because of it, Einstein rather suddenly developed a passionate zeal for Judaism. "He was so fervent in his feelings that, on his own, he observed Jewish religious strictures in every detail," his sister recalled. He ate no pork, kept kosher, and obeyed the strictures of the Sabbath. He even composed his own hymns, which he sang to himself as he walked home from school.

Einstein's greatest intellectual stimulation came from a poor student who dined with his family once a week. It was an old Jewish custom to take in a needy religious scholar to share the Sabbath meal; the Einsteins modified the tradition by hosting instead a medical student on Thursdays. His name was Max Talmud, and he began his weekly visits when he was twenty-one and Einstein was ten.

Talmud brought Einstein science books, including a popular illustrated series called *People's Books on Natural Science*, "a work which I read with breathless attention," said Einstein. The twenty-one volumes were written by Aaron Bernstein, who stressed the interrelations between biology and physics, and reported in great detail the experiments being done at the time, especially in Germany.

Talmud also helped Einstein explore the wonders of mathematics by giving him a textbook on geometry two years before he was scheduled to learn that subject in school. When Talmud arrived each Thursday, Einstein delighted in showing him the problems he had solved that week. Initially, Talmud was able to help him, but he was soon surpassed by his pupil. "After a short time, a few months, he had worked through the whole book," Talmud recalled. "Soon the flight of his mathematical genius was so high that I could no longer follow."

Einstein's exposure to science and math produced a sudden transformation at age twelve, just as he would have been readying for a bar mitzvah. He suddenly gave up Judaism. That decision does not appear to have been drawn from Bernstein's books because the author made clear he saw no contradiction between science and religion. As he put it, "The religious inclination lies in the dim consciousness that dwells in humans that all nature, including the humans in it, is in no way an accidental game, but a work of lawfulness that there is a fundamental cause of all existence."

Einstein would later come close to these sentiments. But at the time, his leap away from faith was a radical one. "Through the reading of popular scientific books, I soon reached the conviction that much in the stories of the Bible could not be true. The consequence was a positively fanatic orgy of freethinking coupled with the impression that youth is intentionally being deceived by the state through lies; it was a crushing impression."

Einstein did, however, retain from his childhood religious phase a profound faith in, and reverence for, the harmony and beauty of what he called the mind of God as it was expressed in the creation of the universe and its laws. Around the time he turned fifty, he began to articulate more clearly — in various essays, interviews, and letters — his deepening appreciation of his belief in God, although a rather impersonal version of one. One particular evening in 1929, the year he turned fifty, captures Einstein's middle-age deistic faith. He and his wife were at a dinner party in Berlin when a guest expressed a belief in astrology. Einstein ridiculed the notion as pure superstition. Another guest stepped in and similarly disparaged religion. Belief in God, he insisted, was likewise a superstition.

At this point the host tried to silence him by invoking the fact that even Einstein harbored religious beliefs. "It isn't possible!" the skeptical guest said, turning to Einstein to ask if he was, in fact, religious. "Yes, you can call it that," Einstein replied calmly. "Try and penetrate with our limited means the secrets of nature and you will find that, behind all the discernible laws and connections, there remains something subtle, intangible, and inexplicable. Veneration for this force beyond anything that we can comprehend is my religion. To that extent I am, in fact, religious."

Shortly after his fiftieth birthday, Einstein also gave a remarkable interview in which he was more revealing than he had ever been about his religious sensibility. It was with George Sylvester Viereck, who had been born in Germany, moved to America as a child, and then spent his life writing gaudily erotic poetry, interviewing great men, and expressing his complex love for his fatherland. Einstein assumed Viereck was Jewish. In fact, Viereck proudly traced his lineage to the family of the kaiser, and he would later become a Nazi sympathizer who was jailed in America during World War II for being a German propagandist.

Viereck began by asking Einstein whether he considered himself a German or a Jew. "It's possible to be both," replied Einstein. "Nationalism is an infantile disease, the measles of mankind."

Should Jews try to assimilate? "We Jews have been too eager to sacrifice our idiosyncrasies in order to conform."

To what extent are you influenced by Christianity? "As a child I received instruction both in the Bible and in the Talmud. I am a Jew, but I am enthralled by the luminous figure of the Nazarene."

You accept the historical existence of Jesus? "Unquestionably! No one can read the Gospels without feeling the actual presence of Jesus. His personality pulsates in every word. No myth is filled with such life."

Do you believe in God? "I'm not an atheist. I don't think I can call myself a pantheist. The problem involved is too vast for our limited minds. We are in the position of a little child entering a huge library filled with books in many languages. The child knows someone must have written those books. It does not know how. It does not understand the languages in which they are written. The child dimly suspects a mysterious order in the arrangement of the books but doesn't know what it is. That, it seems to me, is the attitude of even the most intelligent human being toward God. We see the universe marvelously arranged and obeying certain laws but only dimly understand these laws."

Is this a Jewish concept of God? "I am a determinist. I do not believe in free will. Jews believe in free will. They believe that man shapes his own life. I reject that doctrine. In that respect I am not a Jew."

Is this Spinoza's God? "I am fascinated by Spinoza's pantheism, but I admire even more his contribution to modern thought because he is the first philosopher to deal with the soul and body as one, and not two separate things."

Do you believe in immortality? "No. And one life is enough for me."

Einstein tried to express these feelings clearly, both for himself and for all of those who wanted a simple answer from him about his faith. So in the summer of 1930, amid his sailing and ruminations in Caputh, he composed a credo, "What I Believe," that he recorded for a human-rights group and later published. It concluded with an explanation of what he meant when he called himself religious: "The most beautiful emotion we can experience is the mysterious. It is the fundamental emotion that stands at the cradle of all true art and science. He to whom this emotion is a stranger, who can no longer wonder and stand rapt in awe, is as good as dead, a snuffed-out candle. To sense that behind anything that can be experienced there is something that our minds cannot grasp, whose beauty and sublimity reaches us only indirectly: this is religiousness. In this sense, and in this sense only, I am a devoutly religious man."

People found the piece evocative, and it was reprinted repeatedly in a variety of translations. But not surprisingly, it did not satisfy those who wanted a simple answer to the question of whether or not he believed in God. "The outcome of this doubt and befogged speculation about time and space is a cloak beneath which hides the ghastly apparition of atheism," Boston's Cardinal William Henry O'Connell said. This public blast from a cardinal prompted the noted Orthodox Jewish leader in New York Rabbi Herbert S. Goldstein to send a very direct telegram: "Do you believe in God? Stop. Answer paid. Fifty words." Einstein used only about half his allotted number of words. It became the most famous version of an answer he gave often: "I believe in Spinoza's God, who reveals himself in the lawful harmony of all that exists, but not in a God who concerns himself with the fate and the doings of mankind."

Some religious Jews reacted by pointing out that Spinoza had been excommunicated from Amsterdam's Jewish community for holding these beliefs, and that he had also been condemned by the Catholic Church. "Cardinal O'Connell would have done well had he not attacked the Einstein theory," said one Bronx rabbi. "Einstein would have done better had he not proclaimed his nonbelief in a God who is concerned with fates and actions of individuals. Both have handed down dicta outside their jurisdiction."

But throughout his life, Einstein was consistent in rejecting the charge that he was an atheist. "There are people who say there is no God," he told a friend. "But what makes me really angry is that they quote me for support of such views." And unlike Sigmund Freud or Bertrand Russell or George Bernard Shaw, Einstein never felt the urge to denigrate those who believed in God; instead, he tended to denigrate atheists. "What separates me from most so-called atheists is a feeling of utter humility toward the unattainable secrets of the harmony of the cosmos," he explained.

In fact, Einstein tended to be more critical of debunkers, who seemed to lack humility or a sense of awe, than of the faithful. "The fanatical atheists," he wrote in a letter, "are like slaves who are still feeling the weight of their chains which they have thrown off after hard struggle. They are creatures who — in their grudge against traditional religion as the 'opium of the masses' — cannot hear the music of the spheres."

Einstein later explained his view of the relationship between science and religion at a conference at the Union Theological Seminary in New York. The realm of science, he said, was to ascertain what was the case, but not evaluate human thoughts and actions about what should be the case. Religion had the reverse mandate. Yet the endeavors worked together at times. "Science can be created only by those who are thoroughly imbued with the aspiration toward truth and understanding," he said. "This source of feeling, however, springs from the sphere of religion." The talk got front-page news coverage, and his pithy conclusion became famous. "The situation may be expressed by an image: science without religion is lame, religion without science is blind."

But there was one religious concept, Einstein went on to say, that science could not accept: a deity who could meddle at whim in the events of his creation. "The main source of the present-day conflicts between the spheres of religion and of science lies in this concept of a personal God," he argued. Scientists aim to uncover the immutable laws that govern reality, and in doing so they must reject the notion that divine will, or for that matter human will, plays a role that would violate this cosmic causality.

His belief in causal determinism was incompatible with the concept of human free will. Jewish as well as Christian theologians have generally believed that people are responsible for their actions. They are even free to choose, as happens in the Bible, to disobey God's commandments, despite the fact that this seems to conflict with a belief that God is all knowing and all powerful.

Einstein, on the other hand, believed — as did Spinoza — that a person's actions were just as determined as that of a billiard ball, planet, or star. "Human beings in their thinking, feeling, and acting are not free but are as causally bound as the stars in their motions," Einstein declared in a statement to a Spinoza Society in 1932. It was a concept he drew also from his reading of Schopenhauer. "Everybody acts not only under external compulsion but also in accordance with inner necessity," he wrote in his famous credo. "Schopenhauer's saying, 'A man can do as he wills, but not will as he wills,' has been a real inspiration to me since my youth; it has been a continual consolation in the face of life's hardships, my own and others', and an unfailing wellspring of tolerance."

This determinism appalled some friends such as Max Born, who thought it completely undermined the foundations of human morality. "I cannot understand how you can combine an entirely mechanistic universe with the freedom of the ethical individual," he wrote Einstein. "To me a deterministic world is quite abhorrent. Maybe you are right, and the world is that way, as you say. But at the moment it does not really look like it in physics — and even less so in the rest of the world."

For Born, quantum uncertainty provided an escape from this dilemma. Like some philosophers of the time, he latched on to the indeterminacy that was inherent in quantum mechanics to resolve "the discrepancy between ethical freedom and strict natural laws."

Born explained the issue to his wife, Hedwig, who was always eager to debate Einstein. She told Einstein that, like him, she was "unable to believe in a 'dice-playing' God." In other words, unlike her husband, she rejected quantum mechanics' view that the universe was based on uncertainties and probabilities. But, she added, "nor am I able to imagine that you believe — as Max has told me — that your 'complete rule of law' means that everything is predetermined, for example whether I am going to have my child inoculated." It would mean, she pointed out, the end of all moral behavior.

But Einstein's answer was to look upon free will as something that was useful, indeed necessary, for a civilized society, because it caused people to take responsibility for their own actions. "I am compelled to act as if free will existed," he explained, "because if I wish to live in a civilized society I must act responsibly." He could even hold people responsible for their good or evil, since that was both a pragmatic and sensible approach to life, while still believing intellectually that everyone's actions were predetermined. "I know that philosophically a murderer is not responsible for his crime," he said, "but I prefer not to take tea with him."

The foundation of morality, he believed, was rising above the "merely personal" to live in a way that benefited humanity. He dedicated himself to the cause of world peace and, after encouraging the United States to build the atom bomb to defeat Hitler, worked diligently to find ways to control such weapons. He raised money to help fellow refugees, spoke out for racial justice, and publicly stood up for those who were victims of McCarthyism. And he tried to live with a humor, humility, simplicity, and geniality even as he became one of the most famous faces on the planet.

For some people, miracles serve as evidence of God's existence. For Einstein it was the absence of miracles that reflected divine providence. The fact that the world was comprehensible, that it followed laws, was worthy of awe.

PICO IYER

The Magic Mountain

FROM *Condé Nast Traveler*

BARELY TWENTY PEOPLE got out when at last the small country train reached the final stop on the line: Gokurakubashi, or the Bridge of Heaven. We disembarked and stepped into a cable car that slowly clanked up a thickly forested slope of pines: a handful of Western couples, an intrepid Japanese matron or two, and I. For five minutes we rose high, high above the woods below, until we were deposited in a clearing about 2,800 feet above sea level. A largely deserted parking lot lay in front of us, and a mountain road so narrow that two buses could not pass at the same time.

Beyond taxis and buses, no vehicles are allowed on the road, I had read. For more than a thousand years, in fact, no woman had even been permitted to ascend the holy mountain. When the mother of the mountain's discoverer, Kobo Daishi, tried to climb the slopes, she was repelled by a "thunderstorm of fire rain."

I took a quiet bus around the curves — there is nothing here but trees, the outlines of temples, and a few walking trails on which yellow signs note the imminence of bears. Then, five minutes later, I got off on the solitary main street of Koyasan. A five-minute walk away to one side of me was a majestic temple complex; ten minutes to the other was the Ichi-no-hashi Bridge, where monks and pilgrims traditionally wash their hands and faces before entering what they believe to be the "pure land," or paradise, of Shingon Buddhism. Across that bridge was a dense grove of giant cedar trees, many of them eight hundred years old, surrounded by more than two hundred thousand graves. And at the very end of the path lay the mausoleum of Kobo Daishi, the "mother of Japanese culture," as the pamphlets describe him, though to us he might better be identified as a founding father (or all the founding fathers combined, since he seems to bring together in one person the merits of George Washington, Thomas Jefferson, and Benjamin Franklin).

Around me in the little town were more than a hundred temples, their high-flying cypress-bark roofs like the prows of seagoing vessels about to sail off into the mist. The air was decidedly cooler than in the blazing Osaka I'd left just two hours before — twenty degrees cooler, I would learn — and although the sun was still in its late summer splendor in the cities of the plain, here, the maple leaves were beginning to turn, six weeks earlier than they would down below, and there was already a sense of coming snow. The holiest place in Japan, as Koyasan is called, offered a sense of solemnity, of gravitas, of overwhelming darkness that I could not remember seeing in my twenty years of living in the country.

You could best say what Koyasan is, in fact, by saying everything it isn't. There are no high-rises on the sacred mountain, no fast-food parlors, no karaoke bars or pinball arcades. There is none of the flash and acceleration of the neon-streaking, crowded, wildly clangorous shopping malls and entertainment complexes that make up the fabric of modern Japan. Mount Koya (as the name would be in English) is consecrated to everything old and changeless and hushed.

You stay, when you stay here, in a temple, one of the 53 (out of 117 in all) that offer *shukubo,* or temple lodgings. You get up at dawn (if you are sensible) to witness the morning chants and *goma* fire ceremonies in which the monks, by burning 108 pieces of wood (108 is a sacred number in Buddhism) and then scattering 108 white sesame seeds on top of them, believe they are purging their illusions and replacing them with spots of enlightenment, bringing the Buddha into their bodies. By seven thirty every evening, the main street in the mountain village is largely silent and all its shops are shuttered. Even in early afternoon, when I arrived, very few figures were visible — only a nun in blue robes and then an abbot in a black gown, clacking away on traditional geta wooden sandals while a shaven-headed young acolyte hurried to keep up with him.

I walked down the little street (the whole town has a population of four thousand — plus a thousand monks — though once there were more than fifteen hundred monasteries here) and stepped through the gates that led into the fourteenth-century temple where I was to stay the night. A head monk called a hello and then, seeing how I took off my shoes in a non-prescribed, non-Japanese fashion, shouted at me, "That's wrong!" Then he led me up to an exquisite four-room, blond-wood tatami suite, complete with a sleek TV, remote-controlled heating, a heated toilet seat, a private shower and bath, and even a cup in which to make café mocha. Drawing back the shoji screens, I could see a classic Japanese garden with a stone lantern and stone bridge.

Dinner would be served at five thirty, he said — it would turn out to consist of twelve lacquer bowls of delectable food cooked in the traditional Japanese Buddhist way, without meat or fish or garlic or onions: the local specialty, sesame tofu; mountain vegetables; and sweet-and-sour seaweed in vinegar sauce. A morning service would be held the next day at dawn. Then there would be a traditional Japanese breakfast.

I went out for a walk after dinner along the chill, silent streets, and when I got to Ichi-no-hashi Bridge, all I could see was a long trail of stone lanterns, each one giving off a faint light, leading through the graves and the tall cedars to where Kobo Daishi is believed to have been sitting in eternal meditation for 1,172 years. I felt as if I had stepped into a whole pulsing, thrumming mandala, or Buddhist diagram of heaven — the rare place in Japan that seemed to turn with a mystical intensity.

Then I hurried back to the temple; its great wooden gates close to the world every night at eight.

In almost any Japanese home you visit, you will find in one corner a little platform that functions as a household shrine of sorts. On it will be a few ceremonial objects, a picture or two of departed loved ones perhaps, maybe a Buddha. Koyasan is like the secret shrine hidden in one corner of the old household that is known as Japan, a repository of the ancestral and the deep, without which, some believe, the modern, bustling country would not be able to function. It sits near the very center of the nation, tucked within a ring of eight outer and eight inner mountains that cradle the town like a hidden treasure within a set of lotus petals. From here you can't see anything of modern Japan below, and the businessmen in their suits, the perky girls in their cowboy hats and miniskirts, can't see you.

I could hardly believe, as I settled into the monastic rhythm — a futon and a hard rice-husk pillow had been laid out on the floor while I walked — how far I'd come. At noon, I'd arrived at the entrance to the Koya Line of the Nankai private railway system, in the Namba section of Osaka. On one side of me was a bite-size McDonald's in which sat a Louis Vuitton girl in a business suit, picking delicately at a Filet-O-Fish, while beside her a young man tried to balance a cell phone, a laptop, and a McFlurry on his small table. Bossa nova music imparted to everything an air of foreign languor. On the other side was a vast underground labyrinth of passageways and staircases that led to a Namba Parks complex of chic Italian restaurants and San Diegan landscaping, a Namba City world of department stores and elegant boutiques. Above us were love hotels and taxis and all the revved-up signs of a modern Japan that believes that to be itself is to be global and generic.

Then, however, I'd passed through the ticket barrier at the station and stepped into a slow-moving country train. Very quickly the featureless, jumbled suburbs of the big industrial city fell away. Concrete gave way to wood, and wood to clustered trees. Green was everywhere, the only gray the rooftops of traditional houses. In ninety-one minutes, the train stopped at fifty-two stations, the platforms themselves emptying out until they were completely deserted, full of the poignancy and nostalgia that the Japanese associate with lonely country stations. It was as if, with each stop, I was less in the company of the bright, chirpy face that Japan is so keen to show the outside world (or maybe even itself) and more in the presence of the Japan that really exists deep down.

The story of Koyasan is a highly detailed one that still shivers on the edge of folktale or creation myth. In the late eighth century, a young Japanese monk called Kukai began studying classic Chinese philosophy and Buddhism in what was then the capital city of Nara, but soon decided that to learn the true secrets of the tradition he would have to go to China itself. In the year 804, at the age of thirty-one, he set sail for Chang'an, the capital of Tang-dynasty China and then the largest city in the world, three times the size of the new Japanese capital of Kyoto. In Chang'an, he found a master, and within eight months had himself mastered the mysteries of what is called esoteric, or tantric, Buddhism — which was given the Japanese name Shingon, or "True Word."

Then he sailed back to Japan to try to set up a Shingon training center in some quiet space in his home country. He traveled from place to place, looking for an appropriate site, and ten years later (legend has it), he awoke from a deep meditative trance to find himself in a far-off wilderness. Beside him he saw a hunter, accompanied by one black dog and one white dog. The hunter led him up into the mountains, and there he came upon an area where no human tracks could be seen. More remarkable still, he found the *vajra* thunderbolt object that he had flung from the beach in China before leaving, to see where it would land in Japan. After petitioning the emperor of the time, he gained permission to build his meditation retreat complex here.

The Shingon sect is very different from the Zen that many of us associate with Japan, not to mention the Jodo Buddhism of recitations. It is most similar to the swirling, electric intensity of Tibetan Buddhism (not surprisingly, since that is the form of Buddhism that was dominant in China when Kukai visited). Those in this esoteric sect believe that the whole world is a mandala, or drawing of enlightenment. They practice Tibetan mudras, or hand gestures; they recite mantras to draw closer to the secret rhythm of the universe; and they believe that if you master many secret, ascetic practices, you can attain enlightenment in a single lifetime. "Buddha can be here in this very body," as one Koyasan monk explained to me.

In 835, the first temple that Kukai built, Kongobuji (or Diamond Peak Temple), received official recognition from the emperor, and in the following month, Kukai died, leaving his followers to continue settling the mountain. Eighty-six years after his death, another emperor gave him the honorific title of Kobo Daishi, or "Great Master Who Spread the Buddhist Teaching." To this day, Kongobuji oversees the 3,600 Shingon temples and more than ten million practitioners scattered across Japan.

Perhaps the first thing you notice when you get to Koyasan is a dark, collected power that could not be farther from everyday Japan, in which even most Buddhist temples are unexceptional places associated with funeral rites. Manners on the mountain are brusque, unfussy; the faces I saw as soon as I arrived were wild-bearded, grizzled — much rougher than in manicured, eyebrow-plucked Kyoto. At the central tourist information center, where I booked my temple rooms, the staff were not women, who lavish helpful attention on foreigners in every other such office in the country, but men, many of whom spoke no English and did not look at all delighted to see visitors.

In cities like Kyoto, a recorded voice sings out "Welcome" when you enter even a video store; in Koyasan, the message, refreshingly, seemed to be "Keep your distance. And remember where you are."

Yet very soon that air of weightedness and remoteness began to feel like the source of the area's power. Even now there are, by one count, more than two thousand stupas, shrines, and pagodas on top of the mountain, and on the cable car up, the final announcement had told us, in Japanese and English, that there are fifty thousand cultural and historical treasures among the tall cedars and cypress trees. A sign at the entrance to the cable car had proclaimed that Koyasan, as of 2004, had been named a UNESCO World Heritage Site. And as I began walking around the settlement my first morning, I heard a solemn gong from within a temple nearby, and looked up to see a handsome young Japanese man dressed from head to toe in pilgrim's white, with a ceremonial topknot to keep his long hair under control. As I wandered along the main street — from the graveyard on one side of town, heavy with tombs and weathered headstones, to the bright temple compound on the other — I noticed that many of the visitors were groups of pilgrims, often elderly, also wearing white shirts, on the back of which was written, WE DEVOTE OUR LIVES TO KOBO DAISHI AND WE ALWAYS WALK WITH KOBO DAISHI. Wherever they visited, they stood and let out loud chants while a leader hit a bowl steadily, making a clacking sound, or shook what sounded like bells.

"When you think of a mountain in Europe," a Koyasan monk told me, "what do you see? Blue skies, sunshine, space. But here in Japan, mountains are dark, because of the trees. In Europe, people talk of mountains as 'ladders to heaven.' Here in Japan, people come to the mountains in order to die." Or, I thought, to live again, but in a pure and uncluttered way, guarded by and close to the spirits of those who have died over the past twelve centuries. I had moved, in only two hours, from what might be a comic-book canvas by Lichtenstein into a Rothko land of blacks and deep browns and stripes of gray, the occasional candle or lantern against a dark surface throwing up a blaze of gold.

Mountains are, in fact, the charged hot centers of all Japan, the only places in the often overdeveloped country where you can get in touch with a kind of aboriginal land of spirits and folklore. Perhaps this is true in many places, but in Japan, where nearly every city was rebuilt after the war — and along the Western model — the contrast is especially pronounced. As soon as you drive out of the crowded skyscraper streets of Kyoto, say, and toward the ancient slopes of Mount Hiei, only twenty minutes away, you feel something lift inside you as the landscape clears out and you enter a world of stone gates, thick valleys, and deep snow. In the mountains in Japan, you are in the realm of *kamisama,* or gods who are said to live in streams and hills; the mountains are where you see beautiful women who turn out to be foxes in disguise (the old stories say) or *tanuki,* raccoonlike tricksters who mark the end of the city and the entry into somewhere wild.

Koyasan draws on all this magnetism and concentrates it by keeping out everything else. And the first place to see when you arrive on the mountain is, indeed, the grove of giant cedars (some of them fifty feet in circumference) that surround the graves that lead, on a long path, to the Gobyo — the mausoleum of Kobo Daishi. Somehow the shaded walk seems always quiet, even when several groups of pilgrims are proceeding along it, and however many people there are, they are outnumbered by the small stone statues along the way — representatives, usually, of Jizo, the protective god.

The graves on Koyasan are built in the distinctive five-tiered shape of what are *gorinto* — reserved for high families in Japan, and drawing on the fact that here, as in China, there are five elements, not four (in part because the word for "four" sounds the same as the word for "death"): earth, fire, water, air — and wind. The Jizos often wear red bibs around their necks, and stand on behalf of those children who died too young. In one area near the great mausoleum, a giant stupa has been built from all the small gravestones that have been found discarded or abandoned along the ground here over the years.

For the Japanese, the passage through the graveyard known as Okunoin ("Innermost Sanctum") has something of the solemnity of a walk through the country's history books. Daimyo and samurai, kabuki actor and Korean soldier, are all buried here: on one side is the grave of the legendary fighter Toyotomi Hideyoshi (who, in fact, once wanted to attack Koyasan from his stronghold in Kyoto); on another is the monument that remembers his famous predecessor Oda Nobunaga (who also wanted to attack the strategic mountain). Among Kobo Daishi's many achievements (he is said by his followers to have edited a dictionary, introduced people to the use of coal, and even to have performed rainmaking rites to help those suffering from a drought), he was one of the first religious figures in Japan to bring the animist folk tradition of Shinto together with Buddhism. This means that his cemetery is full of the graves of the leaders and followers of other, rival Buddhist schools, as well as a group of Chinese Christians. There are monuments here recalling those who fell in a siege in Otsu in the year 1600; students killed in World War II; the Australians, Japanese, and Borneo natives who died in North Borneo during the same war.

Indeed, the nature of Buddhism of every kind in Japan is highly inclusive; as a Koyasan monk told me, with evident delight, "We even include hell in our mandalas of enlightenment." At the very least, the line between sacred and profane is drawn very differently here than in the West. Thus, many a newcomer to Japan is startled to find that priests are often married men with families who live in spacious old villas appointed with modern gadgets and kegs of beer, and are driven around town in spotless black Mercedes sedans. The first thing the man at the tourist information center said to me, when making a booking for a night in a temple, was, "You must pay extra for beer!" And, in truth, many of the temples are famous for their sake and beer.

So in the midst of an indefinable sense of entering another world in the cemetery — the smell of incense and cedars intense, small umbrella pines (or Koyamaki) placed at the foot of many tombstones, an enclosure near Kobo Daishi's mausoleum strictly reserved for the remains of nine emperors and their families — there are also startling images of the everyday. One shrine is shaped like a blowfish (though not, I gathered, in honor of someone laid low by the famously poisonous delicacy), and outside the reception hall, near the climax of the walk, a group called the Delight Factory has erected a huge board with children's elaborate cartoons on it and the enigmatic slogans, in English, "I buried a cigarette butt in the beach. It was like burying something in the sandbox" and "You tossed your cigarettes out the window. You looked like you were fleeing the scene of a crime." This all goes well, perhaps, with temples that display the badges of Visa and MasterCard on the windows of their offices; the one I was staying in had gleaming vending machines along its corridors and a comic book thoughtfully placed beside my bed. There is nothing good or bad, as Hamlet had it, but thinking makes it so.

At the most resonant area of all, near the end of the path, there is a row of statues over which petitioners pour water to protect their ancestors in the afterworld, and a small Jizo shrine in which the god of protection doubles as a food taster (akin to those unfortunates who had to sample food before it was served to a ruler). Twice every morning, a senior monk in saffron robes says prayers before this shrine, and then two younger monks, also in saffron robes, transport on a kind of simple palanquin a blond-wood box (a chest, really) that contains fresh food for Kobo Daishi's spirit to eat (since it is believed that the mountain's founder is still sitting in his shrine, meditating). Through typhoon and war and earthquake, Kobo Daishi is served elaborate meals every day for breakfast and lunch, the robed figures often trudging through snow to bring them to him.

Yet as you walk away from this holy spot and back toward the main road, one of the first large shrines you pass in what is called "the new graveyard" depicts two enormous stone coffee cups (in which, if you peer inside, dark marble has been placed to represent coffee). The UCC coffee company has decided that Koyasan is the perfect place to catch the eye — perhaps to win the affection — of some of the million or so pilgrims who visit every year. Nearby is a glossy shrine with two fresh-faced young men walking as to war (though when I looked closer, I saw the Nissan logo and realized that it was consecrated to those who had died building Nissan cars). A pantyhose company shows off its well-known mascot on one plot of land, and a great marble slab put up by the Sharp company, on which you can see your reflection as you pass, is said to represent a high-definition TV screen. There is even one shiny, very tall rocket ship in the new cemetery: the shrine was initially disallowed by the Koyasan authorities, I was told, but then the resourceful aeronautical company assured the graveyard's keepers that the rocket was built in five stages to represent the five tiers of a classic *gorinto*.

For all these reminders that in Japan nothing is sacred (or maybe everything is, if you see things differently), I really did feel, very often, as if I had stumbled into a prior Japan here, a kind of family heirloom kept in a dusty attic of the country. I slipped into a coffee shop late one afternoon to find a man in a suit, in the sepulchral open space, massaging a very elderly man in yellow robes (a retired monk, perhaps), while a dog wailed and barked. Women sell special mushrooms and persimmons along the main road, and once I saw an old lady pad into a café and drop three fresh persimmons on the counter.

Another day I was sitting in Bon On Sha, a stylish "international café" run by a young Japanese traveler who, after spending twelve years in China, India, and Paris, decided to return to Japan with his French wife but wanted to find a place that felt nothing like the Japan he had fled (somewhere traditional, in short, and old and deep). As the two dished up the daily special of Thai curry, homemade pear tart, and delicious chai, one of the three customers at the counter — a vivid, decidedly unretiring Westerner in robes — caught my eye and came over to introduce himself.

Kurt Kübli was a full-time monk on Koyasan — though born in Zurich and trained in the arts — and the two people he was eating with were a Shingon nun from Croatia and her husband, a monk from Germany. "The whole of life here is sometimes like a drawing," the Swiss monk said. "Everything is a mandala. This is all paradise. Why live anywhere else?"

I had already heard him speaking fluent French, Japanese, Italian, and German, and now he proceeded to deliver Buddhist teachings, in English, on the architect Tadao Ando, the fourteenth Dalai Lama, classic Indian philosophy, and the eccentric German film director Werner Herzog. He had been fascinated with Asia for forty years, he said, and as soon as he visited Koyasan twenty-seven years before, he had realized that it was the place to make his life's retreat. He had been living as a monk in Muryokoin, around the corner, for ten years now.

"When is the best season to visit?" I asked.

He looked at me, astonished, and said, "Can you say the trees are not beautiful when they are bare? I have taken photographs when the snow is in the temples. Big wedges of it, but so soft. And through the snow you can see a thousand little points of light. And then in the spring, there are cherry blossoms, and then rhododendron . . ." He proceeded to annotate the beauties of every month of the year. The best time to visit Koyasan, clearly, was any time.

The one other sight that it is essential to see on the sacred mountain — which is alive with private graves, little nunneries (to accommodate the women who were first allowed to visit in 1872), and even a stone marking the spot where a girl chose to turn into a Jizo statue — is the Garan. This is a huge compound linking nineteen separate buildings, including the exquisite Reihokan Museum, alight with perfectly serene Buddhas and almost fire-breathing temple guardians, and Kongobuji itself. Inside Kongobuji, as in a great Kyoto temple, are elegant rooms with painted walls depicting the seasons and Kobo Daishi's journey to China; outside is the largest rock garden in Japan, made of 140 great slabs of granite representing a male and a female dragon.

The whole of Koyasan still has this masculine force and uncompromising assertiveness, which puts it in a different universe from the ornamental courtesies of Kyoto. The old capital, for all the two thousand shrines and temples that ring it, is largely a place of grace notes that seem feminine to us — flower arranging, kimonos, samisen playing, and of course geisha — and its very language is softened to give it a refined and delicate air. Koyasan, by comparison, is unhesitatingly male, unfrilly. Where Mount Fuji is the poster peak for Japan, showing the serene image the country likes to project for public purposes, it comes with none of the sacramental history of Mount Koya.

And yet even here, in this temple with huge vats that can serve seven hundred bowls of rice, and the small room with willow panels where Toyotomi Hideyoshi's nephew committed ritual suicide (Koyasan opens out onto what seems a Kurosawa movie), there is, in places, a slightly more lyrical and feminine cast to things. As the sign explaining one room puts it, in delicate English, "Koyasan is particularly lovely in the autumn. Red and yellow autumn leaves, fallen from the maple trees, growing here and there among the

misty Japanese cedars, drift like pieces of brocade on the Tamagawa River, inviting people to enter the perfect mandala of Shingon Buddhism. Hearing the gentle turtledove's cry among the
trees, the faithful visiting Shingon recall the dear voices of their departed parents."

And so my days on the mountain went on, gaining weight, letting me fall into a monkish spell, clearing out the clutter from my
mind so I could concentrate at last on essentials, appreciate the
fullness of the empty rooms I found myself in, notice the intricacy
of the drawings on the doors in Kongobuji (where even sketching
is forbidden). Suddenly, from one wooden entrance one afternoon, twelve shaven-headed men in black tumbled out, with large
white shoulder bags over their arms and white, spotless, split-toe
tabi socks. Against the slopes, the pine trees in the misty mornings
looked like ink strokes on an ancient scroll. The pilgrims, all in
white, had arrived in Koyasan as a culmination after visiting eighty-
eight temples across the island of Shikoku.

At times, I felt almost as if I were living inside a Kobo Daishi divinity center (or a kind of Shingon Disneyland). The hero of Japan
is said to have founded the first public school in the country and to
have created the hiragana script that makes Japanese readable. He
is said to have discovered hot springs, to have been a calligrapher
and a healer; his book *Ten Grades of Human Mentality* is one of the
formative works of Buddhism. "Kobo Daishi was also a civil engineer," Teruko Yasukawa, a kindly local woman who was showing me
around one day, volunteered. "He invented a system for an irriga-
tion pond. He was also a geologist — he found mercury." It almost
seemed plausible that he had built the whole mountain with his
own hands by the time I saw a caption in the museum noting, matter-of-factly, "The morning star went into Kobo Daishi's mouth."

Yet just as I was feeling myself too much inside a single being's
cult — even the magnolia is said to resemble the infant Kobo Daishi, seated amid lotus petals — I looked up and saw monks going
about their punishing routines, which include bathing in the freez-
ing Tamagawa, chanting all night one day of the year, and so deeply
visualizing the Buddha and looking at their mandalas that they can
become a Buddha in the process. Many of the iconic photographs
of Koyasan show mysterious figures in white — hooded monks —

walking at high speed through the cedar trees as part of their ascetic discipline, or sitting in a dark hall lit by candles as if they had
themselves become just shapes on a mandala. When one monk,
greeting me at a temple I was to stay in, said, "I am reading you," I
was ready to believe almost anything of him — until I realized that
he merely had problems with his *l*'s.

As the days passed, I walked again and again to the Okunoin,
sometimes descending below the Hall of Lanterns to see where fifty
thousand tiny statues of Kobo Daishi are all lined up in rows, shelf
after shelf of them in an underground chamber. And soon I began
to register that the real time to see Koyasan is winter, when there is
snow everywhere and the night falls early and the great dark buildings represent bold slashes of calligraphy against the white. But
even in less sonorous seasons, the time to see Koyasan is dusk. It is a
vespers place — it often feels like late afternoon there long before
night falls — and as my stay deepened, I found myself going out
night after night, sometimes to the beautifully illuminated buildings of the Garan, all great white lanterns and silence across the
white-gravel courtyard, or, more often, in the direction of the Okunoin. To step across the first bridge after dark is to walk into a whis-
pered allegory.

Even on the main street, almost no figures were to be seen after
dark: only a kimonoed spirit slipping past on high wooden sandals
and, another time, a man with a triangular bamboo hat and a cane
— another pilgrim — stomping off into the dark. And in the grove
of great cedars and graves, almost nothing was to be heard, except
on the occasion when, just outside Kobo Daishi's mausoleum, I
came upon a man standing by himself, in the dim light of a few candles, shouting out the unearthly syllables of the Hannya Shingyo,
or Heart Sutra.

The final bridge you cross before coming to the mausoleum is
called the Bridge of Ignorance, because it is believed that when you
issue forth into the vicinity of Kobo Daishi, you are in a world of il-
lumination. Two lights in the Hall of Lanterns are said to have
been burning continuously for almost a thousand years, and the
very presence of light is all the more potent for the crowding dark
all around. "When you are living in a world of typhoon, of fire and
lightning," the Swiss monk had told me (Koyasan has been as-
saulted at least four times by major fires), "you are living in the sec-

ond. You don't wait for anything. You go out and use the day right now."

For many Japanese, of course, the presence of the graves is so intense that the place is terrifying after dark. After I came down the mountain, I showed my Japanese sweetheart some pictures of Koyasan at its most potent, and she shivered, seeing a spirit behind every tree or hiding in every shrine. But for a foreigner less at home in the old, the atmosphere was just unworldly: all I could hear as I walked among the graves was the scuffling of small animals in the dark, the hiss of a fluorescent light above the line of stone lanterns as it flickered out, the last of the year's crickets. In one place, the reflection from the lamps gave two golden eyes to a small stone statue.

On my last evening in Koyasan, as I was standing in front of the Hall of Lanterns, pondering its agelessness, I saw a movement nearby: a small, raccoon-faced creature was foraging among some pebbles for food. A tanuki, I realized — the almost legendary badger-dog that is more often seen in stories than in real life. It looked at me intently and then went on scrabbling.

The next day, I woke up at first light, splashed some water on my face from a rough communal basin (my nighttime walks had gotten in the way of using the traditional Japanese bath available only in the evenings), and walked into a prayer hall where monks sat in the near-dark, barely lit by occasional tapers, while in an adjoining room a figure sat stock-still for half an hour and then began building a fire in the small wooden space.

Three hours later, I was back in central Osaka, and around me were plate-glass offices, beeping cell phones, trucks, and giggling girls. Flashing lights gave off the time, people rushed to commuter trains, and in McDonald's the cash registers were clicking hectically. Like Rip Van Winkle, or so it seemed, I had awoken to a world several decades out of sync. So soon, so soon, I thought, the fire turns into ash again.

HEATHER KING

The Closest to Love We Ever Get

FROM *Portland*

> There is another world, and it is this one.
> — Paul Eluard

I'M A PERSON WHO CRAVES quiet and solitude, yet I've lived in the crowded, noisy Los Angeles neighborhood of Koreatown for eleven years. I tell myself it's because I have a spacious, beautiful apartment and a gated courtyard filled with hibiscus and pomegranates. I tell myself it's because I pay only $760 a month — half as much as almost anywhere else in the city. But the longer I stay, the more I see it's not just the apartment that keeps me here: it's the challenges, the dilemmas, the paradoxes. People blast *ranchera* music at three in the morning but they also prune bougainvillea into glories of cascading blooms. They spray-paint gang slogans on my garage door by night and scrub the sidewalks clean by day. As I hang out my clothes on the line by the lemon tree, my back is to a busted washing machine; across the alley, a brand-new down comforter, still in its package, sits on top of a dumpster.

Part of my impulse living here is to hide out from the rest of the city — from the cell phones and SUVs, the hipsters, the people writing screenplays in too-cool-to-care coffeehouses — but in Koreatown I can't hide out from myself. Here I come face to face every day with the cross of my irritation, my anger, my racism, my fear. Here I am plunged into the deepest contradictions: between abundance and scarcity, community and solitude, sin and grace, my longing for wholeness and my resistance to it.

Here, I have no voice, no particular power. At Mass at St. Basil's, at 24-Hour Fitness, at Charlie Chan's Printing, at Ralph's Grocery, at the Vietnamese shop where I get my pedicures, I am often the only white person present. When I call out my window to Jung, the kid next door, to keep it down, he yells back: "We were here first! Why don't *you* move?" His nine-year-old face contorted by hate; hurt and fury rising in my own throat; I don't have to read the headlines on Iraq to know how wars start, how the battle lines are drawn.

I have driven from Koreatown to Death Valley, to Anza Borrego, to the East Mojave. I am pulled to the desert as if by a magnet; I'm forever scheming to escape there for a week, or two, or a month; I devour books about the desert, and yet I am uneasy with the nature writers who leave human beings out, who see us as a blight on the landscape. As a human being, and a Catholic, I see the cross everywhere: in actual deserts and, in the middle of one of the most densely populated sections of Los Angeles, in the desert of my own conflicted heart. Living in Koreatown has fortified my sense of apartness, allowed me to be in the city but not always of it, shaped me as a writer. But a writer has to be fully engaged: emotionally, spiritually, physically; has to mingle his or her body and blood with the rest of the world, the people in it, the page; has to find a way to cherish that world even as he or she struggles to endure it — Flannery O'Connor's phrase — which is perhaps the best definition of the cross I know. How can you be Catholic? people ask, and I want to ask back, but am afraid to, How can you write unless in some sense you have died and been resurrected and, in one way or another, are burning to tell people about it? How can you bear the sorrow of a world in which every last thing passes away without knowing that Christ is right up there on the cross with you? How can you be spiritual in LA? someone from back East once asked, and, as a car alarm blared, a leaf blower blasted, and I looked out my window at the children hanging out the windows of the six-story apartment building across the street and screaming, I thought, *How can you deal with this ceaselessly pulsing aorta of life with anything but spirituality?*

Sometimes I have coffee with my friend Joan, who waitresses at Langer's Deli, or my friend Larry, a janitor at Kaiser. Here is what feeds me: sitting on the corner of Wilshire and Serrano with traffic streaming by while Joan tells me about her troubles with the cook at work, or while Larry, who did time at every mental health facility from Camarillo to Norwalk before he stopped drinking, reminisces about his "nuthouse romances." What feeds me is the miracle of flesh-and-blood, of stories, of the daily struggles that "break, blow, burn" and make us new, as John Donne put it, that give us compassion for the struggles of others.

Inching out into Oxford Avenue on foot, headed to the library, I can barely make it across, there are so many cars barreling down from either direction: honking, cutting each other off, jostling for space. It's so easy to feel besieged, so easy to think *Why are there so many of them?* instead of realizing I'm one of "them" myself; that nobody else likes being crowded either. *How can a person live a life of love?* I ask myself as I reach the opposite curb: not love tacked on, added as an afterthought, but shot through every second; flaming out, "like shining from shook foil," as Gerard Manley Hopkins described the grandeur of God.

Wending my way home with my books, my vision temporarily transformed, I'm not seeing the refrigerators abandoned on the sidewalk, the triple-parked ice cream trucks, the overflowing trash cans. I'm seeing flashes of colorful Mexican tile, the 98-cent-store mural of waltzing Ajax cans and jitterbugging mops, my favorite flowers: the heliotrope on Ardmore, the wisteria near Harvard, the lemon on Mariposa. Or maybe it's not that I'm seeing one group of things instead of another but, for one fleeting moment, all simultaneously: the opposites held in balance a paradigm for the terrible tension and ambiguity of the human condition; the dreadful reality that we can never quite be sure which things we have done and which things we have failed to do, the difference between how we long for the world to be and how it must be a kind of crucifixion in the darkest, most excruciating depths of which we discover — the rear windows of the parked cars I'm walking by now covered with jacaranda blossoms — it's not that there's not enough beauty; it's that there's so much it can hardly be borne.

Monday morning, putting out the garbage as the sky turns pink above the salmon stucco façades, I bend my face to the gardenia in the courtyard, knowing that every shabby corner, every bird and flower and blade of grass, every honking horn and piece of graffiti, every pain and contradiction, deserves a song of praise. *O sacrament most holy, o sacrament divine . . . ,* we sang at Mass yesterday. The kids are coming in droves now, making their way to Hobart Middle School — pushing, yelling, throwing their candy wrappers on the sidewalk — and that is a kind of hymn, too. We're all doing our part, their exuberant shouts mingling with the thoughts I'll shape into an essay, all drifting like incense, raised aloft and offered up to the smoggy air above Koreatown. Maybe that's exactly as it should be. Maybe I need their noise and they need my silence; maybe the song we make together — all of us — is the closest to love we ever get.

"What are we here for?" Annie Dillard asks in *The Writing Life*. "*Propter chorum,* the monks say: for the sake of the choir."

MAXINE KUMIN

The Domestic Arrangement

FROM *The Southern Review*

From Dorothy Wordsworth's journals

Wm went into the wood to alter his poems
writes Dorothy. *I shelled peas, gathered beans,
and worked in the garden.* This is Grasmere

where she picked and boiled gooseberries,
two lbs. of sugar in the first panfull
while *Wm went into the wood to alter his poems*

a trip he makes almost daily, composing
the lines she will later copy. Mornings
she works in the garden at Grasmere

*which looked so beautiful my heart
almost melted away,* she confides
while Wm's in the wood altering his poems.

On one of their daily walks she observes
helpful details of Wm's famed daffodils.
Then it's back to the garden at Grasmere

where she ties up her scarlet runner beans
and pulls a bag of peas for Miss Simpson.
Leave Wm in the wood to alter his poems;
praise Dorothy in the garden at Grasmere.

URSULA K. LE GUIN

About a Poem

FROM *Shambhala Sun*

A Shropshire Lad: XXXII

> *From far, from eve and morning*
> *And yon twelve-winded sky,*
> *The stuff of life to knit me*
> *Blew hither: here am I.*
>
> *Now — for a breath I tarry*
> *Nor yet disperse apart —*
> *Take my hand quick and tell me*
> *What have you in your heart.*
>
> *Speak now, and I will answer;*
> *How shall I help you, say;*
> *Ere to the wind's twelve quarters*
> *I take my endless way.*

A. E. HOUSMAN WAS a classics scholar with a rare, particular gift: in an ancient text in which words or lines had been garbled or mis-copied or lost, he could see what they must have been and correct the error, fill the gap. Such a gift must rise from an uncanny sense for the right, the inevitable word. In the three brief volumes of his own verse you can see that gift fulfilled.

Modernism, which became the dominant style during Hous-man's lifetime, turned us away from regular beat and full rhyme. But that's all he wrote. Jog jog, his poems go, three- or four-beat lines in quatrains or other stanzas familiar from ballads and hymns, always rhymed. It's so simple. Nothing to it. Anybody can do it. Just try!

What he did makes you realize the infinite suppleness and subtlety of simple forms when used by a great poet.

Rhythm of beat, of stress, of rhyme goes so deep in us; it answers a human need. Last month I saw a baby not yet a year old whop a stick against a chair in perfect time, laughing and singing out: Wow! — Wow! — Wow! — Wow! This is the origin of music, and poetry.

True rhythm gets into your head, your bones. I can't recall more than a line or two of any free-verse poem, even those I love. But when I'm sick or wakeful in the dark, I invite Housman's poems to sing in my head and find solace in their pure, uncompromised music.

Housman was god-free. His was the world of Lucretius and scientific materialism — not presided over by a deity either vengeful or loving, not containing anything humanly attainable beyond physical reality, yet vast, full of mystery. In this world death takes us not to heaven but to earth — to dust, to "the wind's twelve quarters." Human love and pain are all the deeper for their brevity; human honor burns all the brighter because it has no reward.

That a poem may draw from such apparently bleak realism a warm, urgent morality — "Take my hand quick / How shall I help you?" — this is something to ponder.

JAMES LONEY

Cell Group

FROM *Christian Century*

TOM FOX, *fifty-four, a peace activist and a member of Langley Hill Friends Meeting in McLean, Virginia, was kidnapped in Iraq in November 2005 along with three other members of Christian Peacemaker Teams — Norman Kember, seventy-four, of Britain; and James Loney, forty-one, and Harmeet Singh Sooden, thirty-two, both of Canada. Their captors, a group called the Swords of Righteousness Brigade, accused the four of spying for Western governments. Fox was eventually separated from the others; his dead body was discovered in Baghdad on March 9, 2006. The other hostages were rescued two weeks later. The following article is excerpted from Loney's account of the team's time in captivity.*

In the beginning stages of the captivity, Tom Fox was our anchor, our stalwart. He had learned a lot about Iraq's kidnapping industry: how the field was played by both criminals and insurgents; how they were organized in a hierarchical network of power and influence; how hostages were put up for auction and sold up the ladder until the highest bidder secured the rights to extort princely ransoms — or murder their ideological prey in executions recorded on grainy videos. He knew all the most important Arabic words, like *hamam* (bathroom), *my* (water), *mumkin* (could I please), *Ia* and *nam* (no and yes), the numbers, the days of the week, various references to time. He knew a great deal about Iraqi culture, history, and politics. His calm judgment was an invaluable resource.

During those first days of relentless, terrifying, excruciating uncertainty, Tom dove into prayer the way a warrior might charge into battle. He turned his captivity into a sustained, unbroken meditation. The chain that bound his wrist became a kind of rosary, or *sebha* (the beads Muslims use to count the names of God). He would picture someone: a member of his family, a member of the Iraq team or the CPT office, one of the captors — whoever he felt needed a prayer. Holding a link of the chain, he would breathe in and out, slowly, so that you could hear the air gushing in and out of his lungs, praying for the person he was holding in his mind. With the completion of each breath, he would pass a chain link through his thumb and index finger. During his first breath he would say to himself, *with the warmth of my heart.* In the second, *with the stillness of my mind.* In the third, *with the fluidity of my body.* And in the fourth, *with the light of my soul.* At the end of each series of four breaths, he would pause and simply rest in the light with the person he was praying for.

Tom's vigilance in prayer was astounding. I sometimes felt ashamed. My mind would wander helplessly in self-preoccupation and garish tableaux in absurd cycles of repetition. His unrelenting focus called me back to prayer again and again, almost as if someone had suddenly taken hold of my shoulders, was gently shaking me and telling me, "Wake up! Come back to your senses."

Tom would exhort us to live in the present moment. The past and the future did not exist, he would say, we only have the now. He would remind us, despite assurances from our captors that release was imminent, that we could be held for months, even years.

On day 8, the second Saturday following our abduction, the captor we called Medicine Man paid us a visit. He earned that name when he brought blood-pressure medication for Norman. Medicine Man announced that we were going to be moved, one by one, in the trunk of his car: Tom first, then Norman, then me, then Harmeet. We would be separated and held in different locations.

Though my mind was perfectly clear, my body began to shiver uncontrollably. I hated when fear possessed my body, and my mind was helpless to disguise or control it. Tom intensified his meditations. Just before they took him, he said, "I've been preparing for this for a year — thinking about it, praying about it, meditating about it," and then, "The way I feel now, I could do this forever." I turned to look at him, astonished that he could say such a thing. Serene determination illuminated his face. "Be strong," he said to us as they led him away, blindfolded and handcuffed.

Tom always took the hardest place. You couldn't argue him out of it. It was part of the fierce stubbornness that kept him going. Take our pillow collection, for example. We had five of them — three that were sufficiently comfortable and clean to rest your head on, and two that were so flat and grimy with body oils they were hardly fit to use underfoot (which we did, day and night, to protect our feet from the greedy, heat-sucking cold of the tile floor). Norman, Harmeet, and I each had the luxury of our own pillow — only because Tom insisted on using the sweater he bundled into a makeshift headrest. From time to time we would check with him. "Tom, are you okay with not using a pillow? We can easily take turns."

"No," he would say, "I'm fine. I'm actually very comfortable with what I'm doing." I didn't believe him, but I didn't argue: one, there was no way of winning, and two, I loved my pillow and was secretly pleased I didn't have to share it.

And then there was the matter of blankets. There weren't enough of those either. The one blanket we had, a fire engine red, double-lined fleece monstrosity (it had to weigh fifteen pounds!), was just big enough to cover three of us, as long as someone didn't pull an unfair portion in his direction. This meant that someone had to sleep outside the communal blanket. Our ever resourceful captors, seeking an immediate solution that didn't involve spending money, unceremoniously yanked two dust-laden, ceiling-length curtains off the wall and thrust them into Tom's arms. One of the curtains looked like a bridal train. Without blinking an eye, Tom fashioned them into a makeshift mummy bag and slid beneath them. Again we would check. "Tom, are you sure you're okay? Why don't we share sleeping in those things?"

"No, no," he'd say, "really, I'm okay. I'm a hot sleeper and I've got myself a system here that's working really well." But when the nights got cold in January and as our metabolisms slowed from lack of food, Tom found it impossible to keep warm. The lack of sleep began to take a visible physical and psychological toll. Still, the course had been set, and Tom was going to keep to it.

On December 23, day 29 of captivity, we began the discipline of a daily check-in in which we talked about how we were doing physically, emotionally, and spiritually. I led our first worship service, and Tom led our first *de memoriam*, Bible-less Bible study. The for-mat was simple. The leader would recall as best he could a Bible passage, and we would reflect together on it according to a series of four questions: What is the main point of this passage to me? Is it true in my experience? What is difficult, challenging, or confusing about the passage? How might this passage change my life?

We took turns rotating through a schedule, so that the days became more like regular days. There were tasks, responsibilities, decisions to make (when shall we have worship today — before or after lunch?) — a little structure to mark our progress through the endless gray-wash of time. And perhaps most important, through our prayer together we could reach outside the paint-peeling walls of our second-story dungeon, reach with our hearts and our souls to all those imprisoned by despair, poverty, and violence. It was a way for us to counteract the creeping self-absorption that inevitably accompanies captivity.

Tom's prayers were profound. They brought our suffering into dialogue with the vast suffering of the world. Again and again his prayers brought to mind other prisoners — security detainees in Iraq, illegal combatants in Guantánamo, the lost and forgotten souls in American penitentiaries. And every time we heard a bomb explode, near or far, Tom would stop to pray for those whose lives had just been destroyed. Every time, without fail.

Between Christmas and New Year's, something shifted in Tom. Perhaps it was the lack of protein his body craved, the absolute lack of solitude, or the relentless cold. Perhaps it was his inability to sleep, the burden of fear that came with his U.S. citizenship, or the extreme boredom. The intransigent strength and unflagging leadership of those first weeks evaporated. He asked for a sedative to help him sleep, and the captors obliged.

Tom took one, then two pills each day and still complained of being unable to sleep. His mind lost its suppleness. He seemed to be more fixed on his own ideas, less able to incorporate new information, his perceptions more rigid. We would frequently have to repeat things. He was either stone-silent or helplessly garrulous. His emotional life, which heretofore he carefully guarded, became an open book. "You know," he once said, "I've shared more with you guys than I have with anyone else in my life." Sometimes his sharing sounded more like verbal floundering.

We started to worry. Tom no longer seemed himself. Something had to be said. As if on cue, he voluntarily cut back to one capsule a day. He'd discerned that the sedation was pulling him deeper into a vortex of depression. "I don't like what it's doing to me," he said. I was relieved because his realization saved us from a confrontation.

Of course, none of us was at his best. Each of us, in our respective struggles to cope with the confinement, fear, and hunger, took turns carrying, and being carried by, the others.

At the end of a check-in one day, I embarked on a carefully prepared speech. "Early on, I figured out that there's no way I can defeat this boredom. It's just too big, too vast. It doesn't matter how many mental puzzles I do, how many prayers or meditations I say, there's just no way to win against it. I don't have enough will, or enough strength, or enough creativity, or enough of whatever it takes to manage or control or moderate what we're going through, or my reaction to it. It's just too big. If I'm going to get through this, it's going to have to come from something outside of me, something beyond me. It'll be because God carried me, and not because of anything I did."

Tom's theology was unfamiliar to me. In comparison, I found myself in the unusual position of feeling rather old-fashioned and orthodox in believing that Jesus is the Son of God, the unique incarnation of God's love; that we are destined to live in communion with a God who loves and knows each of us by name; that the place (or state of being) where that happens forever is called heaven; and that salvation is an unmerited consequence of God's unconditional love.

For Tom, God was a kind of nonpersonal energy, an energy of love, perhaps best described as light that suffuses and imbues everything. There is no limit to this energy, this light. It can — and wants to — grow and expand infinitely. We each have a little bit of that light. Or, as Quakers say it, "There is that of God in everyone." While not the Son of God, Jesus had a unique and privileged understanding of his connection to God. Though this spiritual connection is accessible to all of us, Jesus perfected that connection by going all the way in the spiritual life. Our task is to follow the example of Jesus and work to increase the amount of love energy in the universe as much as we can, so that one day everything will be transformed into love. This task requires tremendous effort, sacrifice, and hard work so that we can grow into a perfect understanding of our connection to God. It was effort, not grace, that seemed to animate Tom's ceaseless spiritual quest.

It's my hunch that Tom was haunted by a dread fear that the stresses and privations of captivity would irrevocably sever his connection to the divine, that he would eventually succumb to the temptation to hate and dehumanize his captors, and thus everything he worked for in the spiritual life would be lost. In our desperate circumstances, his answer was to strive harder, to hold fast with every last ounce of strength lest he fall helpless into the abyss of negativity.

It pained me to watch him in this struggle. I wanted to tell him, "You don't have to fight. God loves you more than you can possibly imagine. You don't have to *do* anything. Your connection with God is permanent and irrevocable. You cannot not be in the light."

The morning after Tom was taken, the commonplace routine of folding away our bed and arranging our chairs against the wall for the long day of sitting changed. Now, instead of four chairs, we needed only three.

A great hole opened in our lives. It was like the soul had gone out of our group. We labored through the day in a collective stupor. None of us wanted to acknowledge the horrible implication of Tom's departure.

I remember going into the bathroom and seeing only three toothbrushes. I had always enjoyed looking at them when there were four. There was something complete about them standing together in their square, grungy Tupperware container, each a different color (chosen purposely by Medicine Man so we wouldn't confuse our toothbrushes — red, green, blue, and purple — there was so little color in our lives!). They somehow represented our individuality. But now the purple one, Tom's, was gone. For just a moment, grief broke through. That little forest of toothbrushes I loved had been decimated.

Check-in, worship, and Bible study ceased. After a handful of days, I suggested that we resume check-in. After another handful of days, we returned to daily worship. Neither was ever the same. It always felt to me like we were merely going through the motions. As for Bible study, without Tom it was impossible.

On March 7, day 102, Medicine Man made a house call. "Do you have any news about Tom?" I asked.

"Yes, he is still at the other house. We have some problems so we separate him. You know his government will not negotiate for him. The CIA is trying to prevent the negotiation. They do not want the [prisoner] exchange to happen, so the negotiations are going very slow. We will make some announcement that we kill him — to separate your case. They do not know he is still alive. But we not kill him — he will be released with you. We make this announcement to the media, to put pressure on your governments, but we not kill him."

I said nothing. I looked at Medicine Man, nodded, received his news with a blank face. A poker face.

The next clue came four days later, on March 11. We were watching TV in our captors' living quarters. It had become something of a routine — they would unlock us around seven P.M., take us downstairs, and feed us supper. That was nice because we could eat with our hands free, like regular human beings. If we were lucky they'd have a pirate-edition DVD for us to watch. Otherwise it was an evening of Arabic channel surfing. At ten they'd return us to our room and lock us up for the night after we brushed our teeth.

We were watching TV when we saw it, a preview of the day's top news story, a poster board with each of our pictures, a close-up of Tom's picture, a cut to the last, ghostly video image of Tom in captivity. Then a road under construction, a piece of heavy equipment in the background, a close-up of a particular spot on the ground. That was all we saw before they changed the channel. I involuntarily shivered. Harmeet asked the captor we called Nephew why Tom was on TV. "Oh, this is normal," he said. "They are showing about your life on the news. Every night a different one of you. Tonight they are showing Tom." We knew he was lying. We stopped asking about Tom after that.

We didn't know for sure until the day of our rescue, fourteen days after Tom's body was found. It was the first question I asked the British soldiers who busted us out. "Where's Tom? Is he free or has he been killed?" I still clung to the hope that he might have been released.

"No, he was killed." The voice was hesitant, apologetic.

"Are you sure? Did they find his body?"

"Yes. They found his body."
"They found his body? You're sure?"
"Yes, they found his body."

Why are we here? It's the ultimate question, really. Whether we're cleaning up after dinner or facing a captor's gun, the earth turns, the sun rises and sets, the seasons come and go. We all have to find our way through, to somehow make sense of the turning, the rising and the setting, the coming and going of our lives, whatever the here is that we've been given to live. It's the task that God has breathed into us.

On this Tom was clear, as he tried to be about anything that was important. Clear in the sense of being open, seeing, paying attention, pushing the clutter away. Clear in the sense of letting the light within him shine. He reflected on that question in something he wrote titled "Why Are We Here?" on November 25, 2005, the evening before we were kidnapped.

The answer, he wrote, is "that we are to take part in the creation of the Peaceable Realm of God," a realm we help create when we love God, our neighbors, even our enemies, "with all our heart, our mind, and our strength."

In the context of Iraq, where "dehumanization seems to be the operative means of relating to each other," and where U.S. forces kill innocent Iraqis in "their quest to hunt down and kill" those they've dehumanized as "terrorists," Tom defined love positively as "a profound respect for all human beings simply for the fact that they are all God's children," and negatively as "never thinking or doing anything that would dehumanize one of my fellow human beings.

"The first step down the road to violence," he said, "is taken when I dehumanize a person . . . As soon as I rob a fellow human being of his or her humanity by sticking a dehumanizing label on them, I begin the process that can have, as an end result, torture, injury, and death.

"Why are we here?" he asked again. It was not a rhetorical question. "We are here to root out all aspects of dehumanization that exist within us. We are here to stand with those being dehumanized by oppressors and stand firm against that dehumanization. We are here to stop people, including ourselves, from dehumanizing any of God's children, no matter how much they dehumanize their own souls."

Every time I read these words, shivers ride up and down my arms. Amplified by their uncanny timing, these words were his last will and testament. His will, fierce and indomitable, to root out all aspects of violence within himself was the unceasing struggle of his captivity. His testament, what the arc of his life pointed to, the why of his "why are we here," was what he called the Peaceable Realm of God, where the lion lies down with the lamb, where every division is healed and fear is banished from every heart, and where rich and poor feast together at God's banquet table. That vision was the light that guided Tom Fox.

NANCY LORD

I Met a Man Who Has Seen the Ivory-billed Woodpecker, and This Is What He Told Me

FROM *Fourth Genre*

The Woods

THE SWAMP FOREST is only corridor between rice fields, but the ancient cypress tower there. Winds the week before had bared the trees, laying a carpet of tupelo golds, sweet-gum reds, the rusty cypress needles. It was possible to walk dry-footed among the fluted trunks and spreading knees, the wet-season watermarks waist-high on a man.

Woodpeckers

The usual woodpeckers were all there: their bouncing flight, the sounds of rapping, scrabbling on bark. They called *keer-uck* and *querrr-querrr, pik* and *peek, yucka, yucka yucka.* The downy and the hairy were there, the red-bellied, the yellow-bellied sapsucker. The pileated was there, the largest of them, the red crest, drumming like the pounding of mallets, loud. It was a birdy place: the wildness of trees in every aspect of life and death, with pecked-out cavities, with beetles, with peeling bark.

Woodpecker!

This is the word he let out as he grabbed for his wife's arm. He knew what he was seeing, and he could not believe that he was, in fact, seeing it. If for sixty years something has been missing, it takes more than the sight of a large, utterly distinct flying bird to convince a man of what is possible.

Eight Seconds

One for the bird flying toward him from deep forest. Two for the bird landing twelve feet up a cypress trunk and clinging there in profile. Three for the bird sliding around to the back of the tree, hiding itself. Two for the bird flashing back the way it came, a single whomping wing beat and all that white.

Color

The colossal male crest, of course — the brilliant flame so inescapably, unignorably red and pointedly tall. The white was more the surprise, down the neck and across the shoulders like a saddle, and the two large wedges shaped by folded wings. And the black, the black that was not charcoal, not ebony, only the absolutest of all blacks, and blacker still beside white.

Sound

He never heard the bird, not the *henk, henk* of its call, not its tooting, staccato song, not the double rap that distinguishes its tree knocking from any other woodpecker's. The early naturalists described ivory-bills as social and raucous, but whatever birds have survived have had to be shy and wary, as quiet as bark. They live by stealth.

What He Missed

Not the bill, not the length, which he showed me, holding his fingers apart — "Three inches." Not the thickness of the bill — this time, making a fat circle of forefinger and thumb. What he for-

got to notice was the pale color of the bill, the look of ivory. In the
blitz of recognition, he missed that, as he missed the very yellow eye.

The Quote

No puny pileated but a whacking big bird, he said, quoting Roger
Tory Peterson, who witnessed the ivory-bill in 1941 and called that
occasion the greatest birding moment of his long birding career.
Peterson kept a page for the bird in his guidebooks, hope against
hope, for years after others had shifted it to the extinct category.
But a decade ago, even Peterson concluded that the bird had
reached its end, like the woodlands it had inhabited, and no longer
existed except in memory.

After

For a long time, he had to sit on a log and not say anything. He
played the image of the bird over and over and over in his mind. It
was too great a thing to comprehend — that he was there, and the
bird was there, and he and the bird were breathing the same air. After the descriptions and illustrations by Catesby, Audubon, and Wilson; and after the photos and films from the Louisiana swamps
in the 1940s; and after the late but extensive Tanner scholarship
about life history and habitat; and after Peterson's passion and despair; and after the fleeting white of new video and all the talk
about the ghost bird and the grail bird and the Lord God bird; and
after his dead father's lifetime of desire and his own matching but
far-fetched desire and all the desire of the world; after all that, the
ivory-billed woodpecker was still more than a person could imagine. It was as beautiful and as perfect as only it itself, its living being,
could be.

THOMAS LYNCH

Into the Oblivion

FROM *Harper's Magazine*

MY EXPERIENCE WITH bodies and the parts of bodies over the past thirty-five years has taught me that our dead are precious to us because ours is a species, for better or for worse, that has learned to deal with death, the idea of the thing, by dealing with our dead, the thing itself. It casts my imagination back to forty or fifty thousand years ago, when the first human widow awakened in that cave to the dead lump of protein next to her and said, "My, he's very quiet this morning," or words to that effect. Depending on the season and the weather, sooner or later she would begin to sense — actually, she'd begin to smell — that this stillness was a different stillness than she had ever experienced before. She knew she'd have to do something about it. She knew she'd have to leave the cave to him, in which case, I suppose, it would become his tomb. Or maybe she thought she'd drag him out by the ankles and kick his sorry self over the cliff, in which case we could call him "consigned to the oblivion," or maybe she'd build a fire and burn his body, or she'd scratch a hole in the ground and tip him into it.

Whatever she did, whatever oblivion she consigned him to, the questions that quickened in her looking into that void became, I think, the signature of our species, what separates us from rock bass and rhododendrons and cocker spaniels and other living things that die. Looking into whatever oblivion she consigned that first dead thing to, she asked the standard questions. I hear them asked by widowed people today: "Is that all there is? Can it happen to me? Why is it cold? What comes next?" The dead do not care. I've spent a fair amount of time around cadavers, corpses, dead neighbors,

dead friends and family, and never once has one of them said anything like, "I want the blue pinstriped suit" or "the cherry casket"
or "the mum plants, please." They say nothing. They are mum on
the subject. The dead don't care, you can take that to the bank. But
the dead do matter. They matter to the living in ways that we're
only beginning to understand.

And so as you discuss bodies and the parts of bodies, I would encourage you to take on more the notion that whether we are talking about the parts of bodies of dead gangsters, buried maybe in
Milford, Michigan, where last month they went digging for whatever is left of Jimmy Hoffa at Hidden Dreams Farm, or whether we
are looking for our dead at the Fresh Kills landfill site, where their
bodies are commingled with those of their murderers on September 11, the dead are with us. We are all haunted, properly and hap-
pily in some cases, not only by their memories but also by their rem-
nants.

There are distinctions to be made between the notions of medical
death or metabolic death, social death, spiritual death, and actual
death as far as your family is concerned. I might know, for example,
that after a cremation, we end up with, say, fourteen pounds of
bone fragment and desiccated tissue that we can put in a box and
hand to the family, but when you see the elderly sister come to
claim the ashes of a sister whose own children couldn't come and
get her, when she bears that box like viaticum, when she walks out
the door, flips the button to open the trunk, and then reconsiders
and goes to the back door and opens it up, and then thinks better
of it and closes it again, when she goes to the front-seat passenger
door, opens it up, places the box on the front seat, and then clicks a
seat belt around it, you can see that whether we are remnant or
icon or relic is not up to you or me. It's up to the living who bear us
in their memory and, in fact, bear our mortality, because we are humans, tied to this humus, this layer of earth from which our monuments and our homes and our histories rise up.

The market, the retail event of organ and tissue procurement, is
something that may have medical consequences, but to most families it remains a mystery, tied up in issues of personhood, not parts.
There's this "just a shell" theory of how we should relate to dead
human bodies. You hear a lot of it from young clergy and old family

friends, well-intentioned in-laws, folks who are unsettled by the fresh grief of others. You hear it when you bring a mother and a father in for the first sight of their dead daughter killed in a car wreck or left out to rot by some mannish violence. It is proffered as a kind of comfort in the teeth of a comfortless situation, consolation to the inconsolable. Between the inhale and exhale of the bone-racking sob such hurts produce, some frightened and well-meaning ignoramus is bound to give out with "It's okay, it's not her. That's just a shell."

I once saw an Episcopalian deacon nearly decked by the swift slap of a mother of a teenager dead of leukemia to whom he had tendered this counsel. "I'll tell you when it's just a shell," the woman said. "For now and until I tell you otherwise, she's my daughter." The woman was asserting the long-standing right of the living to declare the dead dead. Just as we declare the living alive through baptisms and lovers in love by nuptials, funerals are the way we close the gap between the death that happens and the death that matters. It's how we assign meaning to our little histories. And the rituals we devise to conduct the living and the beloved and the dead from one status to another have less to do with performance than they do with meaning. In a world where "dysfunctional" has become the operative adjective, a body that has ceased to work has, it would seem, few useful applications beyond those we are talking about here this morning. It's dysfunction more manifest than the sexual and familial forms that fill our tabloids and talk shows. A body that doesn't work is, in the early going, the evidence we have of a person who has ceased to be, and a person who has ceased to be is as compelling a prospect as it was when the first hominid dug holes for his dead and set our species apart from the others.

So I encourage you, as you wrestle with these difficult issues, to consider the traffic between the living and the dead, because in most of these situations, there is no medicine or math, no bottom line or Bible verse, that will explain the mystery we behold when we behold someone we love dying or dead. I know this not only because of my professional and personal experience but also because I sense it in the lives of people all around me. The bodies of the newly dead are not debris or remnant, nor entirely icon or essence.

They are rather changelings, incubates, hatchlings of a new reality that bear our names and dates, our images and likenesses, as
surely in the eyes and ears of our children and grandchildren as
did words of our birth in the ears of our parents and their parents. It is wise to treat such new things tenderly, carefully, and with
honor.

From remarks to the President's Council on Bioethics, June 2006.

ADAM MINTER

Keeping Faith

FROM *The Atlantic Monthly*

ON A JUNE DAY in 1982, Father Aloysius Jin Luxian, a sixty-six-year-old Jesuit just released from prison, walked into Shanghai's St. Ignatius Cathedral for the first time in twenty-seven years. In his youth, the building had been one of the great churches in East Asia, celebrated for its delicate Gothic arches and colorful stained glass. Now the color was gone, replaced by clear glass and harsh sunlight that bleached the cracked columns and tiled floor. The steeples, once among the tallest in Shanghai, were missing, as was the altar beneath which he'd been ordained, in 1945. Jin had spent nearly three decades under house arrest, in reeducation camps, and in prison, so he had few illusions about the Chinese Communist Party's attitude toward religion. But the damage to the church was still hard to bear. St. Ignatius, he learned, had been converted to a grain warehouse during the Cultural Revolution, and the authorities had spent three days burning most of the diocese's Catholic books in front of the church.

Now services were being held again. But open prayers for the pope were strictly prohibited, and scant mention of the Holy Father could be found in any of the crudely printed books used in the cathedral. Mass was still in Latin, unintelligible to most Chinese. The current bishop had been ordained without approval from Rome, by a Communist government determined to erase the memory of Shanghai's still-incarcerated bishop, Ignatius Kung (Gong) Pin-mei. Everything was under the direct control of the Chinese Catholic Patriotic Association, the twenty-five-year-old government agency that oversaw Chinese Catholic life.

Yet on Saturday nights, the church was packed, its pews filled with 2,500 or more parishioners. Morning Mass wasn't quite as crowded, but it *happened*, and regularly. Elsewhere in Shanghai, four more Catholic churches were holding services, and they, too, were packed on Saturday nights. All these parishioners were attended to by sixty elderly priests, who'd submitted to living together in a single house, under strict CPA supervision, because they were determined to live openly as Catholic priests.

Priests had other options, including a nascent "underground" movement, whose members refused to worship in churches registered with the Religious Affairs Bureau, which oversaw the CPA. During the later years of his incarceration, Jin had become familiar with several priests who belonged to this movement, and he'd been impressed by their courage and piety. But the catastrophe that befell China's Catholics in the 1950s had convinced him that the underground movement, with its determination to confront the Communist Party, would never be able to provide a stable spiritual home for the thousands of Catholics who openly attended Mass in Shanghai every week.

Jin had once hoped that a distinctively Chinese Church would replace the missionary Church of his youth, reconciling his devout Roman Catholicism with his Chinese identity. The old attempts at reconciliation had failed because they'd emphasized one identity over the other, leaving a church that seemed neither authentically Catholic nor Chinese. But now, with Rome separated from its Chinese followers, there was an opportunity to create a truly Chinese Church — for Jin, and for the Catholics he aspired to lead.

Twenty-five years later, Father Jin — now bishop of Shanghai — sat across from me in his third-floor office, facing the cathedral's restored steeples. "It was heartbreaking," he said of the day he returned to the cathedral, and threw up his hands. "But what could I do?" We were talking in English, one of the five languages he speaks fluently. At ninety-one, he's a slight man, maybe five and a half feet tall, but his stiff posture gives him a sturdy presence, and when he took my hand to emphasize a point, I felt the metal of his bishop's ring.

Though largely unknown outside of China, Jin is arguably the most influential and controversial figure in Chinese Catholicism of the last fifty years. He played a leading role in persuading the authorities to allow a prayer for the pope to be said during Masses in China's registered, or "open," churches and in developing a Chinese-language liturgy, and he was single-handedly responsible for training more than four hundred priests — including several who became Vatican-recognized bishops — in Shanghai's seminary. He's also been an unabashed supporter of dialogue and compromise with the Communist government. He accepted ordination as a bishop without Vatican approval and has taken a leading role in China's open churches, all of which still have to register with the Religious Affairs Bureau and are overseen by bishops appointed by the CPA in consultation with local congregations.

Defying canon law, as Jin has done on several occasions, is no small matter for a Catholic bishop. But Rome has tolerated his disobedience, largely because of what he's accomplished in Shanghai. From his modern office, Jin looks out over a diocese that includes 141 registered churches, 74 priests (most under the age of forty), 86 nuns, 83 seminarians, and 150,000 laypeople. In Shanghai, at least, there's been a significant rapprochement between the underground Church and the open one, particularly on the leadership level: Jin is the most prominent Chinese open-Church bishop who recognizes, albeit quietly, the authority of the pope.

Indeed, the line between China's open and underground churches has been blurring for some time. There are members of the underground Church who still refuse to worship in open churches or to recognize the legitimacy of open-Church bishops. The open Church tends to be much more in line with the reforms of the Second Vatican Council, which translated the Mass into the vernacular and elevated the role of the laity; the underground Church tends to be nostalgic for the more hierarchical pre–Vatican II Church. But the reality of day-to-day life in the underground Church is more complex than the popular image of Christian believers hidden in Chinese catacombs would suggest. At least 90 percent of open-Church bishops have quietly reconciled with Rome, just as Jin did. In at least one diocese, a priest who served in the open Church was also ordained as an underground bishop. In other dioceses, underground priests have been known to hold Mass in open churches, often using missals and Bibles that Jin had translated and printed.

Nevertheless, the underground Church continues to be targeted by local governments wary of any social movement that refuses to recognize their authority (the national government is more tolerant). The harassment is most pronounced in rural areas, where many Catholics don't have access to priests or registered churches. But Catholics are sometimes still persecuted in the cities, and today more than two dozen underground priests and bishops are reportedly in government custody.

Jin does not dismiss the suffering of underground Catholics, but he seems to believe it's unnecessary, now that the sacraments are available in open churches. Explaining why accommodation, rather than resistance, is the right path for Chinese Catholics, he says his flock is in no position to confront the Chinese government, particularly at the behest of the wealthy overseas supporters of the underground Church. "I don't wait for [the Communist] collapse," he says. "I get things done now." Besides, he adds, from the 1950s onward, he realized that Communist secret police "are everywhere, like God. So we can't do secret activities. It's stupid."

Cardinal Theodore McCarrick of Washington, D.C., a friend and admirer of Jin for nearly two decades, told me, "What I like about Jin is that he's very Chinese and very Catholic at the same time." It's why McCarrick calls him "one of the most important churchmen in China of our time." Jin isn't so optimistic about his legacy. "The Vatican thinks that I don't work enough for the Vatican, and the government thinks that I work too much for the Vatican," he says. "It is not easy to satisfy both."

Jin says that from the beginning his primary interest has been poor Catholics in China, "my Catholics." Neither Beijing nor Rome has always had their best interests at heart, he suggests, and so he's tried to step into the breach. In the process, he's become a different sort of Catholic than he was when he was ordained (by a *French* priest, he points out) — a personal transformation that's mirrored by the changes at work in China's growing population of Catholics, both underground and open.

Christianity first reached China in the seventh century, carried by Nestorians via the Silk Road, but it wasn't until the mid-sixteenth century, with the arrival of the Society of Jesus, that the Catholic Church established a permanent presence in the Middle Kingdom.

After that, the faith made substantial inroads, thanks to Matteo Ricci, a brilliant Italian Jesuit who abandoned traditional evangelization techniques in favor of an "enculturated" approach that accommodated traditional Chinese beliefs and rituals, including the commonplace practice of venerating one's ancestors.

The Jesuits' tolerance for these "Chinese rites" generated controversy back in Rome, and in 1704, after a century of debate, Pope Clement XI was persuaded by the Jesuits' rivals to condemn them as hopelessly tainted by superstition. The Chinese emperors, who'd been tolerant of the missionaries, were outraged — as Jin notes, "To be Chinese, it was most important to venerate ancestors" — and during the 1720s missionaries and then Christianity itself were banned in China.

Catholic missionaries reentered China a century later, thanks to the 1842 treaties that opened the Chinese mainland to both opium and European Christians. French Jesuits built their headquarters on the edge of the small fishing village of Shanghai, and soon after raised Shanghai's first cathedral, a wooden predecessor to St. Ignatius that was completed in 1910. Catholicism — and Christianity in general — grew steadily in China throughout the nineteenth and early twentieth centuries, and by the outbreak of World War I, Chinese Catholics numbered 1.2 million.

Jin claims that the first members of his family converted to Catholicism more than ten generations ago, while they were servants in the house of a Shanghai aristocrat. His childhood was beset by tragedy: at ten he lost his mother, at fourteen his father, and at eighteen his only sibling, an older sister. ("And yet I live to a very old age," he observes. "Very curious, yes?") His family had enrolled him in Shanghai's Jesuit-run schools, and he entered the order in 1938, the year he turned twenty-two. "I had lost everyone," he says. "So I looked to be a soldier for God."

Jin had always seen similarities between Catholicism and Chinese culture. Like many Chinese Christians, he was attracted to the Gospel of John and its mystical concept of Logos — or "the Word," as embodied in Christ. "The Logos is like Chinese philosophy," he says, referring to the Tao, a concept sometimes translated as "the Way." Both the Tao and Logos, he explains, suggest a rational order in the universe, though in the case of Catholicism, that order is revealed physically in the figure of Christ.

Reconciling Chinese philosophy with Catholic theology was eas-ier than reconciling the political demands of his two masters in this world. The year after Jin entered the Jesuit order, Pope Pius XII ended most of the restrictions on the Chinese rites, and in 1946 he established an independent hierarchy for China's Church, so that it was no longer a missionary project. But there was still tension be-tween being Catholic and being Chinese. As late as 1949, more than 80 percent of China's dioceses remained under the control of European bishops who had little interest in relinquishing their sees to the Chinese. Like the pope and the Vatican hierarchy, many of these bishops — under the direction of Archbishop Antonio Riberi, the papal internuncio to China — supported Chiang Kai-shek's Chinese Nationalists, even after 1949, when the Commu-nists triumphed and Chiang's government fled to Taiwan. That created an identity crisis for Catholics on the mainland, many of whom shared Jin's perception that the Communist victory marked "the recovery by China of full independence as well as her national self-respect." As Jin remarked in a 1987 speech to German Catho-lics, "To remain Catholic, they could not remain Chinese."

When the Communists swept into power, Jin was in Rome work-ing on his doctorate in theology at the Pontifical Gregorian Univer-sity. By the time he graduated, in 1950, Beijing had begun to re-strict religious freedoms and expel foreign missionaries. "I knew that I would be arrested if I returned to China," Jin says matter-of-factly. He returned anyway. "The missionaries were leaving, and China needed pastors."

In 1951, in an attempt to persuade the Communists not to view the Church as a hostile, foreign-controlled entity, Jin proposed cre-ating a conference of Chinese bishops that would run the Church in a manner that reflected Chinese, not European, interests. He was promptly reported to the papal internuncio, whose response, he says with a laugh, was: "This young priest talks nonsense!" Re-buked, Jin spent the next four years as the rector of Shanghai's ma-jor seminary, training as many Chinese priests as possible to re-place the departed missionaries.

But by then, little could be done to help China's Catholics. The Communists had expelled Riberi in 1951 and officially severed diplomatic relations with the Vatican. Ignatius Kung Pin-mei, the bishop of Shanghai, emerged as China's leading Catholic voice against the Communists. Jin considered Kung a friend but disagreed with his confrontational approach. "Kung believed that the Nationalists would win and come back," he says. "I said, 'No. How? It's a small island — how can they conquer [mainland] China?'"

On September 8, 1955, Kung and Jin were arrested, along with three hundred priests, nuns, and laypeople (an additional eight hundred Catholics were arrested a few weeks later). For the next five years, Jin was kept mostly in solitary confinement in Shanghai, his only human contact with the interrogators and the guards. He was allowed no books or other written materials. When I asked how he survived that period, he smiled and said that he'd memorized the Gospels as a young man. "I kept my faith, by praying and meditating on the Gospels, especially John."

In 1960, Jin was convicted of counterrevolutionary activities and received an eighteen-year sentence. Kung was convicted of high treason and received a life sentence. Jin spent the ensuing years in various prisons and reeducation camps, where he worked as a farmer and, off and on, as a translator of foreign documents for the national Public Security Bureau. Ironically, after he finally got access to newspapers during the Cultural Revolution, his hope was shaken in a way it hadn't been when he was in solitary confinement. "I heard that China was an atheist nation — that the missions, churches, Catholics, Buddhist temples, and Islamic mosques were all gone," he says. "And I nearly lost my hope." He pauses. "Almost." Prayer sustained him, as it does today: every morning, promptly at 7:30, he says a private Mass with a single attendant in the chapel next to his study. "I still pray the rosary," he notes. "Now I have beads, and I didn't in jail."

Though Jin's sentence was completed in the mid-1970s, he remained a political prisoner in northern China until 1982. "I entered [prison] a young man," he says, "and left an old one." He emerged to find a Chinese Church that had been utterly transformed. In July 1957, at the behest of the Communist Party, a small group of Chinese Catholic leaders had held the first meeting of the Catholic Patriotic Association, whose stated policy was to ensure that "Chinese Catholics, cleric and lay, take charge of their own affairs and no longer act contrary to the interests of their country." A year later, two Chinese bishops were ordained without papal approval, and over the next seven years, forty-nine more would be — until the Cultural Revolution ended the government's limited toleration for religion.

The Vatican saw the ordinations as an affront, and Pope Pius XII wrote an encyclical letter reasserting his right to select bishops — and to excommunicate anyone who circumvented him. However, neither he nor his successors excommunicated any of the bishops consecrated under Communist supervision. Instead, the Vatican quietly recognized that, despite the illicit procedure, the bishops had been ordained by valid prelates, and thus were valid themselves. According to Anthony S. K. Lam, a scholar of the Chinese Church at Hong Kong's Holy Spirit Study Centre, the "illicit but valid" designation is well known. "If you are ordained by an illicit but valid bishop, you are a valid bishop," he says. "But only the pope can say you are the bishop of Shanghai."

When Jin emerged from prison in 1982, Shanghai had two bishops: Ignatius Kung Pin-mei, who was still incarcerated, and Aloysius Zhang Jiashu, a ninety-year-old Jesuit who'd been consecrated under Communist supervision in 1960. Many in the city's elderly Catholic community held Kung in the highest regard, but Zhang was a more controversial figure. The situation epitomized the larger dilemma facing Chinese Catholics: how to reconcile the Church that had spent more than a generation underground with the Church that was tainted by its links to Communism and estranged from the Holy See.

But an important fact was pushing the two churches toward reconciliation, or at least coexistence: Catholicism was growing. In 1980, China officially had three million Catholics (likely an underestimate due to poor census data), the same number it had had in 1949. Today, the best estimates place the Catholic population between twelve million and fifteen million. No single explanation accounts for this increase, which is mirrored by the growth of other Christian denominations, but many people, including Jin, think that religion has been filling the vacuum created by the collapse of Marxism's ideological credibility. Whatever the cause, the exploding numbers have reinforced the need to hold the Church in China together, despite the forces that threaten to tear it apart. This is the mission that has defined Jin's career — one that began when he stepped out of prison and onto the tightrope he's walked ever since.

Within a few months of Jin's release, the Communist Central Committee published Document 19, the official policy on religion. Following party dogma, it declared religion to be a historical phenomenon that would disappear once socialism's triumph was complete. In the interim, it called for steps that would strengthen the independence of Chinese religious institutions and insulate them from negative foreign influences, steps that included the reopening of seminaries to train a new generation of patriotic priests.

Under this policy, Jin was asked to take up his old responsibilities as rector of Shanghai's seminary. Though the CPA would be looking over his shoulder, he saw the necessity: in all of China, there were at most four hundred priests to serve three million Catholics. He believed that if the Church was to have any chance of survival, China would need young, well-educated priests, even if they were subjected to Communist propaganda during their training. Through a "foreign friend," Jin requested permission from Rome. The response was that he should "wait for the collapse" of the Communist Party, then reopen the seminary. "They underestimated the Chinese Communist Party," says Jin. And so, after "much prayer," he acted in what he believed to be the best interests of China's Catholics. "I didn't obey the directive of Rome. I said, 'Let the Catholic Church survive.'"

Initially at least, there was little to suggest that the seminary was Catholic. Without Vatican support, Jin had to look elsewhere for books and Bibles. "I had to go to Protestants," he says. That set a precedent, and though he says he tries to obtain support and funding from Roman Catholic organizations whenever possible, since the early 1980s the Shanghai diocese has received significant funding for religious publishing and book purchases from non-Catholic Christian organizations sympathetic to his desire "to proclaim the word of God."

Such developments didn't help Jin's already tenuous standing in Rome. "Once, I was present when John Paul [II] was given testimony on the dramatic suffering of the underground in Shanghai," recalls Jeroom Heyndrickx, a Belgian priest who has served as an informal Vatican emissary to the Chinese Church since the early 1980s. "And then you hear that a man like Jin comes out and is officially recognized. That puts him in a very bad light."

Jin's fellow Jesuits in Taiwan were particularly critical of his approach. "In the early eighties they accused me of being a traitor," he says. "They said I was a secret Communist. They accused me of becoming a party member in prison and being a traitor to the

Church." Sighing, he adds, "Rome believed it" — for most of the 1980s, "people abroad considered me a Judas."

Despite the negative reports that made their way to Rome, John Paul II showed a strong sympathy for China's Church. As a former bishop of Krakow, he seemed to understand instinctively the compromises made by China's Catholics, and in several speeches and encyclicals, he indicated his support for open as well as underground believers. According to Heyndrickx and two other people who closely observed Vatican China policy in the 1980s, John Paul II and his inner circle developed a positive perception of Jin in the mid-'80s, mostly as a result of reports emanating out of the newly reopened seminary. Heyndrickx recalls being asked by the pope to assess Jin's character, and responding, "If he is not faithful, then neither am I."

Jin's loyalty was put to the test in January 1985, when he was chosen by Shanghai's priests and the CPA to be ordained an auxiliary bishop (an assistant and possible successor) to Bishop Zhang. Few inside or outside of Shanghai believed that it was possible for Jin to remain a faithful Catholic — at least, a *Roman* Catholic — if he accepted the ordination. Yet Jin believed that to reject the appointment would not only place the seminary at risk but also open the Shanghai hierarchy to a priest more inclined toward the CPA and the Communist Party. Reluctantly, he accepted, and he says that on the day of the ordination, he was in need of "consolation."

It arrived from an unlikely source: with Pope John Paul's knowledge and tacit approval, Laurence Murphy, a past president of Seton Hall University and an informal intermediary and adviser to the Vatican on the Chinese Church, and Father John Tong, now the auxiliary bishop of Hong Kong, attended the ceremony. "That was kind of delicate," Murphy told me, recalling that St. Ignatius was filled with "brass from the CPA." Jin concedes that there might have been serious consequences had the CPA been aware of a Vatican-approved presence, and he admitted that Murphy and Tong had attended the ordination only after I asked him to confirm Murphy's account. "It was not encouraged by me," he said defensively. "I did not apply for that." After a pause, he added, "They encouraged me, and it was helpful and consolation."

In 1982, shortly after he was released from prison, Jin petitioned the government to allow him to visit the imprisoned Bishop Kung.

He was allowed to make three visits before Kung was released, in 1985 (with Jin signing a personal guarantee of his good behavior). Kung lived in Shanghai under house arrest, accepting visitors and maintaining friendly relations with Jin, who says Kung was "like a brother" at the time. Then in 1988, the same year that Bishop Zhang died and Jin succeeded him as the government-approved head of the Shanghai diocese, Kung received permission to seek medical treatment abroad, and after it was completed, he went into exile, living at his nephew's home in Connecticut.

According to an American Church official involved in making the Vatican's China policy, the Vatican strongly preferred that Kung remain in China, because it believed that he was uniquely positioned to heal the rift in China's Church. Instead, against the wishes of John Paul II but with the tacit support of high-ranking Vatican officials who sympathized with the underground, Kung, working with his nephew, began deepening the rift. The situation grew even more confused when it was revealed that the pope had named Kung a cardinal *in pectore* — "in secret" — in 1979, during his imprisonment. Kung and his nephew formed the Cardinal Kung Foundation, a U.S.-based nonprofit that supports and agitates on behalf of the underground Church. For Jin, a favorite target of foundation attacks, Kung's status and activities were an affront. "Cardinal Kung pushes all of the Catholics against the Chinese Communist Party, then he moves to the United States," he says. "Very nice for him." Jin has traveled abroad extensively (the government allows him to go anywhere but Rome), and he likes to point out that he too has plenty of "foreign friends" who could support him in exile if he chose that.

Instead, Jin used his standing as a bishop to begin the reforms that he'd wanted to see in China's Church since the 1940s. In 1988, he made six trips to Beijing in hopes of persuading the Religious Affairs Bureau to, among other things, allow him to include a prayer for the pope in his diocese's services; he obtained permission on the sixth visit. The next year, he received permission to have two Hong Kong priests and an American priest teach at the seminary. Soon after their arrival, the priests began preparing the seminarians to say Mass in the vernacular, and on September 30, 1989, the first Chinese-language Mass was celebrated in Shanghai. Father Joseph Zen, a Shanghai native and now the cardinal archbishop of Hong Kong, was the celebrant. The risk was significant:

China's religious authorities reserved the right to approve changes to the liturgy, and they'd long preferred Latin, largely because it couldn't be understood by most Chinese.

Over the next several months, Jin says, he quietly ordered his priests and seminarians to take the new liturgy to Shanghai's other churches. "Jin was the one who had the guts to implement the Mass," says Father Thomas Law, a Hong Kong liturgist who was involved in the Mass at the chapel. "Nobody else." The Chinese-language Mass wasn't officially authorized on a national level until 1993. Soon afterward, the Shanghai diocese published its own translation, which was quickly disseminated throughout the country.

It was characteristic Jin. He has keen political instincts, and throughout his career he's been able to use his standing as an open-Church bishop to achieve things that he never could have done in the underground Church. Though Jin won't discuss his relationships with Chinese officials, those close to him claim that he has good relations at a very high level in Beijing and Shanghai. It's a delicate balancing act, says Jeroom Heyndrickx: "He had to say things that sound correct to the regime that also protect his church."

During one of our interviews, Jin contrasted himself with the outspoken Joseph Zen, who has become a well-known agitator against the CPA since taking over as archbishop of Hong Kong. "You cannot speak out as a bishop in a Communist country," Jin says. "I can't freely speak like Zen, because I must protect my diocese." Withholding criticism of China's religious authorities and their policies is perhaps the greatest compromise that the open-Church bishops choose to make.

At the same time, there are lines that Jin won't cross. In the early 1990s, for instance, he was offered the chairmanship of the government-organized Chinese bishops' conference, but declined the overture because he thought it would compromise his independence. The role was later assumed by Beijing's Bishop Fu Tieshen, who, after his death in April 2007, was widely criticized for being little more than a mouthpiece for the Communist Party.

In conversation, Jin exhibits few doubts about his decisions, but occasionally his answers turn defensive. During one of our interviews, I asked about his impressions of the underground Church.

He began to answer, then suddenly interrupted himself. "[The members of the underground Church] say they are loyal to the pope," he said. "But I am as loyal as them. Why become bishop? I led the [Chinese] Catholics to pray for the pope and even printed the prayer! I reformed the liturgy. Before me, it was all in Latin. But the underground Church did nothing. If I stayed with them, I would do nothing, too."

Cardinal McCarrick told me that he and Jin had a routine during the 1990s: "I would tell him, 'I am going to visit the Holy Father soon. Is there anything that you would like me to tell him?' And he would answer, 'Tell the Holy Father that he has my prayers and blessings.' And I would ask, 'Anything else?' And he would answer, 'And the blessings of my priests, sisters, and congregations.' And anything else? And he would pause and say, 'Not at this time.'"

During the 1990s, according to several of his friends, Jin was frustrated that despite his accomplishments, he could not be recognized as the rightful bishop of Shanghai. (By 2000, roughly two-thirds of the open-Church bishops were reconciled with Rome.) Laurence Murphy says the reason was that Jin was unwilling to communicate, in writing or orally, that he was loyal to the pope. "Along with many others, he believed that the Vatican had been infiltrated by the Communists," says Murphy. "And they didn't want to trust anything to that bureaucracy, because they thought, 'In twenty-four hours it will be known in Beijing.'"

Many in the Vatican doubted Jin's loyalties well into the 1990s, in part because of allegations made by the Kung Foundation and others sympathetic to the underground Church. Kung himself ultimately refused to meet Jin in the United States, even though the Vatican had asked them to sit down together and try to repair the divide. Kung died in exile in 1999, and his auxiliary, Fan Zhongliang (who lived in Shanghai), succeeded him.

In 2000, at the behest of the Vatican, Fan visited Jin at his office in the basilica near the seminary. At the time, both bishops were in their eighties, and the Vatican had asked them to agree upon a successor. Their candidate would be submitted to the pope, then presented to the diocese's priests for election and to the CPA for approval. At the very least, the Vatican intended to make clear that the auxiliary bishop would be an open-Church bishop, and that

Fan — as an underground bishop — would have no successor. And if all went as planned, the two faces of Shanghai's Church could be officially unified.

Fan proposed a priest who Jin says "didn't know the diocese, and the diocese didn't know him." Jin's preferred candidate, Joseph Xing Wenzhi, was unacceptable to Fan. During the years that followed, Fan became incapacitated by Alzheimer's, a turn of events that Heyndrickx says gave the Vatican the opportunity to secretly recognize Jin as the de jure bishop of Shanghai (in the Vatican's eyes, Jin is officially the coadjutor of the diocese). Jin will neither confirm nor deny that status, but it's unquestioned among Church leaders in Europe and North America, and it was tacitly acknowledged at the June 2005 public consecration of Xing as Jin's auxiliary. Had Jin not been reconciled with Rome, Xing's ordination would have been declared illicit. Instead, it was attended by Vatican emissaries, hundreds of laypeople from the underground Church, several underground priests, and more than a dozen government representatives.

In the months surrounding Xing's ordination, Beijing hinted that the ascension of Pope Benedict XVI might offer an opportunity for a deal with Rome, and Benedict seemed to signal a desire to work with the Communist government. That September, he personally invited four mainland Chinese bishops, including Jin, to attend the Synod of the Eucharist in Rome the following month. The government refused on the bishops' behalf, decrying Vatican interference in China's affairs, but the point had been made: Jin and the two other open-Church bishops were legitimate in the eyes of the new pope. Jin left the Vatican's letter of invitation on his desk for a month, explaining to anyone who asked that it "justified everything [he] had done."

Then, as now, Beijing had two conditions for normalizing relations with the Vatican: the severing of the Vatican's diplomatic ties with Taiwan (and as a consequence, the transfer of its embassy to the mainland) and an agreement not to interfere in China's internal affairs. The Vatican has indicated that it's prepared to meet the Taiwan condition, but the second issue, which encompasses the selection of bishops, is more difficult. Informally, the Vatican might be satisfied with a compromise similar to the process used to nominate Xing in Shanghai. However, public declarations to the contrary, it's been suggested that both the government and the underground Church have a tacit interest in preventing a deal, since it would inevitably empower the open bishops and their conference, diminishing the government's influence and the underground Church's prestige.

Whether an immediate way can be found through the impasse may depend on what Benedict XVI has to say in a promised letter to Chinese Catholics.* Leaked reports and the impressions of a source close to the drafting of the letter suggest that it will call, as John Paul II did, for reconciliation between the open and underground churches, and focus largely on pastoral concerns. Ultimately, it's expected to portray China's Catholics as largely united after a half century and to acknowledge that any diplomatic solution will need to accommodate both the vitality of the open Church and the struggles of the underground one.

Jin has watched the diplomatic ebb and flow between Rome and Beijing for twenty years, and he's pessimistic about the short-term prospects for a deal. If he's wrong, and rapprochement occurs suddenly, China's Church could change dramatically: the Chinese hierarchy — still split between underground and open bishops in many dioceses — would be reunited, which could smooth over divisions within the Church, but also reopen old wounds. For now, though, Jin's attempt at an intermediate way still seems likely to chart the future for China's Catholics.

Of the many goals that Bishop Jin set for himself after leaving prison, none was more personal than the restoration of Shanghai's cathedral. Over the two decades that followed, the steeples were replaced, the walls and columns were repaired, and a new altar was built. But cost constraints meant that the hundreds of Gothic window frames had to be filled with clear, rather than stained, glass. Even so, Jin did not give up hope that he might once again see the church lit with a mysterious glow, as it had been in his youth.

In 1991, while in Beijing on Church business, Jin was introduced to Wo Ye, the then twenty-eight-year-old daughter of Communist Party officials and a recent convert to Catholicism. Trained as a traditional porcelain painter, Wo was working as a newspaper art di-

---

*Pope Benedict's letter was released on June 30, 2007, and conformed to the description in this paragraph.

rector. The two became fast friends, and Jin invited her to work for the Shanghai diocese as an artist. Since she had no training in church art, he offered to send her abroad for nearly a decade of study at Catholic institutions in Italy and the United States. Wo agreed, a first step toward restoring the stained glass.

In 2001, after Wo returned to China, formal planning for the project began. Work started the following year, with Wo supervising a staff of nuns from the diocese, and in the fall of 2006, they completed the first stage: forty-four windows in ground-level nave chapels depicting the life of Jesus.

The results look nothing like the stained-glass windows of Europe. Images of Christ's life are executed as variations on traditional Chinese paper cutouts, and the surrounding grillwork is based on Qing-dynasty window designs found in a busy Shanghai market. Chinese iconography complements the Gospel story — a magpie represents the birth of Christ, a coiled phoenix represents the risen Christ — and blazing Chinese characters explain the scenes. Over the next several years, the plan is to fill the upper-level windows with a golden bamboo garden meant to represent paradise and the middle level with figures important to China's Church, rendered in a fashion that suggests traditional Chinese painting. "The old church appealed to three million Catholics," says Jin. "I want to appeal to a hundred million Catholics."

During my last interview with Jin, Wo stopped by the office to say hello, settling into a chair beside the bishop. The conversation drifted, and Jin told a story that neither Wo nor I had heard before. In the late 1980s, he said, the Italian government invited him to Rome. Zhou Ziyang, then China's prime minister, gave him permission to go. "The Chinese say, 'Go and get the real feeling of the Holy See toward China,'" Jin said. "At the time, Zhou Ziyang was ready to normalize relations." The Vatican was not. "Rome refused me."

A priest close to the Vatican later wrote to me to say that he'd heard this "rumor" and speculated that Rome had refused permission because of Jin's poor standing with people in Shanghai's underground Church. Jin didn't tell me this. Instead, he looked across the room at Wo, smiled, and asked when the cathedral would be completed.

"In time," she answered.

RICHARD JOHN NEUHAUS

A University of a Particular Kind

FROM *First Things*

VALPARAISO UNIVERSITY HAD an inestimable part in shaping my understanding of the Church and its mission in the world, as it did for many Lutherans of the time. There at Valparaiso was the Lutheran Human Relations Association under the leadership of the sainted Andrew Schulze. There was the annual Liturgical Institute, which strove to advance a Lutheran understanding of what Valparaiso's Ernest Koenker described as "The Liturgical Renaissance in the Roman Catholic Church." There was the journal the *Cresset,* under the skillful editorships of John Strietelmeier and, later, of my cherished colleague at *First Things,* James Nuechterlein.

But, above all, Valparaiso was O. P. Kretzman. Please permit a measured indulgence of nostalgia. As a young boy in a Lutheran parsonage, I avidly read his column "The Pilgrim," and in it I glimpsed a world of faith and devotion joined to learning and beauty. Always with O.P., as he was called, the autumn leaves seemed to be falling to the strains of Bach's Mass in B Minor, and a melancholic wisdom was tempered by the shimmering promise and high good humor reflected from a light and a light yet to be.

In luce tua videmus lucem. "In your light we see light." The words of Psalm 36 and the motto of Valparaiso University. Which raises the inescapable questions: Is that still Valparaiso University? And will that be Valparaiso twenty-five or forty years from now?

In his 1990 apostolic constitution on Christian education, John Paul II insisted that the university is *ex corde ecclesiae* — from the heart of the Church. He spoke of the Catholic university, of course, but the vision challenges every Christian university. In *Ex Corde*

Ecclesiae, John Paul wrote: "With every other university [the Christian university] shares that *gaudium de veritate,* so precious to Saint Augustine, which is the joy of searching for, discovering and communicating truth in every field of knowledge. [Such] a university's privileged task is to unite existentially by intellectual effort two orders of reality that too frequently tend to be placed in opposition as though they were antithetical: the search for truth, and the certainty of already knowing the fount of truth."

There are — or there should be — different kinds of universities. At least that is the case if there is no such thing as a university pure and simple. John Henry Newman's much and rightly admired *The Idea of a University* is the idea of *a* university, which is a way of saying that a decision must be made, and constantly remade, to be a particular kind of university. It is sometimes said that a Christian university has a "dual identity," one by virtue of being a university and another by virtue of being Christian. I suggest that is seriously mistaken, since it assumes that the term "university" is neutral or self-explanatory. Every university is, whether by careful deliberation or by accident, a university of a particular kind.

The origins of the university are *ex corde ecclesiae.* From the Middle Ages to the present — from Bologna and Oxford to Yale and Princeton — the university was explicitly constituted and inspired by Christian faith. In Harvard Yard one can still see the original seal with the word *veritas* surrounded by the words *pro Christo et ecclesia,* "for Christ and the Church." By the beginning of the twentieth century, that motto was reduced to just the one word, *veritas,* and at Harvard there is obviously no consensus on what that truth might be, or even on whether there is such a thing as truth. (The long and steady retreat of American universities from their Christian founding is brilliantly analyzed in James Burtchaell's *The Dying of the Light,* a book that must be read by everyone who cares about the future of the Christian university.)

When Harvard changed its seal and the constituting conviction reflected in that seal, it did not become more of a university. Nor did it become less of a university. It became a different kind of university. It became what we are accustomed to call a "secular university." A secular university is not a university pure and simple. "Secular" is not a synonym for "neutral." Secular, which easily turns into the ideology of secular*ism,* is more often than not a repudiation of an institution's constituting understanding of *veritas.*

When a university decides not to say that Jesus is the way, the truth, and the life, it is not saying nothing. Rather, it is saying that adherence to *this* way, *this* truth, and *this* life is not necessary to, or is a hindrance to, being the kind of university it wants to be. The idea that the word "university" has a univocal meaning results in an American circumstance in which all universities are measured by Harvard, Yale, Princeton, Stanford, and perhaps a few others, such as Duke and Berkeley. All other universities are in the second, third, and fourth tiers. They are, not to put too fine a point on it, second, third, or fourth rate. This way of thinking is both reflected and reinforced by the way that faculty members calculate the arc of their academic successes or, as the case may be, of their failures. The achievements of the great research universities are not to be belittled. But they are not universities pure and simple.

It is a pleasant thing when *U.S. News & World Report* ranks a school in "the top twenty" or "the top fifty" in the country. But what does *U.S. News & World Report* know about what that school intends to be? What does *U.S. News & World Report* know about what Valparaiso University intends to be? Of course, if it is merely a matter of recruitment and marketing, or of developing what is called a niche market, there is no problem with such rankings. There is, however, an unattractive word for people who can be bought on the market, and the same word applies to universities that are for sale. If I may be permitted to paraphrase: what does it profit a university to attain the second tier but lose its soul?

Institutions have souls that reflect the souls of those who brought them into being with a definite intention and reflect the souls of those who keep faith with, and build upon, that intention. A university born *ex corde ecclesiae* — from the heart of the Church — must decide, and then decide again every day, whether or not to keep faith with the Church of Jesus Christ. Many schools describe themselves as being church-related. "Church-related" — it is a phrase suggestive of tenuousness and ambivalence. Some Catholic schools that are uncertain about Catholicism delicately describe themselves as being "in the Catholic tradition" or, even more tenuously, "in the Jesuit tradition."

Some years ago, *First Things* sponsored a conference on higher education. One of the participants was the president of a major university tenuously affiliated with the United Methodist Church. He said that, in speaking to certain audiences, he sometimes referred to the school as a Methodist university, but, he added, "If I said we were a Christian university, all hell would break loose." Any talk about being church-related frequently refers to something vestigial; it says something about the school's past rather than its future, something about what the school used to be rather than what it hopes to be. It can present itself as Methodist merely by pointing to its history, while to present itself as Christian it must believably point to its governing convictions.

That president and his constituency are made nervous by the phrase "Christian university," for it brings to mind Jerry Falwell's Liberty University or Pat Robertson's Regent University, with their lingering taint of fundamentalism. But should we let schools such as Liberty and Regent have a monopoly on the venerable title of "Christian university"? Without denigrating those schools, which are to be respected for their determination to be a particular kind of university, one may suggest that leaders who have a firmer and more comprehensive understanding of the Christian intellectual tradition have the responsibility to demonstrate a different way of being a Christian university.

It is not enough to be a church-related university. Governing conviction is more important than church affiliation, but church affiliation can help sustain governing conviction. In 1967 — in what is called the Land O' Lakes Statement — a number of Catholic universities declared that they were not accountable to any authority outside the institutions of the academy. They were born *ex corde ecclesiae*, but now they declared that they were cutting the umbilical cord. In the past ten years or so — prompted by the pope's exhortation of 1990, or by alumni discontent and recruitment problems, or by a mix of these and other considerations — many of the more than two hundred Catholic colleges and universities in this country have been scrambling to reassert what is called their "Catholic identity." Catholic identity is usually something short of governing Catholic conviction. For Catholics and other Christians, the community of conviction is the church, however variously structured.

The Christian university requires a structured form of conversation, both affirmative and critical, with a particular community of Christian faith. In the absence of such accountability — an accountability that is not imposed but freely sought — the Christian university will most likely succumb to the institutional and ideological dynamics of other kinds of universities. It is not enough that there be a department of theology or a vibrant student chaplaincy. Indeed, as James Burtchaell's research demonstrates, the schools that ended up in repudiating their Christian founding began by assigning the responsibility to be Christian to theology departments and the chapel. The result was that they lost their connection with "the Church's heart for learning" and, along with it, the responsibility of inviting students to enter on the high adventure of the Christian intellectual tradition — a tradition ever so much richer than the reductionist Enlightenment embraced by schools that claim to be universities pure and simple.

A prominent professor at an Ivy League school recently wrote on the op-ed page of the *New York Times* that he tells his students that "if they are not more confused and uncertain at the end of my courses than they were at the beginning, I have been a failure." Imagine that: a well-credentialed and tenured grownup whose purpose in life is to increase confusion and uncertainty in the minds of undergraduates.

It seems to me that the great majority of young people entering college are sufficiently confused and uncertain as it is. The idea that it is the task of the university to debunk the certitudes and orthodoxies of young people is quite wrong-headed — unless, of course, one means by certitudes and orthodoxies the intellectual incoherence and mindless relativism that the young imbibe from the general culture. The task of the university is to form and inform minds by arousing curiosity about, as Matthew Arnold put it, the best that has been thought and said. The goal of the Christian university is to arouse and direct such curiosity about the unparalleled synthesis of Athens and Jerusalem, of faith and reason, that is the Christian intellectual tradition. Faith and reason, John Paul said in his encyclical *Fides et Ratio,* are the two wings by which the mind rises toward wisdom. The goal of the Christian university is wisdom. This is as true of those parts of the university that are most in danger of becoming merely trade schools as it is of the humanities and arts.

A Christian university is not a church, although, absent a vital relation with a particular community of faith, it can become a church unto itself. (Of course, a church that is designed to graduate its members, and that observes Holy Communion chiefly through alumni donations, is not much of a church.) A church has many tasks, including worship, evangelizing, catechesis, and works of mercy. All these tasks may be pursued within a university, but the specific task of the university is the cultivation of the life of the mind.

There are those who say that the phrase "Christian university" is an oxymoron, and, if the life of the mind is not understood as an integral part of Christian discipleship, they are right. And if forming the minds of disciples is not integral to the university's mission, that mission will — sooner or later, but inexorably — become alien to the mission of the Church. Most Christian universities today have "mission statements," and they trend toward ever-increasing vagueness and generality, reflecting a desire to be a university pure and simple. A student of the contemporary academy tells me that when a school is haggling over its mission statement, it is a sure sign it has already lost its way. That may be saying too much, but it is not without an element of cautionary truth.

At the same time, the worry is expressed that anything smacking of Christian mission is an "imposition" on the integrity of the university. John Paul II notes, in his encyclical *Redemptoris Missio,* that some are offended by the very idea of communicating the faith. "Who are you," they say, "to impose your religion on me?" To which John Paul responds, "The Church imposes nothing. She only proposes." She proposes respectfully, winsomely, persuasively. What she proposes she believes to be the truth, and the truth does impose itself, for human beings endowed by God with the gift of reason are, as it were, hard-wired for the truth.

Let me put it bluntly: a student at a Christian university who has not encountered the proposal of the Christian intellectual tradition — from Paul to Augustine, from Irenaeus to Dante, Aquinas, Luther, Milton, and moderns such as Lewis and Polanyi, along with those who have challenged and now challenge that tradition — such a student has been grievously shortchanged in his or her university education. This is true not only for students majoring in theology, philosophy, or the liberal arts. It is true, to varying levels of intensity, for all students. If, that is, the *Christian* in the claim to be a Christian university refers to governing conviction and not merely to a hangover of historical accident.

Of course, there is no university without the faculty. *Ex Corde Ecclesiae* says a majority of the faculty should be Catholic, but that hardly seems sufficient. More important, I would suggest, than whether faculty be Catholic, Lutheran, Baptist, or even Christian is the consideration that faculty support, or at least do not actively oppose, the idea of a Christian university. Certainly, the institution-defining decisions must be made by those who understand and support the nature of the institution. Discrimination — a much-abused but invaluable term — must be exercised in faculty appointments; not necessarily discrimination on the basis of religious belief but discrimination on the basis of belief in the great good of being a Christian university. The university is better served by an agnostic who understands and supports the idea of a Christian university than by a devout believer who does not.

The Christian university is unqualifiedly devoted to the truth. Jesus said, "You will know the truth and the truth will make you free." Academic freedom and freedom of inquiry are not in tension with truth but are themselves grounded in truth. Contrary to Pontius Pilate and many thinkers of our time, the question "What is truth?" does not preclude but invites the search for truth. When academic freedom is divorced from truth, it is no longer possible to make a truthful argument for academic freedom. One may suggest that the only person disqualified from teaching in a Christian university is a person whose truth, so to speak, is that there is no truth to be sought and known and served. But of course this assumes that there is a critical mass of faculty composed of those who persuasively propose the truth of Christianity and those who believe that truth should be proposed.

Today there is an intense interest, almost an obsession some would say, in diversity and pluralism. Within the world of higher education, a Christian university serves the great good of diversity and pluralism by being a different kind of university. It does not mimic the false pluralism and diversity that pretends our deepest differences make no difference. Rather, it engages within the bond of civility the differences that make the deepest difference. The Christian university, if I may use today's academic jargon, does not fear the otherness of the Other. It very deliberately *is* the Other. As the Other, it respectfully engages and defines itself in relationship to the other kinds of universities to which it is other.

A Christian university is a profoundly humanistic university that embraces, far beyond what are called the humanities, all knowledge of the three transcendentals — the good, the true, and the beautiful. No humanism is so radical as the humanism premised on the truth that God became a human being. This does not mean that everybody will agree on the meaning of these transcendent realities. On the contrary, the Christian university nurtures thoughtful disagreement. As Father John Courtney Murray observed, disagreement is a rare achievement; most of what we call disagreement is simply confusion.

A Christian university will have no truck with the dichotomies that pit truth against truth. In this connection, there is an often unrecognized alliance between anti-intellectuals in church communities outside the university and intellectuals within the university. Both subscribe to there being a dichotomy between faith and reason, between heart and mind, between facts and values, between belief and knowledge, between devotion and learning. The most foundational premise of the Christian university is that all truth and all ways to truth are one because the Author and the End of truth is One.

Ex Corde Ecclesiae insists that "it is essential that we be convinced of the priority of the ethical over the technical, of the primacy of the person over things, of the superiority of the spirit over matter. The cause of the human person will only be served if knowledge is joined to conscience. Men and women of [learning] will truly aid humanity only if they preserve the sense of the transcendence of the human person over the world and of God over the human person."

If the truth of Christianity does not support, illumine, and elevate every quest for truth, it is questionable that Christianity is true. The God who gave us reason and who keeps faith with the orders of his creation requires us to respect the integrity of every way of knowing. Different subjects and different disciplines have their own integrity. It is neither possible nor desirable to teach Christian mathematics, or Christian geology, or Christian chemistry. But a Christian university will not lose sight of the truth that these and other disciplines have their own integrity because they are an integral part of the Creator's order. That at least is the Christian proposal that, in the Christian university, is ever present — sometimes explicitly, sometimes tacitly, but never ignored. As is evident in the breadth and depth and variety of the Christian intellectual tradition, that proposal is not a conversation-stopper but a conversation-starter, and not least in the conversation about what it means to be a university.

Today the Christian university is in crisis. At least in many institutions, there is a dying of the light. The crisis is often described as a crisis of secularization. But that, I would suggest, is not quite right. The secular, the *saeculum,* is the world of God's creation and redeeming love. The crisis of the Christian university is more accurately described as a crisis created by the ambition to imitate other kinds of universities that falsely claim to be universities pure and simple. It is a crisis created by competing to belong to the second tier, or even the third tier, of schools that do not aspire to be Christian universities. It is a crisis created by envying excellence divorced from truth. Enough can never be said in favor of excellence, but it is small comfort for a Christian university to be recognized as being moderately good at being what it did not set out to be in the first place.

The crisis is most accurately described, I believe, as a crisis of faith. The question that those who lead a Christian university must answer, and answer again every day, is whether the Christian proposal limits or illumines the university's calling to seek and to serve *veritas* — to seek and to serve the truth.

In speaking about the crisis of the Christian university, I have been generalizing, and I am assured by some that Valparaiso University is an exception — that it is determined to be what it was founded to be. I pray this is the case, for I cannot forget the Valparaiso that helped form me and innumerable others in the high adventure of responding to the Church's heart for learning. I cannot forget those chords of the Mass in B Minor and O. P. Kretzman's pilgrim pondering of the falling autumn leaves, prelude to winter and the promise of a new springtime. Yes, this is in part nostalgia, but it is in much greater part hope and anticipation of what a Christian university can be in imaginative fidelity to its motto — "In your light we see light."

This essay is adapted from the Albert G. Huegh Lecture on Church-Related Higher Education, given at Valparaiso University in February 2007.

ROBERT PINSKY

XYZ

FROM *The Atlantic Monthly*

The cross the fork the zigzag — a few straight lines
For pain, quandary and evasion, the last of signs.

RICHARD RODRIGUEZ

Atheism Is Wasted on the Nonbeliever

FROM *Image*

ATHEISM IS WASTED on the nonbeliever.

That thought occurred to me recently as I watched Christopher Hitchens push his book *God Is Not Great* on a cable television show hosted by Bill Maher. Mr. Hitchens proposed to Mr. Maher that the human race would be better off trusting science instead of religion. Mr. Maher agreed. Neither Mr. Hitchens nor Mr. Maher mentioned Hiroshima — or that the problem with religion or science might be the human race.

I remember, some years back, writing about Christopher Hitchens on the occasion of his sleazy exposé of Mother Teresa, *The Missionary Position*. Mr. Hitchens revealed that the woman popularly regarded as a saint had extended her begging bowl under the noses of corrupt men and women; she laundered money to serve the unwashed.

I had always assumed saints are tainted, as most of us are tainted. Graham Greene taught me that holiness must dwell in a tarnished temple. (There is no other kind.)

I do not, in any case, need this latest book by Mr. Hitchens, or any of the books by the other best-selling "New Atheists," to persuade me to disbelief. Atheism seems to me a deeply persuasive response to the night. But then again, faith seems to me a deeply persuasive response to the night.

A few days after Mr. Hitchens conferred with Mr. Maher, the Democratic Party presidential front-runners took turns professing religious belief. (Democrats are unwilling to cede heaven to the Republicans and their politically active supporters in the Protestant right.) The curtain of secular discretion that has made religion nobody's business in America was cast aside for political advantage.

Listening to Hillary Clinton describe her faith in Jesus Christ from a political dais was a disheartening experience. There was not a hint of spontaneity in her confession. Doubtless, her every adjective had been tested by handlers.

In American lore, the village atheist is an eccentric soul at odds with conventional propriety. But in truth, atheism has governed American intellectual life for most of the twentieth century. Atheism has long been the orthodoxy of the university faculty club, the New York journals, and most fiction. (For every Flannery O'Connor I can name ten Mary McCarthys.)

Now, thanks in no small part to the political ambitions of Low-Church Protestants and to the deceptively distant cry of the muezzin, religion looms, as never before, over American public life.

Americans who have never known religious war now routinely hear U.S. armed forces in Iraq and Afghanistan identified as "crusaders" by angry Muslims. And as Islam gathers force in Europe, American Protestants gather equal public confidence in Colorado Springs and Washington, D.C.

It occurred last year to some faculty members at Harvard that the overwhelming importance of theism throughout the shrinking world might suggest that a religion course be required of their undergraduates. The atheists on the faculty quickly disapproved, and the proposal was tabled at a faculty senate meeting. In the name *veritas*.

I am enough of an atheist to be horrified by examples of religious extremism on the evening news from the Middle East: honor killings, Shiah murdering Sunni today in revenge for yesterday's Sunni murder of Shiah, exploding mosques, Moqtada al Sadr addressing his piratical band at Friday prayers, and on and on.

Any Christian — Orthodox, Protestant, Catholic; especially Catholic — should be embarrassed, in the face of Islamic extremism, by the memory of the violence within our own history: the holy wars, the torture and murder of the heretic, the attack on the Jew, the Muslim, and the pagan — all in the name of a loving God.

What is that line of Anne Sexton's? *God is only mocked by believers.*

The great temptation for the believer, it seems to me, is not atheism; it is the arrogance of claiming to know God's will. It is therefore with some measure of irony and necessary caution that I say I
believe in God.

I believe in Jesus Christ, the Christ who was a loser in human history — destroyed by this world — whose life reveals in its generos-
ity and tragedy the most complete and challenging version of theism I know. What the New Atheists do not comprehend is that the
crucifix cannot be mocked. It is itself mockery.

As a Christian, I worship the same God as the Jew and the Muslim, a revealed God. I share with the atheist and the agnostic a
sense of a God who is hidden. (I say hidden; an atheist would say
never there in the first place.)

And more: I believe the monotheistic religions would be health-
ier, less inclined to extremism and violence, if those of us who pro-
fess belief in God were able also to admit our disbelief.

It seems to me not inappropriate that I take my inner atheist with
me to church every Sunday. The atheist within me is as noisy as my
stomach, even when I am standing in the Communion line. But
never is the atheist within me so quarrelsome as during the homily.

While I am blessed by belonging to a welcoming and consoling
parish community, I have not heard from the pulpit what I desperately needed to hear in the aftermath of September 11, 2001 —
the implication for faith posed by terrorists who prayed to Allah
even as they aimed Boeing jets into the World Trade Center.

The sound of the chanting within those planes has haunted my
prayers, overwhelmed my own prayers like an engine's roar.

This is my prayer: *Dear God, I believe in you. Please strengthen my disbelief.*

OLIVER SACKS

The Abyss

FROM *The New Yorker*

IN MARCH OF 1985, Clive Wearing, an eminent English musician and musicologist in his midforties, was struck by a brain infection — a herpes encephalitis — affecting especially the parts of his brain concerned with memory. He was left with a memory span of only seconds — the most devastating case of amnesia ever recorded. New events and experiences were effaced almost instantly. As his wife, Deborah, wrote in her 2005 memoir, *Forever Today*:

> His ability to perceive what he saw and heard was unimpaired. But he did not seem to be able to retain any impression of anything for more than a blink. Indeed, if he did blink, his eyelids parted to reveal a new scene. The view before the blink was utterly forgotten. Each blink, each glance away and back, brought him an entirely new view. I tried to imagine how it was for him . . . Something akin to a film with bad continuity, the glass half empty, then full, the cigarette suddenly longer, the actor's hair now tousled, now smooth. But this was real life, a room changing in ways that were physically impossible.

In addition to this inability to preserve new memories, Clive had a retrograde amnesia, a deletion of virtually his entire past.

When he was filmed in 1986 for Jonathan Miller's extraordinary documentary *Prisoner of Consciousness*, Clive showed a desperate aloneness, fear, and bewilderment. He was acutely, continually, agonizingly conscious that something bizarre, something awful, was the matter. His constantly repeated complaint, however, was not of a faulty memory but of being deprived, in some uncanny and terrible way, of all experience, deprived of consciousness and life itself. As Deborah wrote:

It was as if every waking moment was the first waking moment. Clive was under the constant impression that he had just emerged from unconsciousness because he had no evidence in his own mind of ever being awake before . . . "I haven't heard anything, seen anything, touched anything, smelled anything," he would say. "It's like being dead."

Desperate to hold on to something, to gain some purchase, Clive started to keep a journal, first on scraps of paper, then in a notebook. But his journal entries consisted, essentially, of the statements "I am awake" or "I am conscious," entered again and again every few minutes. He would write: "2:10 P.M.: This time properly awake . . . 2:14 P.M.: this time finally awake . . . 2:35 P.M.: this time completely awake," along with negations of these statements: "At 9:40 P.M. I awoke for the first time, despite my previous claims." This in turn was crossed out, followed by "I was fully conscious at 10:35 P.M., and awake for the first time in many, many weeks." This in turn was canceled out by the next entry.

This dreadful journal, almost void of any other content but these passionate assertions and denials, intending to affirm existence and continuity but forever contradicting them, was filled anew each day, and soon mounted to hundreds of almost identical pages. It was a terrifying and poignant testament to Clive's mental state, his lostness, in the years that followed his amnesia — a state that Deborah, in Miller's film, called "a never-ending agony."

Another profoundly amnesic patient I knew some years ago dealt with his abysses of amnesia by fluent confabulations. He was wholly immersed in his quick-fire inventions and had no insight into what was happening; so far as he was concerned, there was nothing the matter. He would confidently identify or misidentify me as a friend of his, a customer in his delicatessen, a kosher butcher, another doctor — as a dozen different people in the course of a few minutes. This sort of confabulation was not one of conscious fabrication. It was, rather, a strategy, a desperate attempt — unconscious and almost automatic — to provide a sort of continuity, a narrative continuity, when memory, and thus experience, was being snatched away every instant.

Though one cannot have direct knowledge of one's own amnesia, there may be ways to infer it: from the expressions on people's faces when one has repeated something half a dozen times; when one looks down at one's coffee cup and finds that it is empty; when one looks at one's diary and sees entries in one's own handwriting. Lacking memory, lacking direct experiential knowledge, amnesiacs have to make hypotheses and inferences, and they usually make plausible ones. They can infer that they have been doing *something*, been *somewhere*, even though they cannot recollect what or where. Yet Clive, rather than making plausible guesses, always came to the conclusion that he had just been "awakened," that he had been "dead." This seemed to me a reflection of the almost instantaneous effacement of perception for Clive — thought itself was almost impossible within this tiny window of time. Indeed, Clive once said to Deborah, "I am completely incapable of thinking."

At the beginning of his illness, Clive would sometimes be confounded at the bizarre things he experienced. Deborah wrote of how, coming in one day, she saw him

> holding something in the palm of one hand, and repeatedly covering and uncovering it with the other hand as if he were a magician practicing a disappearing trick. He was holding a chocolate. He could feel the chocolate unmoving in his left palm, and yet every time he lifted his hand he told me it revealed a brand-new chocolate.
>
> "Look!" he said. "It's new!" He couldn't take his eyes off it.
>
> "It's the same chocolate," I said gently.
>
> "No . . . look! It's changed. It wasn't like that before . . ." He covered and uncovered the chocolate every couple of seconds, lifting and looking.
>
> "Look! It's different again! How do they do it?"

Within months, Clive's confusion gave way to the agony, the desperation, that is so clear in Miller's film. This, in turn, was succeeded by a deep depression, as it came to him — if only in sudden, intense, and immediately forgotten moments — that his former life was over, that he was incorrigibly disabled.

As the months passed without any real improvement, the hope of significant recovery became fainter and fainter, and toward the end of 1985 Clive was moved to a room in a chronic psychiatric unit — a room he was to occupy for the next six and a half years but which he was never able to recognize as his own. A young psychologist saw Clive for a period of time in 1990 and kept a verbatim record of everything he said, and this caught the grim mood that had taken hold. Clive said at one point, "Can you imagine one night five years long? No dreaming, no waking, no touch, no taste, no smell, no sight, no sound, no hearing, nothing at all. It's like being dead. I came to the conclusion that I was dead."

The only times of feeling alive were when Deborah visited him. But the moment she left, he was desperate once again, and by the time she got home, ten or fifteen minutes later, she would find repeated messages from him on her answering machine: "Please come and see me, darling — it's been ages since I've seen you. Please fly here at the speed of light."

To imagine the future was no more possible for Clive than to remember the past — both were engulfed by the onslaught of amnesia. Yet, at some level, Clive could not be unaware of the sort of place he was in, and the likelihood that he would spend the rest of his life, his endless night, in such a place.

But then, seven years after his illness, after huge efforts by Deborah, Clive was moved to a small country residence for the brain-injured, much more congenial than a hospital. Here he was one of only a handful of patients, and in constant contact with a dedicated staff who treated him as an individual and respected his intelligence and talents. He was taken off most of his heavy tranquilizers, and seemed to enjoy his walks around the village and gardens near the home, the spaciousness, the fresh food.

For the first eight or nine years in this new home, Deborah told me, "Clive was calmer and sometimes jolly, a bit more content, but often with angry outbursts still, unpredictable, withdrawn, spending most of his time in his room alone." But gradually, in the past six or seven years, Clive has become more sociable, more talkative. Conversation (though of a "scripted" sort) has come to fill what had been empty, solitary, and desperate days.

Though I had corresponded with Deborah since Clive first became ill, twenty years went by before I met Clive in person. He was so changed from the haunted, agonized man I had seen in Miller's 1986 film that I was scarcely prepared for the dapper, bubbling figure who opened the door when Deborah and I went to visit him in the summer of 2005. He had been reminded of our visit just before we arrived, and he flung his arms around Deborah the moment she entered.

Deborah introduced me: "This is Dr. Sacks." And Clive immediately said, "You doctors work twenty-four hours a day, don't you? You're always in demand." We went up to his room, which contained an electric organ console and a piano piled high with music. Some of the scores, I noted, were transcriptions of Orlandus Lassus, the Renaissance composer whose works Clive had edited. I saw Clive's journal by the washstand — he has now filled up scores of volumes, and the current one is always kept in this exact location. Next to it was an etymological dictionary with dozens of reference slips of different colors stuck between the pages and a large, handsome volume, *The One Hundred Most Beautiful Cathedrals in the World*. A Canaletto print hung on the wall, and I asked Clive if he had ever been to Venice. No, he said. (Deborah told me they had visited several times before his illness.) Looking at the print, Clive pointed out the dome of a church: "Look at it," he said. "See how it soars — like an angel!"

When I asked Deborah whether Clive knew about her memoir, she told me that she had shown it to him twice before, but that he had instantly forgotten. I had my own heavily annotated copy with me, and asked Deborah to show it to him again.

"You've written a book!" he cried, astonished. "Well done! Congratulations!" He peered at the cover. "All by you? Good heavens!" Excited, he jumped for joy. Deborah showed him the dedication page: "For my Clive." "Dedicated to me?" He hugged her. This scene was repeated several times within a few minutes, with almost exactly the same astonishment, the same expressions of delight and joy each time.

Clive and Deborah are still very much in love with each other, despite his amnesia. (Indeed, Deborah's book is subtitled *A Memoir of Love and Amnesia*.) He greeted her several times as if she had just arrived. It must be an extraordinary situation, I thought, both maddening and flattering, to be seen always as new, as a gift, a blessing.

Clive had, in the meantime, addressed me as "Your Highness" and inquired at intervals, "Been at Buckingham Palace? . . . Are you the prime minister? . . . Are you from the U.N.?" He laughed when I answered, "Just the U.S." This joking or jesting was of a somewhat waggish, stereotyped nature and highly repetitive. Clive had no idea who I was, little idea who anyone was, but this bonhomie allowed him to make contact, to keep a conversation going. I suspected he had some damage to his frontal lobes, too — such jokiness (neurologists speak of *Witzelsucht,* joking disease), like his impulsiveness and chattiness, could go with a weakening of the usual social frontal-lobe inhibitions.

He was excited at the notion of going out for lunch — lunch with Deborah. "Isn't she a wonderful woman?" he kept asking me. "Doesn't she have marvelous kisses?" I said yes, I was sure she had.

As we drove to the restaurant, Clive, with great speed and fluency, invented words for the letters on the license plates of passing cars: *JCK* was Japanese Clever Kid; *NKR* was New King of Russia; and *BDH* (Deborah's car) was British Daft Hospital, then Blessed Dutch Hospital. *Forever Today,* Deborah's book, immediately became *Three-Ever Today, Two-Ever Today, One-Ever Today.* This incontinent punning and rhyming and clanging was virtually instantaneous, occurring with a speed no normal person could match. It resembled Tourettic or savantlike speed, the speed of the preconscious, undelayed by reflection.

When we arrived at the restaurant, Clive did all the license plates in the parking lot and then, elaborately, with a bow and a flourish, let Deborah enter: "Ladies first!" He looked at me with some uncertainty as I followed them to the table: "Are you joining us, too?"

When I offered him the wine list, he looked it over and exclaimed, "Good God! Australian wine! New Zealand wine! The colonies are producing something original — how exciting!" This partly indicated his retrograde amnesia — he is still in the 1960s (if he is anywhere), when Australian and New Zealand wines were almost unheard-of in England. "The colonies," however, was part of his compulsive waggery and parody.

At lunch he talked about Cambridge — he had been at Clare College, but had often gone next door to King's, for its famous choir. He spoke of how after Cambridge, in 1968, he joined the London Sinfonietta, where they played modern music, though he was already attracted to the Renaissance and Lassus. He was the chorus master there, and he reminisced about how the singers could not talk during coffee breaks; they had to save their voices ("It was often misunderstood by the instrumentalists, seemed standoffish to them"). These all sounded like genuine memories. But they could equally have reflected his knowing *about* these events, rather than actual memories of them — expressions of "se-

mantic" memory rather than "event" or "episodic" memory. Then
he spoke of World War II (he was born in 1938) and how his family
would go to bomb shelters and play chess or cards there. He said
that he remembered the doodlebugs: "There were more bombs in
Birmingham than in London." Was it possible that these were genuine memories? He would have been only six or seven, at most. Or
was he confabulating or simply, as we all do, repeating stories he
had been told as a child?

At one point, he talked about pollution and how dirty petrol en-
gines were. When I told him I had a hybrid with an electric motor
as well as a combustion engine, he was astounded, as if something
he had read about as a theoretical possibility had, far sooner than
he had imagined, become a reality.

In her remarkable book, so tender yet so tough-minded and realistic, Deborah wrote about the change that had so struck me: that
Clive was now "garrulous and outgoing . . . could talk the hind
legs off a donkey." There were certain themes he tended to stick
to, she said, favorite subjects (electricity, the Tube, stars and plan-
ets, Queen Victoria, words and etymologies), which would all be
brought up again and again:

> "Have they found life on Mars yet?"
>
> "No, darling, but they think there might have been water . . ."
>
> "Really? Isn't it amazing that the sun goes on burning? Where does it
> get all that fuel? It doesn't get any smaller. And it doesn't move. We
> move round the sun. How can it keep on burning for millions of years?
> And the Earth stays the same temperature. It's so finely balanced."
>
> "They say it's getting warmer now, love. They call it global warming."
>
> "No! Why's that?"
>
> "Because of the pollution. We've been emitting gases into the atmo-
> sphere. And puncturing the ozone layer."
>
> "OH NO! That could be disastrous!"
>
> "People are already getting more cancers."
>
> "Oh, aren't people stupid! Do you know the average IQ is only 100?
> That's terribly low, isn't it? One hundred. It's no wonder the world's in
> such a mess."

Clive's scripts were repeated with great frequency, sometimes three or
four times in one phone call. He stuck to subjects he felt he knew something about, where he would be on safe ground, even if here and there
something apocryphal crept in . . . These small areas of repartee acted
as stepping stones on which he could move through the present. They
enabled him to engage with others.

I would put it even more strongly and use a phrase that Deborah used in another connection, when she wrote of Clive being poised upon "a tiny platform . . . above the abyss." Clive's loquacity, his almost compulsive need to talk and keep conversations going, served to maintain a precarious platform, and when he came to a stop the abyss was there, waiting to engulf him. This, indeed, is what happened when we went to a supermarket and he and I got separated briefly from Deborah. He suddenly exclaimed, "I'm conscious now . . . Never saw a human being before . . . for thirty years . . . It's like death!" He looked very angry and distressed. Deborah said the staff calls these grim monologues his "deads" — they make a note of how many he has in a day or a week and gauge his state of mind by their number.

Deborah thinks that repetition has slightly dulled the very real pain that goes with this agonized but stereotyped complaint, but when he says such things she will distract him immediately. Once she has done this, there seems to be no lingering mood — an advantage of his amnesia. And, indeed, once we returned to the car, Clive was off on his license plates again.

Back in his room, I spotted the two volumes of Bach's *Forty-eight Preludes and Fugues* on top of the piano and asked Clive if he would play one of them. He said that he had never played any of them before, but then he began to play Prelude no. 9 in E Major and said, "I remember this one." He remembers almost nothing unless he is actually doing it; then it may come to him. He inserted a tiny, charming improvisation at one point, and did a sort of Chico Marx ending, with a huge downward scale. With his great musicality and his playfulness, he can easily improvise, joke, play with any piece of music.

His eye fell on the book about cathedrals, and he talked about cathedral bells — did I know how many combinations there could be with eight bells? "Eight by seven by six by five by four by three by two by one," he rattled off. "Factorial eight." And then, without pause: "That's forty thousand." (I worked it out, laboriously: it is 40,320.)

I asked him about prime ministers. Tony Blair? Never heard of him. John Major? No. Margaret Thatcher? Vaguely familiar. Harold Macmillan, Harold Wilson: ditto. (But earlier in the day he had seen a car with *JMV* plates and instantly said, "John Major Vehi-

cle" — showing that he had an *implicit* memory of Major's name.)
Deborah wrote of how he could not remember *her* name, "but one
day someone asked him to say his full name, and he said, 'Clive David Deborah Wearing — funny name, that. I don't know why my
parents called me that.'" He has gained other implicit memories,
too, slowly picking up new knowledge, like the layout of his residence. He can go alone now to the bathroom, the dining room, the
kitchen — but if he stops and thinks en route, he is lost. Though
he could not describe his residence, Deborah tells me that he un-
clasps his seat belt as they draw near and offers to get out and open
the gate. Later, when he makes her coffee, he knows where the
cups, the milk, and the sugar are kept. He cannot *say* where they
are, but he can go to them; he has actions, but few facts, at his disposal.

I decided to widen the testing and asked Clive to tell me the
names of all the composers he knew. He said, "Handel, Bach, Bee-
thoven, Berg, Mozart, Lassus." That was it. Deborah told me that at
first, when asked this question, he would omit Lassus, his favorite
composer. This seemed appalling for someone who had been not
only a musician but an encyclopedic musicologist. Perhaps it reflected the shortness of his attention span and recent immediate
memory — perhaps he thought that he had in fact given us dozens of names. So I asked him other questions on a variety of topics
that he would have been knowledgeable about in his earlier days.
Again, there was a paucity of information in his replies and sometimes something close to a blank. I started to feel that I had been
beguiled, in a sense, by Clive's easy, nonchalant, fluent conversation into thinking that he still had a great deal of general information at his disposal, despite the loss of memory for events. Given his
intelligence, ingenuity, and humor, it was easy to think this on
meeting him for the first time. But repeated conversations rapidly
exposed the limits of his knowledge. It was indeed as Deborah
wrote in her book, Clive "stuck to subjects he knew something
about" and used these islands of knowledge as "steppingstones" in
his conversation. Clearly, Clive's general knowledge, or semantic
memory, was greatly affected, too — though not as catastrophically
as his episodic memory.

Yet semantic memory of this sort, even if completely intact, is not
of much use in the absence of explicit, episodic memory. Clive is
safe enough in the confines of his residence, for instance, but he

would be hopelessly lost if he were to go out alone. Lawrence Weiskrantz comments on the need for both sorts of memory in his 1997 book *Consciousness Lost and Found*:

> The amnesic patient can think about material in the immediate present . . . He can also think about items in his semantic memory, his general knowledge . . . But thinking for successful everyday adaptation requires not only factual knowledge, but the ability to recall it on the right occasion, to relate it to other occasions, indeed the ability to reminisce.

This uselessness of semantic memory unaccompanied by episodic memory is also brought out by Umberto Eco in his novel *The Mysterious Flame of Queen Loana,* in which the narrator, an antiquarian bookseller and polymath, is a man of Eco-like intelligence and erudition. Though amnesic from a stroke, he retains the poetry he has read, the many languages he knows, his encyclopedic memory of facts; but he is nonetheless helpless and disoriented (and recovers from this only because the effects of his stroke are transient).

It is similar, in a way, with Clive. His semantic memory, while of little help in organizing his life, does have a crucial social role: it allows him to engage in conversation (though it is occasionally more monologue than conversation). Thus, Deborah wrote, "he would string all his subjects together in a row, and the other person simply needed to nod or mumble." By moving rapidly from one thought to another, Clive managed to secure a sort of continuity, to hold the thread of consciousness and attention intact — albeit precariously, for the thoughts were held together, on the whole, by superficial associations. Clive's verbosity made him a little odd, a little too much at times, but it was highly adaptive — it enabled him to reenter the world of human discourse.

In the 1986 film, Deborah quoted Proust's description of Swann waking from a deep sleep, not knowing at first where he was, who he was, what he was. He had only "the most rudimentary sense of existence, such as may lurk and flicker in the depths of an animal's consciousness," until memory came back to him, "like a rope let down from heaven to draw me up out of the abyss of not-being, from which I could never have escaped by myself." This gave him back his personal consciousness and identity. No rope from heaven, no autobiographical memory will ever come down in this way to Clive.

*

From the start there have been, for Clive, two realities of immense importance. The first of these is Deborah, whose presence and love for him have made life tolerable, at least intermittently, in the twenty or more years since his illness. Clive's amnesia not only destroyed his ability to retain new memories; it deleted almost all of his earlier memories, including those of the years when he met and fell in love with Deborah. He told Deborah, when she questioned him, that he had never heard of John Lennon or John F. Kennedy. Though he always recognized his own children, Deborah told me, "he would be surprised at their height and amazed to hear he is a grandfather. He asked his younger son what O-level exams he was doing in 2005, more than twenty years after Edmund left school." Yet somehow he always recognized Deborah as his wife, when she visited, and felt moored by her presence, lost without her. He would rush to the door when he heard her voice, and embrace her with passionate, desperate fervor. Having no idea how long she had been away — since anything not in his immediate field of perception and attention would be lost, forgotten, within seconds — he seemed to feel that she, too, had been lost in the abyss of time, and so her "return" from the abyss seemed nothing short of miraculous. As Deborah put it:

> Clive was constantly surrounded by strangers in a strange place, with no knowledge of where he was or what had happened to him. To catch sight of me was always a massive relief — to know that he was not alone, that I still cared, that I loved him, that I was there. Clive was terrified all the time. But I was his life, I was his lifeline. Every time he saw me, he would run to me, fall on me, sobbing, clinging.

How, why, when he recognized no one else with any consistency, did Clive recognize Deborah? There are clearly many sorts of memory, and emotional memory is one of the deepest and least understood.

The neuroscientist Neal J. Cohen recounts the famous story of Édouard Claparède, a Swiss physician, who, upon shaking hands with a severely amnesic woman,

> pricked her finger with a pin hidden in his hand. Subsequently, whenever he again attempted to shake the patient's hand, she promptly withdrew it. When he questioned her about this behavior, she replied, "Isn't it allowed to withdraw one's hand?" and "Perhaps there is a pin hidden

in your hand," and finally, "Sometimes pins are hidden in hands." Thus the patient learned the appropriate response based on previous experience, but she never seemed to attribute her behavior to the personal memory of some previously experienced event.

For Claparède's patient, some sort of memory of the pain, an implicit and emotional memory, persisted. It seems certain, likewise, that in the first two years of life, even though one retains no explicit memories (Freud called this infantile amnesia), deep emotional memories or associations are nevertheless being made in the limbic system and other regions of the brain where emotions are represented — and these emotional memories may determine one's behavior for a lifetime. A recent paper by Oliver Turnbull, Evangelos Zois, et al., in the journal *Neuro-Psychoanalysis,* has shown that patients with amnesia can form emotional transferences to an analyst, even though they retain no explicit memory of the analyst or their previous meetings. Nonetheless, a strong emotional bond begins to develop. Clive and Deborah were newly married at the time of his encephalitis, and deeply in love for a few years before that. His passionate relationship with her, a relationship that began before his encephalitis, and one that centers in part on their shared love for music, has engraved itself in him — in areas of his brain unaffected by the encephalitis — so deeply that his amnesia, the most severe amnesia ever recorded, cannot eradicate it.

Nonetheless, for many years he failed to recognize Deborah if she chanced to walk past, and even now he cannot say what she looks like unless he is actually looking at her. Her appearance, her voice, her scent, the way they behave with each other, and the intensity of their emotions and interactions — all this confirms her identity, and his own.

The other miracle was the discovery Deborah made early on, while Clive was still in the hospital, desperately confused and disoriented: that his musical powers were totally intact. "I picked up some music," Deborah wrote,

and held it open for Clive to see. I started to sing one of the lines. He picked up the tenor lines and sang with me. A bar or so in, I suddenly realized what was happening. He could still read music. He was singing. His talk might be a jumble no one could understand but his brain was still capable of music . . . When he got to the end of the line I hugged

him and kissed him all over his face . . . Clive could sit down at the organ
and play with both hands on the keyboard, changing stops, and with his
feet on the pedals, as if this were easier than riding a bicycle. Suddenly
we had a place to be together, where we could create our own world
away from the ward. Our friends came in to sing. I left a pile of music by
the bed and visitors brought other pieces.

Miller's film showed dramatically the virtually perfect preservation of Clive's musical powers and memory. In these scenes from
only a year or so after his illness, his face often appeared tight with
torment and bewilderment. But when he was conducting his old
choir, he performed with great sensitivity and grace, mouthing the
melodies, turning to different singers and sections of the choir, cu-
ing them, encouraging them, to bring out their special parts. It is
obvious that Clive not only knew the piece intimately — how all the
parts contributed to the unfolding of the musical thought — but
also retained all the skills of conducting, his professional persona,
and his own unique style.

Clive cannot retain any memory of passing events or experience
and, in addition, has lost most of the memories of events and experiences *preceding* his encephalitis — how, then, does he retain his
remarkable knowledge of music, his ability to sight-read, play the
piano and organ, sing, and conduct a choir in the masterly way he
did before he became ill?

H. M., a famous and unfortunate patient described by Scoville
and Milner in 1957, was rendered amnesic by the surgical removal
of both hippocampi, along with adjacent structures of the medial
temporal lobes. (This was a desperate attempt at treating his intractable seizures; it was not yet realized that autobiographical memory
and the ability to form new memories of events depended on these
structures.) Yet H. M., though he lost many memories of his former
life, did not lose any of the skills he had acquired, and indeed he
could learn and perfect *new* skills with training and practice, even
though he would retain no memory of the practice sessions.

Larry Squire, a neuroscientist who has spent a lifetime exploring
mechanisms of memory and amnesia, emphasizes that no two cases
of amnesia are the same. He wrote to me:

If the damage is limited to the medial temporal lobe, then one expects
an impairment such as H. M. had. With somewhat more extensive me-

dial temporal lobe damage, one can expect something more severe, as in E. P. [a patient whom Squire and his colleagues have investigated intensively]. With the addition of frontal damage, perhaps one begins to understand Clive's impairment. Or perhaps one needs lateral temporal damage as well, or basal forebrain damage. Clive's case is unique, because a particular pattern of anatomical damage occurred. His case is not like H. M. or like Claparède's patient. We cannot write about amnesia as if it were a single entity like mumps or measles.

Yet H. M.'s case and subsequent work made it clear that two very different sorts of memory could exist: a conscious memory of events (episodic memory) and an unconscious memory for procedures — and that such procedural memory is unimpaired in amnesia.

This is dramatically clear with Clive, too, for he can shave, shower, look after his grooming, and dress elegantly, with taste and style; he moves confidently and is fond of dancing. He talks abundantly, using a large vocabulary; he can read and write in several languages. He is good at calculation. He can make phone calls, and he can find the coffee things and find his way about the home. If he is asked how to do these things, he cannot say, but he does them. Whatever involves a sequence or pattern of action, he does fluently, unhesitatingly.

But can Clive's beautiful playing and singing, his masterly conducting, his powers of improvisation be adequately characterized as "skills" or "procedures"? For his playing is infused with intelligence and feeling, with a sensitive attunement to the musical structure, the composer's style and mind. Can any artistic or creative performance of this caliber be adequately explained by "procedural memory"? Episodic or explicit memory, we know, develops relatively late in childhood and is dependent on a complex brain system involving the hippocampi and medial-temporal-lobe structures, the system that is compromised in severe amnesiacs and all but obliterated in Clive. The basis of procedural or implicit memory is less easy to define, but it certainly involves larger and more primitive parts of the brain — subcortical structures like the basal ganglia and cerebellum and their many connections to each other and to the cerebral cortex. The size and variety of these systems guarantee the robustness of procedural memory and the fact that, unlike episodic memory, procedural memory can remain largely intact even in the face of extensive damage to the hippocampi and medial-temporal-lobe structures.

Episodic memory depends on the perception of particular and often unique events, and one's memories of such events, like one's original perception of them, are not only highly individual (colored by one's interests, concerns, and values) but prone to be revised or recategorized every time they are recalled. This is in fundamental contrast to procedural memory, where it is all-important that the remembering be literal, exact, and reproducible. Repetition and rehearsal, timing and sequence are of the essence here. Rodolfo Llinás, the neuroscientist, uses the term "fixed action pattern" (FAP) for such procedural memories. Some of these may be present even before birth (fetal horses, for example, may gallop in the womb). Much of the early motor development of the child depends on learning and refining such procedures, through play, imitation, trial and error, and incessant rehearsal. All of these start to develop long before the child can call on any explicit or episodic memories.

Is the concept of fixed action patterns any more illuminating than that of procedural memories in relation to the enormously complex, creative performances of a professional musician? In his book *I of the Vortex,* Llinás writes:

> When a soloist such as Heifetz plays with a symphony orchestra accompanying him, by convention the concerto is played purely from memory. Such playing implies that this highly specific motor pattern is stored somewhere and subsequently released at the time the curtain goes up.

But for a performer, Llinás writes, it is not sufficient to have implicit memory only; one must have explicit memory as well:

> Without intact explicit memory, Jascha Heifetz would not remember from day to day which piece he had chosen to work on previously, or that he had ever worked on that piece before. Nor would he recall what he had accomplished the day before or by analysis of past experience what particular problems in execution should be a focus of today's practice session. In fact, it would not occur to him to have a practice session at all; without close direction from someone else he would be effectively incapable of undertaking the process of learning any new piece, irrespective of his considerable technical skills.

This, too, is very much the case with Clive, who, for all his musical powers, needs "close direction" from others. He needs someone to put the music before him, to get him into action, and to make sure that he learns and practices new pieces.

What is the relationship of action patterns and procedural memories, which are associated with relatively primitive portions of the nervous system, to consciousness and sensibility, which depend on the cerebral cortex? Practice involves conscious application, monitoring what one is doing, bringing all one's intelligence and sensibility and values to bear — even though what is so painfully and consciously acquired may then become automatic, coded in motor patterns at a subcortical level. Each time Clive sings or plays the piano or conducts a choir, automatism comes to his aid. But what happens in an artistic or creative performance, though it depends on automatisms, is anything but automatic. The actual performance reanimates him, engages him as a creative person; it becomes fresh and perhaps contains new improvisations or innovations. Once Clive starts playing, his "momentum," as Deborah writes, will keep him, and the piece, going. Deborah, herself a musician, expresses this very precisely:

> The momentum of the music carried Clive from bar to bar. Within the structure of the piece, he was held, as if the staves were tramlines and there was only one way to go. He knew exactly where he was because in every phrase there is context implied, by rhythm, key, melody. It was marvellous to be free. When the music stopped Clive fell through to the lost place. But for those moments he was playing he seemed normal.

Clive's performance self seems, to those who know him, just as vivid and complete as it was before his illness. This mode of being, this self, is seemingly untouched by his amnesia, even though his autobiographical self, the self that depends on explicit, episodic memories, is virtually lost. The rope that is let down from heaven for Clive comes not with recalling the past, as for Proust, but with performance — and it holds only as long as the performance lasts. Without performance, the thread is broken, and he is thrown back once again into the abyss.

Deborah speaks of the "momentum" of the music in its very structure. A piece of music is not a mere sequence of notes but a tightly organized organic whole. Every bar, every phrase arises organically from what preceded it and points to what will follow. Dynamism is built into the nature of melody. And over and above this there is the intentionality of the composer, the style, the order, and the logic that he has created to express his musical ideas and feelings. These, too, are present in every bar and phrase. Schopenhauer wrote of melody as having "significant intentional connection from beginning to end" and as "one thought from beginning to end." Marvin Minsky compares a sonata to a teacher or a lesson:

> No one remembers, word for word, all that was said in any lecture, or played in any piece. But if you understood it once, you now own new networks of knowledge, about each theme and how it changes and relates to others. Thus, no one could remember Beethoven's Fifth Symphony entire, from a single hearing. But neither could one ever hear again those first four notes as just four notes! Once but a tiny scrap of sound; it is now a Known Thing — a locus in the web of all the other things we know, whose meanings and significances depend on one another.

A piece of music will draw one in, teach one about its structure and secrets, whether one is listening consciously or not. This is so even if one has never heard a piece of music before. Listening to music is not a passive process but intensely active, involving a stream of inferences, hypotheses, expectations, and anticipations. We can grasp a new piece — how it is constructed, where it is going, what will come next — with such accuracy that even after a few bars we may be able to hum or sing along with it. Such anticipation, such singing along, is possible because one has knowledge, largely implicit, of musical "rules" (how a cadence must resolve, for instance) and a familiarity with particular musical conventions (the form of a sonata, or the repetition of a theme). When we "remember" a melody, it plays in our mind; it becomes newly alive.

Thus we can listen again and again to a recording of a piece of music, a piece we know well, and yet it can seem as fresh, as new, as the first time we heard it. There is not a process of recalling, assembling, recategorizing, as when one attempts to reconstruct or remember an event or a scene from the past. We recall one tone at a time, and each tone entirely fills our consciousness yet simultaneously relates to the whole. It is similar when we walk or run or swim — we do so one step, one stroke at a time, yet each step or stroke is an integral part of the whole. Indeed, if we think of each note or step too consciously, we may lose the thread, the motor melody.

It may be that Clive, incapable of remembering or anticipating events because of his amnesia, is able to sing and play and conduct music because remembering music is not, in the usual sense, remembering at all. Remembering music, listening to it, or playing it, is wholly in the present. Victor Zuckerkandl, a philosopher of music, explored this paradox beautifully in 1956 in *Sound and Symbol:*

> The hearing of a melody is a hearing *with* the melody . . . It is even a condition of hearing melody that the tone present at the moment should fill consciousness *entirely*, that *nothing* should be remembered, nothing except it or beside it be present in consciousness . . . Hearing a melody is hearing, having heard, and being about to hear, all at once . . . Every melody declares to us that the past can be there without being remembered, the future without being foreknown.

It has been twenty years since Clive's illness, and, for him, nothing has moved on. One might say he is still in 1985 or, given his retrograde amnesia, in 1965. In some ways, he is not anywhere at all; he has dropped out of space and time altogether. He no longer has any inner narrative; he is not leading a life in the sense that the rest of us do. And yet one has only to see him at the keyboard or with Deborah to feel that, at such times, he is himself again and wholly alive. It is not the remembrance of things past, the "once" that Clive yearns for, or can ever achieve. It is the claiming, the filling, of the present, the now, and this is only possible when he is totally immersed in the successive moments of an act. It is the "now" that bridges the abyss.

As Deborah recently wrote to me, "Clive's at-homeness in music and in his love for me are where he transcends amnesia and finds continuum — not the linear fusion of moment after moment, nor based on any framework of autobiographical information, but where Clive, and any of us, *are* finally, where we are who we are."

NICK SAMARAS

I'm Never Sure about the Word "Apotheosis"

FROM *The Southern Review*

Each time, I transliterate its root into "from becoming God"
but swear the word must mean like the opposite of that.
Outside the window is 1:00 A.M. and I'd rather let threaded light

sew its body before I succumb to opening the dictionary again.
Outside, black trees spoke their winter branches upward
for the web of constellations. Upstairs, I peck at these keys, working

unpaid while my children sleep purely, growing into their bodies.
To my son, I am the largest man. To God, I am amusing.
What holds me from becoming divine, or just saintly, is nothing

more than my willful self, staying up late and not deigning to look
up an annoying word or gaze out into dark light to join the bare
trees stretching upward, the stars lighting my children's sleep.

MATHEW N. SCHMALZ

The Saint of Worcester

FROM *Commonweal*

JOHN MADE HIS last pilgrimage to see Audrey in April 2007. He took an overnight bus from Philadelphia and arrived in Worcester, Massachusetts. John then made his way to the Cathedral of St. Paul, where Audrey's wake was being held. Audrey Marie Santo was dressed in white, her long black hair sweeping behind her, with a sparkling tiara set upon her brow. The first mourners kissed Audrey's wrists as they filed past her casket. After a velvet rope was set up to guide others paying their respects, John moved forward. He stood motionless before Audrey's casket, repeating names of saints in a hushed litany. John had always placed Audrey's name in the roll of saints, but he hoped that the Catholic Church would soon make it official. As he beheld Audrey this last time, John said he saw a halo-like glow around her. The halo grew and filled the entire cathedral with light. It was a vision of tranquillity, as John later reflected, a parting gift from Audrey who had brought tranquillity to his once troubled mind.

It was at Audrey's home in Worcester where I first met John several years earlier. I noticed him when I overheard him talking about his robot collection. He had thirty-one of them, all blessed by a priest. My eyes were drawn to the tattoos on John's neck: CHRIST inscribed in black, BIBLE in blue, SOUL in red, and HOLY in yellow. It was John's first pilgrimage to see Audrey, and she was twenty-two at the time. For over a decade, visitors had been coming to Audrey's home, drawn by stories of her stigmatic wounds and of healings attributed to her intercession. Statues in her home were reported to weep tears of blood and oil, and several Eucharistic hosts had been found bloodstained after being consecrated in her presence.

The story of how Audrey Santo became an object of veneration begins in 1987 when she was three years old. Momentarily separated from her brother while playing outside, Audrey fell into her family's backyard pool. Although paramedics revived her, Audrey could no longer move or speak — a condition that doctors rather matter-of-factly called "akinetic mutism." Although her institutionalization was presented as the only real option for the Santo family, Audrey was brought home. People started coming to the Santo home to pray for Audrey's healing and to help the Santo family. Soon reports of unexplained phenomena began to circulate, and the Santo home became a site for pilgrimage. Although Audrey never regained the ability to move or speak, pilgrims understood her to be fully conscious and able to pray for those seeking relief from maladies of mind and body. Indeed, many came to believe that Audrey was a "victim soul" who would not only intervene for the afflicted, but also would offer up her own sufferings in restitution for sin.

Along with medical support and his family's love, it was Audrey's supernatural intervention that John saw playing a decisive role in his own healing and recovery. Diagnosed as a paranoid schizophrenic, John was tortured by the voices in his head until they stopped ten years ago. Around that time, John learned about Audrey and began praying to her. But it wasn't until several years later that he was able to make the pilgrimage to see Audrey herself. On that first pilgrimage day, John arrived at the Santo home and stopped in a small chapel that had once been the Santo family's garage. The chapel walls were streaked by streams of fragrant oil, as were the many statues of Jesus and the Virgin Mary. This oil, along with that leaking from numerous other statues, would be collected, infused into cotton balls, and sent to people like John for their personal rituals of anointing and healing. John always thought of the chapel as giving witness to Audrey's incomparable sanctity: there were pictures of Audrey with priests; displays of her pink plastic rosary beads along with tissues touched by her tears; and, quite stunningly, formal exhibit of a bloody kerchief reportedly soaked with blood from her stigmatic wounds. Most affecting for John and other pilgrims was a large photograph of four hosts that were found bloodstained after being consecrated near Audrey. A final bloodstained host was discovered approximately a year before Audrey's death, bringing the total to five: five hosts representing the five wounds of Christ.

As his first pilgrimage continued, John and several other pilgrims left the chapel to see Audrey. As always, Audrey lay in her bedroom, attached to a respirator and a feeding tube, with a nurse at her side. The religious images on the wall behind her were arranged in a semicircular pattern resembling a halo. On one side of the bed were relics of several saints, and opposite her bed was a tabernacle. John approached the clear plastic curtain that screened off the entrance to Audrey's room and bowed his head, as did the other pilgrims. Reverential silence then followed, punctuated only by the intermittent sounds from the monitors at Audrey's bedside.

I met John on that first pilgrimage day as part of my academic research into the devotional activities surrounding Audrey Santo. As John began to share his life story with me, our relationship changed into something different from the traditional pairing of observer and informant. John told me about his upbringing in a traditional Catholic family, and his years as a gunner's mate in the navy. He told me how the voices in his head began as whispers and later became screams. He told me how hard he tried to escape the voices, sometimes fleeing by bus to a distant part of the country and often hitchhiking when his money ran out. He told me of nights sleeping under cars and in abandoned buildings. He also told me how the voices led him to set fire to his parents' apartment and how his life eventually became a seemingly endless series of hospital confinements. But in reflecting on his ordeals, John never told me that he ever asked what might be the most obvious question: "Why has God made me this way?"

This was what I asked immediately after being diagnosed with obsessive-compulsive disorder. While I never heard voices, my strong compulsions and obsessive ruminations were akin to hearing voices because they had an independent and often irresistible power. But as disabling as my disorder was, I came to realize that it could be empowering, at least when the vise lock of obsession loosened just enough to allow slightly more reasoned reflections. In the academic world, the ability to follow an idea relentlessly, to check and recheck scholarly work in ritualistic fashion, is a sign of professional commitment. In the classroom, as I came to understand my own anxiety-fueled obsessions, I became more attuned to the fear and mental chaos many students struggle with. Mental afflictions are strange things: along with strong bouts of suffering, they may also bring measures of unconventional insight and ability.

The tattoos on John's neck are only a hint of the series of thirty-one that cover his body. For him, thirty-one is not just a number but a symbol of completeness that should be read as $3 + 1$ or $3 = 1$, indicating "three persons and one Lord." The number 3 is the structuring element in much of John's discourse: at every meal he says three prayers, one before, one during, and one after; in his letters to me, significant words are underlined three times; when he describes periods spent in the hospital, he presents them in multiples of three: a confinement of nine months, followed by one of twelve, and another of fifteen. John's name for the Trinity and the saints is "God's Teams" — an ever-expanding relationship in which the Father, Son, and Holy Spirit seek to bring all within their divinely balanced union. John's tattoos display the names of the "captains" of God's Teams: Jesus, Mary, Moses, and, of course, "Saint" Audrey Santo. These intercessory figures, John explains, are responsible for maintaining the silence and calm in his mind and heart. He links various aspects of his identity to these members of God's Teams — an integrated unity-in-diversity that expresses a dynamic but coherent sense of self.

John's robot collection expresses a similar desire for integration. Since the main schizophrenic voice he heard was robotic, having his collection of thirty-one robots blessed by a priest helped John to reintegrate aspects of his schizophrenic experience into a religiously meaningful whole. Catholicism is often thought of as static in both its institutional structure and its emphasis on doctrinal conformity. But in John's vision, Catholicism is about motion: the motion of the Trinity and God's Teams toward a greater encompassing union; the motion of people through life toward communion with God; the motion of our internally fractured selves to wholeness. For John, robots and tattoos have an almost sacramental power. They express, connect, and sanctify not only the diverse aspects of human experience, but also the diverse voices of the restless mind.

In thinking of robots and tattoos as religiously meaningful, it is tempting to cultivate a detached fascination, such as that wryly depicted by the avant-garde writer J. G. Ballard. In *The Atrocity Exhibition*, Ballard describes a showing of paintings by schizophrenics who themselves were not allowed to attend the display. In addition to suffering the illness itself, schizophrenics experience social exclusion and isolation: as human curios, as clinical exemplars of illness, or, most simply and painfully, as objects of fear or pity. John describes his own isolation as a "purgatory" of internal chaos filled with sound and fear. During the most severe phase of his illness, John felt that only he was real, while all others were phantoms. It wasn't until the voices stopped that he finally grasped that the world around him had a reality of its own. Still, his sense of isolation remained because the voices had been his only friends. And so colorful tattoos became John's way of reaching out to others by giving visual testimony to his identity and inviting conversation about God's healing power.

John would eventually add three more tattoos, bringing the total to thirty-four. As John explained it to me, thirty-four means 3 + 4, which equals 7, the number of the sacraments. John understands his flesh not only as a witness to the sacraments, but also as an embodiment of them. Indeed, John often links significant moments in his life to individual sacraments: the silencing of the voices becomes both a "baptism" and an "anointing," the tattoos a "confession," talking about his illness a mission or "holy order," his devotion to God's Teams a "matrimony," and the publication of this article about him a "confirmation." While John certainly does not understand his body as sacramental in the sense of representing Christ's body, he does understand it as giving witness to the many ways the divine touches the human. Interestingly, a crucial theme in Catholic ecclesiology is the idea of the Church as a "sacrament" of Christ. For this reason, we all potentially have "sacramental bodies" as we endeavor to live out and thus "embody" sacramentality in our choices and actions. Of course, the observation that Catholicism is "sacramental" has become an almost empty slogan, given the wide variety of contexts in which it's made. But a fundamental aspect of the Catholic understanding of sacramentality is that symbols "make real" what they symbolize. John's robots and tattoos not only symbolize the healing of his fragmented self, but also participate in — and make real — the healing process itself.

In 1998, thousands attended a Mass in Audrey's honor at the

College of the Holy Cross football stadium. Pilgrims could view Audrey though a large window in a specially designed room resembling a small house that had been towed to the service. (It was built by a relative of the man who made the popemobile.) Some faculty members objected to the public display of a disabled woman, and many voiced concerns that Holy Cross would become associated with a particularly ostentatious form of Catholic supernaturalism. Some commentators have raised questions about claims of supernatural phenomena and healings associated with Audrey. In 1999, the Diocese of Worcester published an initial report on the case, which stated that the real miracle was the dedication the Santo family has shown to Audrey's care. The report held that, while there was no evidence of fraud, more investigation was needed, especially concerning the nature of the oil stains and the state of Audrey's consciousness. The diocese did not make another formal statement about Audrey's case until the days following her death. Bishop Robert McManus, like his predecessors, praised the devotion of the Santo family but also offered his own view: "We may never fully understand the causes of various paranormal events which have been reported" at the Santo home. A group of priests and laypersons has recently retained a postulator in Rome and applied to the Worcester diocese for recognition as a foundation to promote "the cause of beatification and canonization of Little Audrey Santo." It would thus be difficult to say that Audrey has "passed away," since her presence remains quite dynamic indeed.

As the story of Audrey Santo continues to evolve, there can be no denying that the entire phenomenon raises a series of difficult religious and ethical questions. Indeed, for some the whole affair seems "bizarre" and "repulsive," to quote a letter written in response to the initial magazine publication of this piece. Such strong reactions are to be expected when Catholic devotionalism touches issues regarding proper treatment and respect for those who suffer. But where some see an opportunity for polemics, others see an opportunity for togetherness. John told me about a dream he had in which Audrey presented him to thousands of cheering people in a football stadium. For John, Audrey and the devotion surrounding her opened a space for community he otherwise would not have experienced. In the year before her death, Audrey was removed from public view. But in spite of this, John continued to travel to the Santo house because it was one of the few places he felt acknowledged as a full person. He was not alone in thinking that Audrey emitted a protective halo of acceptance that extended beyond her Worcester bedroom. The Apostolate of a Silent Soul, the ministry that grew up around Audrey and still promotes her case, used to publish a newsletter containing letters from people touched by her. Some letters were simply petitions, while other letters testified to healings and other supernatural experiences. But most letters were intended simply to express moments of anxiety and suffering along with the unexpected consolations that everyday life sometimes brings. Through and in Audrey's silence, John and other devotees found voice for their own otherwise silent sufferings.

"John" is a pseudonym of his own choosing. "It refers to John the Baptist — the man who lost his head," he explained. *To lose one's head* is an appropriate metaphor to describe the experience of mental illness. But losing one's head can also mean being dis- and reoriented: to see things differently, beyond the ordinary categories that shape our perceptions of the world. After all, as John reminded me, John the Baptist saw beyond the external appearance of Jesus to recognize him as the messiah. Part of the sacramental quality of Catholic spirituality is openness to a reality that may lie behind external appearance. For example, the Thomistic understanding of "transubstantiation" explains how the presence of Christ is realized, literally "made real," under the external appearance, or "accidents," of bread and wine. Similarly, the "external signs" of John's tattoos and robot collection help him to "realize" rich and complex religious and spiritual meanings.

There can be a tendency to romanticize mental illness by portraying it exclusively as an altered state of consciousness without acknowledging its often overpowering pain. John would have none of that. Nor would I. Like schizophrenia, obsessive-compulsive disorder can be a horrible and imprisoning experience. There is a famous print by M. C. Escher depicting ants on a Möbius band: they walk on and on, forever looping back on an endless journey to nowhere. That's what it's like when you cannot "turn off" your mind. Yet, by going over the same ground again and again, the mind becomes sensitive to subtle changes in the shape and texture of thought and feeling. Sacraments and sacramentals also take form within a very circumscribed set of ritual parameters. Still, in their constant, formalized repetition and presentation, one can find ever new meanings and imaginative possibilities.

I do not know whether John was alone in seeing pure light surrounding Audrey during her wake at the Cathedral of St. Paul. But I do know many others who have told me of similar experiences when they saw Audrey at her Worcester home. Light can be associated with sanctity, just as it can be connected with tranquillity, as it was in John's reflections on his last viewing of Audrey. But light, at its very brightest, also envelops and blurs visible distinctions. Once isolated by their distinctive sufferings, pilgrims like John met and blended together under the glow of sanctity they saw and felt at the Santo home. There John and many others were able to realize a powerful range of religious meanings through the "sacramentals" of suffering and silence associated with the young Audrey Santo. Of course, many view the Audrey Santo phenomenon as yet another example of Catholic exoticism. But the exotic and the familiar, not to mention the holy, are often the same thing refracted differently through the prism of our expectations and experience. The power of the Catholic sacramental imagination is that it allows us to see all three at the same time.

KURT SHAW

Only a Mother's Love

FROM *Harvard Divinity Bulletin*

WORKING WITH STREET CHILDREN, gangsters, and thieves, I've had ample opportunity to see any number of tattoos. Among all of the words and images that young people choose to inscribe on their bodies, I have noticed one common thread among Crips and Bloods in New York, *sicarios* in Medellín, and gang members in Brazil. One message stands out among all of the rest, perhaps best expressed in a tattoo I saw in the Brazilian city of Recife last year: *"Amor só de mãe,"* "Only a mother's love."[1]

Most essays on crime and violence try to use academic knowledge to solve the problems of the inner city or the shantytown, but here I want to do the opposite. When we put the phrase "only a mother's love" in dialogue with the psychoanalytic and theological traditions, we see that "gangstas"[2] have something to teach the academy — and the broader society. In their thought about mothers and love, they have discovered an important route out of postmodern violence.

Last August, during a workshop in Argentina, I taught a young man — once a street kid and petty thief — how to make documentary films.[3] For the central symbol of his movie, Alejandro chose the passage through the sewers under the city of Córdoba, where he and his friends had always fled "after we swiped old ladies' purses." He managed to escape this tunnel — both the literal and the metaphorical one — only after his mother became ill. "Because of the things I was doing — things that make me feel awful now, bad things I was doing like robbing and sniffing glue — she suffered an aneurysm in her brain," he said. "If something worse had happened, I don't know if I would have been able to forgive myself for doing that to her." The break with his past — the moment when he "came out into the light," as he puts it in his video — emerged only when he saw how his actions had made his mother suffer.

Amparo, a conflict mediator in the Kennedy neighborhood of Medellín, in Colombia, told me a similar story. In her neighborhood, the gang leader was Jhonny, a killer and dealer of the worst kind, but a man with a great and sincere affection for his mother. He bought one thing after another for her: clothes, household appliances, and a house. Jhonny knew that what he was doing wasn't good, but everything he did was to improve his mother's life. Amparo met Jhonny's mother through a neighborhood association, and began talking to her about life in the neighborhood, about violence, justice, and exclusion. Amparo found out that Jhonny's mother didn't like what her son was doing, but she didn't want to criticize him because she thought that she could lose her son if she did so. Aware of how her own life had changed after she read Gandhi's autobiography, Amparo gave a copy of the book to Jhonny's mother.

In the following weeks, Amparo and Jhonny's mother talked about Gandhi, reflecting on the possibility of fighting against violence with peace and ethics. Jhonny's mother admitted that she was part of the problem: after all, her accepting his presents encouraged her son to lead the unjust life of a criminal and a killer — it was the act that offered expiation, or at least justification, for his sins. Mother's Day, perhaps the most important holiday in Medellín, arrived, and Jhonny came over in the morning with a special present for his mother: an expensive gold watch. The mother gathered her courage and said: "I don't want it, my dear son. But when you bring me a present that you earn with your own sweat, that will be the best day of my life."

Jhonny, the brutal gang boss, cried loudly enough for the whole neighborhood to hear. Within a week, he left the gang and went abroad, where he is now the director of a conflict-resolution program for youth. He writes to his mother from his new home.

While working with children and teenagers from the most violent favelas of Recife, Brazil, I was stunned by their ability to memorize long and complex rap lyrics. One of the songs that every child knew was "Desculpa Mãe" ("Forgive me, Mother"), by the group Facção Central, which includes these lines: "I don't deserve the tear that runs down your cheek / When you see the table empty for dinner . . . / Forgive me, Mother, for stealing the smile from your lips."

Whether among gangstas in Brazil, hired killers in Colombia, or thieves in Argentina, a mother's love is a force capable of transforming her son. I want to show here that this love is also the force that constitutes the ethical subject.

The gangsta life promises a direct path to what the French psychoanalytic tradition calls *jouissance* (badly translated in English as "enjoyment"): the pleasures of drugs, of promiscuous sex, and of other people's fear and respect. What strikes me most about this criminal *jouissance*, however, is that its pleasures do not emerge from the traditional dynamic of desire and satisfaction, but from the more perverse Freudian logic of the *Treib*, the drive. For Jacques Lacan and Slavoj Žižek, the difference between desire and drive lies in their relationship with the mysterious thing — whatever it may be — that inspires and centers what I want. With the drive, one gains access to *jouissance* exactly through the *failure* to get the desired object, by the endless circulation around it.[4] Think of the shopping mall: buying more and more commodities isn't about having, but about the strange joy of returning home, and then several days later saying: "You know, this isn't exactly what I wanted. Let's go back to the mall."

Teenage heroin addicts have told me that the first time they used the drug, it was like arriving in paradise, but that every other time they used the drug, it was merely a vain attempt to recapture that first experience. What turns the drug into an addiction isn't so much physiology as ritual: surreptitious buying, cleaning the needle, tying the band on the arm — and always knowing that it isn't going to work, that the paradise of the first experience will never happen again. At first, the *jouissance* comes from the heroin, but after that it comes from the *failure* of the drug, the constant, pointless circulation around the object, like a planet trapped by the gravity of a black hole.

Gang life plays by the same rules, finding its *jouissance* in the failure of drugs, power, and sex. The Comando Vermelho — the most powerful drug mafia in Rio de Janeiro — takes as its slogan "the

right side of the errant life" *("O lado certo da vida errada"),* a powerful description of the drive. "Errant" means wrong and failed, but
it still preserves traces of its original meaning as "wandering" or
"lost," like the knight errant or the *judeu errante.*⁵ The "right side of
the errant life" means that one finds his *jouissance* in the act of er-
ring, in the vain and wandering circulation around the absent or
unattainable object that inspires desire.

If we frame this issue in theological terms — a language in which
gang members would feel more comfortable than in that of Lacan-
ian psychoanalysis — we might say that the gangsta sins much in order to escape original sin. The gun offers almost unlimited power
to a child or teenager, providing the delusion of omnipotence, as
does the easy road to bliss provided by drugs and sex. As Augustine
knew quite well, lack and impotence structure what it means to be
human, the incompleteness that the theological tradition names
"original sin." The gangsta's sins endeavor to cover this gap in being; the gangsta wants to delude himself into believing that bliss
and completeness are possible.

Ever since Plato wrote *The Symposium,* one metaphor has dominated the way that the West has seen love: the story that Plato puts
in the mouth of Aristophanes. In the time of myth, humans were
whole, complete, and round, but in a great tragedy, these beings
were split, and now we spend our lives looking for our "other
halves" so that we can be whole again. The gangsta's "errant life"
plays the same role as the object of love in Aristophanes' myth: it is
supposed to make us whole, to give direct access to *jouissance,* to
overcome original sin.

The mistakes in this theology don't escape gang members and
drug addicts. They know quite well that drugs and sex and guns do
not make them whole, but instead send them into an endless spiral
of failure around the thing that they want: we should take seriously
their metaphors of "going nowhere" and "going around in circles"
as a way to describe the dynamics of the drive. "The people who sell
drugs also know right from wrong," as a young Brazilian rap artist
told me. "They just know it in a different way."⁶ The fundamental
question becomes, then, what can break the circular *jouissance* of
the drive? Alejandro, the young man in Argentina, described it perfectly when he said, "If something worse had happened, I don't
know if I would have been able to forgive myself for doing what I

did to her." For him, a mother's suffering was the only power strong enough to tear apart the drive, the illusion of completeness. In forgiving ourselves (or blaming ourselves), we fold ourselves over. One part of us forgives, while the other is forgiven. This folding or doubling permits us to look at ourselves, reflect, examine ourselves: it is as if we stood outside looking in. Here we find the philosophical definition of consciousness, the birth of the subject. When a gangsta's mother begins to suffer, his self-contained world breaks down, he takes cognizance of his actions, and he comes to recognize that something real exists outside of his drive. "I heard my conscience, and now I want to support her in any way that I can," Alejandro says in his movie. "And more than anything else, to value life. Life, and the people around us . . ." This "call of conscience" — a call that divides the subject between the active, blaming part and the passive, blamed part — gives birth to the subject. Most important, this subject directs himself toward the other, toward the good of "the people around us."

Much of European theology has come to see grace through the eyes of the Greeks — with their longing for wholeness and union — but gangstas know grace in a much more prophetic, Hebrew way. Just as the pain of a mother breaks the circular drive of crime and drugs, the call of God came to the prophets essentially as a *rupture* in their lives. Gangsta wisdom shows us that the truth of love is exactly the opposite of what Aristophanes and Plato taught: love doesn't make us complete. It *breaks* the economy of the drive. It *divides*. And as such, it allows a person to see himself. When a mother's pain and love forces her son to look at himself honestly, he can become a real subject.

A mother creates the space in which her child can become a subject. First, she teaches her child that he is not omnipotent, that he does not have direct access to *jouissance*, or wholeness. Then, when the child sees himself in his mother's eyes, he also sees his mother looking at him. He sees himself as the *object* of the mother's gaze, but also as a *subject* capable of gazing upon her. In the midst of a mother's love, a child gains a conscience. *"Amor só de mãe"* isn't a cynical slogan, nor is it pessimist or nihilist. It criticizes the myth of love as the encounter of two broken halves, but also insists that though love is not union, it still exists, and that it is powerful enough to force a gangsta to change his life.

Most important, the phrase "only a mother's love" shows us that love doesn't just come from the mother. We could see this same process in a father's love, or a husband's, or a friend's. Love happens when we gain the ability to divide ourselves, criticize ourselves, and look at ourselves from outside. A mother's love gives birth to more than a child: it gives birth to the subject.

This essay is an English adaptation of a presentation to the Escola Brasiliera de Psicanálise, Secçáo Santa Catarina.

Notes

1. In Portuguese, this phrase is much more ambiguous than in English, meaning "only a mother's love," but also "only a mother could love," and even "love only comes from the mother."

2. Here, I use the slang term "gangsta" because it is more common among gang members in the United States, but also because the Brazilian slang for urban bandit (*ganguista*) is a loan word derived from English slang.

3. Available at www.shinealight.org/ElTunel.html.

4. See Slavoj Žižek, *The Parallax View* (Cambridge, Mass.: MIT Press, 2006).

5. In Portuguese and Spanish, this is the phrase used for the anti-Semitic trope of the "Wandering Jew."

6. M. C. Chipan, in *City of Rhyme* (Shine a Light, 2007).

JASON SHINDER

Living

FROM *The New Yorker*

Just when it seemed my mother couldn't bear

one more needle, one more insane orange pill,
my sister, in silence, stood at the end

of the bed and slowly rubbed her feet,

which were scratchy with hard, yellow skin,
and dirt cramped beneath the broken nails,

which changed nothing in time except

the way my mother was lost in it for a while
as if with a kind of relief that doesn't relieve.

And then, with her eyes closed, my mother said

the one or two words the living have for gratefulness,
which is a kind of forgetting, with a sense

of what it means to be alive long enough

to love someone. *Thank you,* she said. As for me,
I didn't care how her voice suddenly seemed low

and kind, or what failures and triumphs

of the body and spirit brought her to that point —
just that it sounded like hope, stupid hope.

SALLY THOMAS

Schooling at Home

FROM *First Things*

ONE MORNING, as the four children and I prepared to start the school day, I consulted the saints' dictionary, as I habitually do, to see whose feast it might be. That day there were two feasts: those of Saint Damascus and Saint Daniel the Stylite, the latter of whom particularly captured everyone's imagination. Saint Daniel's long tenure on his pillar by the Bosphorus is described in my saints' dictionary as "mainly uneventful," an assertion followed by a remarkable catalog of events, including miraculous healings of the sick, the forecasting of a devastating fire, and a visit from a demon-possessed prostitute. After his death, when the monks, having brought him down at last, tried to straighten his body out of its long-accustomed fetal position, "his bones cracked so loudly that an accident was feared."

Eeeeeewwww, said everyone with an appreciative shudder, the four- and three-year-olds leaning raptly against my shoulders. The twelve-year-old and the nine-year-old spent some minutes in serious discussion about potential hermitages in the backyard — the top of the swing set versus the fort — until, with the useful observation of monastic writers that some lives are "worthy of admiration, not imitation," I recalled us all to work.

The night before, we had gone to dinner with old friends, and in the course of the evening the conversation turned to our homeschooling. Our hosts didn't want to argue with the decision my husband and I had made to homeschool; in truth, people do that a lot less often than we had steeled ourselves to expect early on. I suppose they didn't ask how we expected our children to be "socialized" because there the children were, in front of everyone, doing their best impersonations of socialized people. The nine-year-old talked to the grownups about *Star Wars,* the four-year-old helped to carry dishes to the table, the three-year-old played nicely on the floor with our friends' baby granddaughter. The twelve-year-old, away at a ballet rehearsal, proclaimed her socialization by her absence.

In fact, our friends' questions had nothing to do with the welfare of our children, because they could see for themselves that the children were fine. But they were curious, and what they wanted to know was simply this: *What do you do all day long?*

That's never an easy question to answer. When people think of school, typically they think of a day dominated by a roster of discrete subjects. In English, you do reading, writing, spelling, and grammar. In math, you do numbers. In history, you do what's been done before.

In our homeschool, though we cover all these necessary subjects, the delineations among subjects are often far from clear. For example, this fall my math-tutor brother gave us a book entitled *Famous Mathematicians,* a series of little biographies beginning with Euclid and ending with Norbert Wiener in the twentieth century. The nine-year-old asked if he could read it, so twice a week, during our math time, instead of doing regular computational math, I let him read. When he finished the book, he chose one famous mathematician to profile and wrote a little report. As I was describing this exercise for our friends, I kept thinking that we had either done an awful lot of math and given English the short end of the stick, or else had done a lot of English and shafted math. But then I realized that in fact we had done it all. He had learned math concepts, he had learned history, he had practiced reading and writing and spelling and editing — all by reading one book and writing about it.

In recent years, as homeschooling has moved closer to the mainstream, much has been said about the successes of homeschooled children, especially regarding their statistically superior performance on standardized tests and the attractiveness of their transcripts and portfolios to college-admission boards. Less, I think, has been said about how and why these successes happen. The fact is that homeschooling is an efficient way to teach and learn. It's time-effective, in that a homeschooled child, working independently or one-on-one with a parent or an older sibling, can get through more work or master a concept more quickly than a child who's one of twenty-five in a classroom. It's effort-effective, in that a child doesn't spend needless hours over a concept already mastered simply because others haven't mastered it yet. Conversely, a child doesn't spend years in school quietly not learning a subject, under the teacher's radar, only to face the massive and depressing task of remediation when the deficiency is finally caught.

To my mind, however, homeschooling's greatest efficiency lies in its capacity for a rightly ordered life. A child in school almost inevitably has a separate existence, a "school life," that too easily weakens parental authority and values and that also encourages an artificial boundary between *learning* and *everything else*. Children come home exhausted from a day at school — and for a child with working parents, that day can be twelve hours long — and the last thing they want is to pick up books or have conversations. Television and video games demand relatively little, and they seem a blessed departure from what the children have been doing all day. "You know I don't read all that stuff you read," a neighbor child scornfully told my eldest some years ago during one of those archetypal childhood arguments about what to play. Our daughter wanted to play *Treasure Seekers* or *Betsy-Tacy and Tib;* her friend insisted on playing the Disney cartoon character Kim Possible. Book-talk was for school, and she wasn't at school just then, thank you.

At home we can do what's nearly impossible in a school setting: we can weave learning into the fabric of our family life, so that the lines between "learning" and "everything else" have largely ceased to exist. The older children do a daily schedule of what I call sit-down work: math lessons, English and foreign-language exercises, and readings for history and science. The nine-year-old does roughly two hours of sit-down work a day, while the twelve-year-old spends three to four hours. But those hours hardly constitute the sum total of their education.

We spend some time formally learning Latin, for example, but we also say our table blessing in Latin and sing Latin hymns during prayers. Both older children sing in our parish treble choir: still more Latin, which is not a dead language to them but a living, singing one. The twelve-year-old is working her way through an Eng-

lish-grammar-and-composition text, but she is also, on her own,
writing a play, which our local children's theater will produce in
the spring. The nine-year-old has his own subscription to *National
Geographic* and fills us in at dinner on the events of the D-day inva-
sion or the habits of the basking shark. He practices handwriting,
with which he struggles, by writing letters to friends in England,
where we lived when he was small. Last November, the older children and a friend adopted a project for sending care packages to
soldiers in Iraq; they wrote letters, knitted hats, made Christmas
cards, and one Saturday went door to door around the neighborhood collecting funds to cover postage and to buy school supplies
for the soldiers to hand out to Iraqi children. This undertaking
by itself was something of a mini-curriculum, involving reading,
handwriting, composition, art, math, community service, and even
public relations. At their best, our days are saturated with what
school merely strives to replicate: real, substantial, active, useful,
and moral learning.

Most important for us in the ordering of our life is that our
homeschooling day unfolds from habits of prayer. We begin the
day with the rosary and a saint's life; we say the Angelus at lunch-
time; we do a lesson from the catechism or a reading in apologetics
and say the evening office before bed. Our children have internal-
ized this rhythm, and, to my intense gratification, the older children marshal the younger children to prayers even when their father and I are absent. The day is shaped and organized by times of
turning to God.

A lot of unscheduled learning seems to happen during these
times. In saying the rosary, for example, we exercise our skills in
memorization and recitation, as well as in contemplation. The little
children practice sitting still; they also practice counting. In remembering our daily intentions together, we practice the discipline of inclining our hearts and minds toward the needs of others.
Often, too, during devotions we find ourselves plunged into discus-
sions about current events, ethics, and questions about God and
life that have been simmering unasked in some child's mind until
just that moment. The saints, whose dates we record in our family timeline book, provide us not only with examples of holiness
but also with insight into the historical eras in which they lived.
We have even found ourselves doing geography during prayers:

though I now forget why we needed to know this in praying the office, I distinctly recall dragging out the atlas one evening to confirm the exact location of Chad.

On reflection, if I had to give our homeschool a name, as some states require, I might be tempted to call it St. Daniel the Stylite Academy. This would be original and memorable — for one thing, we wouldn't be constantly saying, "No, we're not *that* St. Daniel the Stylite Academy." Moreover, it captures something of what I believe the essence of homeschooling to be: an integrated life of learning, ordered by and emanating from the discipline of prayer. After all, despite the admonition of the monks, Saint Daniel's career may be more worthy of imitation than I had thought.

The homeschooling life often feels like life on a pillar: isolated but visible, removed yet immersed in essential undertakings. We have not so far, in our own "mainly uneventful" life, done single combat with sword-wielding phantoms or been shown off as a "wonder of the empire." And yet, what looks like not that much on the daily surface of things proves in the living to be something greater than the schedule on the page suggests, a life in which English and math and science and history, contemplation and discussion and action, faith and learning, are not compartmentalized entities but elements in an integrated whole from which, we hope and pray, our children will emerge one day so firmly formed that nothing in this world can unbend them.

J. SCOTT TURNER

Signs of Design

FROM *Christian Century*

BECAUSE I AM a biologist, evolution is at the core of virtually everything I think about. Like most of my colleagues, I've kept an eye on the emerging "intelligent design" movement. Unlike most of my colleagues, however, I don't see ID as a threat to biology, public education, or the ideals of the republic. To the contrary, what worries me more is the way that many of my colleagues have responded to the challenge.

ID proponents claim that Darwinism is insufficient to explain the origin and evolution of life on Earth. All is better explained, they say, if there is some kind of designing intelligence guiding things. These assertions are based on two core ideas. The first is essentially a scientific theory of miracles that is the brainchild of philosopher and mathematician William Dembski, one of ID's leading intellectual lights. According to Dembski, one can use rules of probability and information theory to construct "explanatory filters" that can objectively distinguish between purely natural phenomena that come about on their own and phenomena that require some kind of intelligent guidance — a miracle, in a word. Applying an explanatory filter to, say, the origin of life reveals that the probability that life arose by chance is infinitesimal. This in itself is not a particularly novel or controversial idea — no biologist I know would disagree. But Dembski parts company with the rest of us when he insists that a designing intelligence is the only agency that could bring such an improbable event to pass. What heats people up, of course, is that Dembski's "designing intelligence" strikes many as code for "God."

The second core idea comes from microbiologist Michael Behe, who is another of ID's leading lights. He asserts that living systems exhibit a sort of "irreducible complexity" that cannot be derived from the piecemeal evolution that Darwinism demands. The poster child for this argument is the bacterial flagellum, a whiplike device that bacteria use to propel themselves around their environment. This remarkable contrivance, which resembles an electric motor, is built from protein parts and will work only when all the parts are assembled into the complex whole — and this is why Behe calls its complexity irreducible. Whether the flagellum actually is irreducibly complex is questionable: scientists have proposed reasonable models for how its design could have emerged via piecemeal evolution.

Nevertheless, Behe considers irreducible complexity to be proof positive of a designing intelligence at work: how could the flagellum have developed by natural selection if none of its elements by themselves would have made the organism's predecessor more fit to survive? Behe claims that many other attributes of living systems, including the complicated structure of genomes, mechanisms for gene replication, and complex metabolic pathways in cells, are likewise irreducibly complex. What stirs the pot is ID's claim that all this irreducible complexity constitutes a rhetorical dagger pointed at the heart of Darwinism.

If all this sounds familiar, it should: it is essentially natural theology and the argument from design dressed up in modern clothes — William Paley equipped with a computer and electron microscope. Looked at in this way, ID seems not so much like the radical alternative to Darwinism that it claims to be, and more like nostalgia for the Platonic tradition in natural history that prevailed prior to Darwin.

The nostalgia is puzzling: for centuries, the Platonic tradition tied natural history into knots, with some of the most intractable tangles woven around the nature of species and the meaning of the apparent design that abounds in the living world. In a single decisive stroke, Darwin cut a wide path through this Platonic morass with a simple and, most important, reasonable natural explanation for why species exist and why they exist in such marvelous diversity and complexity. To extend Richard Dawkins's famous quip that Darwin made it possible to be an intellectually fulfilled atheist, so too did Darwin make it difficult to be an intellectually credible Platonist.

Nevertheless, ID is as popular as it is controversial, and Platonic nostalgia is not enough to explain why. Something deeper is obviously at play.

To most people who contemplate the natural world, it seems self-evident that the world is a designed place. Despite its many difficulties, the Platonic tradition endured because it offered a satisfying explanation for why: the world reflects God's purposeful design for creation. In dethroning the Platonic tradition, Darwin seemed to take that purpose away, and this has obviously been a difficult pill for many to swallow. It's not so clear, however, that Darwin did divorce design and purpose so decisively from the living world. Indeed, to claim that he did is to misread the history of Darwinism.

Consider, for example, the bedrock concept of Darwinian fitness. Natural selection operates because "fit" individuals are more fecund than "unfit" individuals. This should, over time, produce populations of fitter creatures, even though there is no purpose at work here, no striving for perfection. However, a problem lurks in this seemingly simple explanation. For a scientific idea to be credible, there must at least be the possibility that one can show it to be incorrect. Darwin ran into early difficulty on this score because the conventional depiction of fitness cannot be false — fecundity is fitness, and fitness is fecundity. To Darwin's early critics, a veritable fountain of doubt gushed from this tautology at the heart of his theory.

Edward Drinker Cope, a nineteenth-century American paleontologist, probably expressed the issue best. The problem is not so much the origin of species as it is the origin of fitness: how, precisely, do organisms become well-crafted — *fit* — things? To Cope, and to many of Darwin's contemporary critics, the way out of the tautology was the very purposefulness that Darwin so adamantly insisted we reject.

Interestingly, Darwin himself was a little muddy on the issue. Asa Gray, the Harvard botanist who was Darwin's most energetic advocate in the nineteenth-century United States, actually saw in Darwinian adaptation the vindication of purposefulness in biology —

to Darwin's chagrin. Darwin's most enthusiastic German convert, Ernst Haeckel, did Gray one better, crafting his own theory of evolution by melding Darwinian natural selection with the purposeful *Naturphilosophie* of romantics like Goethe — and leaving Darwin not just exasperated but aghast.

One could argue that Gray and Haeckel simply failed to understand Darwin's elegantly simple idea, but that argument doesn't hold water. Alfred Russell Wallace, who independently conceived the idea of natural selection and whose thinking surely would be most closely aligned to Darwin's own, thought that purpose in some form had to have guided the origin of life and the origin of consciousness in the higher animals, particularly humans. One finds similar doubts cropping up among thinkers throughout the late nineteenth and early twentieth centuries — Freud, Louis Agassiz, Carl Jung, and Henri Bergson, to name a few — and all were concerned about Darwin's insistence that a purposeless materialism is all there is.

To be fair, much of the ambiguity and unease swirling around during Darwinism's early years was fueled by a lack of knowledge about how another core Darwinian concept — heredity — works. For a time, it was thought that we could resolve Cope's question about how organisms came to be fit by clarifying the material nature of the gene, Mendel's "atom of heredity." That quest succeeded spectacularly, culminating in today's remarkable revolution in molecular biology, and engendering along the way our modern answer to Cope's question: the gene-centered conception of Darwinism — neo-Darwinism, as it is called — in which fitness arises by way of the selection of "good-function genes" at the expense of "poor-function genes."

For a time, neo-Darwinism triumphantly swept away quaint notions of purposeful evolution, to the point where Will Provine, the eminent Darwin historian, could confidently say that there are "no designing agents in evolution." That confident pronouncement may have been premature, however. As we discover more about how genes work, the stranger they become; they are far from the simple specifiers of good and poor function that they were classically thought to be. Paradoxically, this has breathed new life into Cope's question, making it more acute, not less so. Indeed, my own scientific work has led me to a conclusion that is precisely the opposite of Provine's: designing agents are in fact everywhere, if only you know how to spot them. The ubiquity of these designing agents may make evolution a far more purposeful phenomenon than neo-Darwinists have been willing to allow.

This puts intelligent design into what I believe is its proper perspective: it is one of multiple emerging critiques of materialism in science and evolution. Unfortunately, many scientists fail to see this, preferring the gross caricature that ID is simply "stealth creationism." But this strategy fails to meet the challenge. Rather than simply lament that so many people take ID seriously, scientists would do better to ask *why* so many take it seriously. The answer would be hard for us to bear: ID is popular not because the stupid or ignorant like it, but because neo-Darwinism's principled banishment of purpose seems less defensible with each passing day.

A more constructive response to the ID challenge would ask whether ID is a credible critique of Darwinian materialism. In my opinion, that judgment should turn on one simple criterion: will ID pose testable answers to Cope's question? By this measure, a fair reading of ID's prospects shows that it is in the game, though it has stepped up to the plate with two self-inflicted strikes against it. The first strike is its philosophical commitment to the argument from design and to the Platonic intelligent designer it implies. The second strike is that the testable ideas it has produced, like Behe's irreducible complexity, have not so far measured up. Whether ID gets a third strike will depend on whether it can come up with a credible and scientific theory of purposeful evolution. Most scientists, including me, doubt that it will be able to, but of all people scientists should know that the world is full of surprising things. ID might surprise us still.

It seems less than sporting, then, to call the pitch while it's still in the air, which is precisely what many of my colleagues insist on doing, sometimes quite vehemently. This, to me, is the most problematic thing about the controversy: it's not ID that keeps me awake at nights, but the tactics and attitudes of certain colleagues who really should know better. In Pogo's immortal words, "We have met the enemy and he is us."

One doesn't have to look far to find examples of conduct unbecoming. There is the recent case of Richard Sternberg, an unpaid staffer at the National Museum of Natural History (part of the Smithsonian), who became the object of a malicious campaign to oust him from the museum. Sternberg's crime? As managing editor of a Smithsonian-affiliated journal, he decided to publish an article that was sympathetic to ID on the seemingly reasonable grounds that a scientific journal is the appropriate venue for an advocate of a controversial theory to state his case. The Justice Department rapped the museum's knuckles for its treatment of Sternberg.

It would be comforting if one could dismiss such incidents as the actions of a misguided few. But the intolerance that gave rise to the Sternberg debacle is all too common: you can see it in its unfiltered glory by taking a look at Web sites like pandasthumb.org or recursed.blogspot.com and following a few of the threads on ID. The attitudes on display there, which at the extreme verge on antireligious hysteria, can hardly be squared with the relatively innocuous (even if wrong-headed) ideas that sit at ID's core. Why, then, are such attitudes commonplace? The only explanation I can come up with is that many biologists regard ID as a dire existential threat. And that is what really troubles me about the ID controversy: the animal that feels threatened is the one most likely to do something irrational and destructive.

Consider, for example, the most emotionally charged issue related to ID — whether it has any place in our classrooms. One can render plausible arguments that it does: even if ID is wrong, students are interested in the issue, and it offers a wealth of teachable moments to explore deeper issues of the philosophical roots of biology and the nature of science. What, then, is the harm in allowing teachers to deal with the subject as each sees fit? Advance this seemingly reasonable proposition, and you are likely to see scientists rolling their eyes; some may even become apoplectic.

When pressed to explain why normal standards of tolerance and academic freedom should not apply in the case of ID, scientists typically reply with all manner of evasions and prevarications that are quite out of character for otherwise balanced, intelligent, and reasonable people. To give just one argument that has turned up frequently in my correspondence with colleagues: because ID has its roots in fundamentalist Christianity (a dubious proposition in itself), admitting it into our classrooms will foster an exclusionary and hurtful climate, as would admitting other exclusionary sins such as racism or sexism.

Even setting aside the numerous head-turning non sequiturs that weave through this argument, a stroll through most modern universities will quickly reveal how hollow the argument is. Each day as I make my way to my office, for example, I pass the usual gauntlet of Bushitler cartoons and "Duck, it's Dick" posters, and doors plastered with lame jokes and cartoons about Republicans, Christians, and conservatives. "Abortion Stops a Beating Heart" posters, on the other hand, are as rare as four-leaf clovers. The display is a stark panorama of what the modern academy is evolving into: a tedious intellectual monoculture where conformity and not contention is the norm. Reflexive hostility to ID is largely cut from that cloth: some ID critics are worried not so much about a hurtful climate as they are about a climate in which people are free to disagree with them.

Such things are easily laughed off as the foibles of the modern academy. My blood chills, however, when these essentially harmless hypocrisies are joined with the all-American tradition of litigiousness, for it is in the hands of courts and lawyers that real damage to cherished academic ideals is likely to be done. This is not mere lawyer-bashing: as universities become more corporatized and politicized, academic freedom and open inquiry are coming under an ever more grave threat. A case in point is the recent federal court decision in *Mayer v. Monroe County Community School Corporation,* which essentially dismisses the notion of academic freedom in high schools. The court found that teachers have no academic autonomy but are only instruments for advancing the interests of school boards.

My university colleagues should not take much comfort in the fact that this decision involved a high school, because it would require only a short step to apply the same logic to them — a step that some administrators are eager to take. A high-level administrator at the prestigious university near my own has gone on record saying that First Amendment rights of free speech do not apply at an "educational corporation" like a private university. We should take heed: courts, ambitious attorneys, and lawsuit-averse administrators are manifestly not academics' friends when it comes to unfettered free speech. Yet the courts are where many of my colleagues seem determined to go with the ID issue. I believe we will ultimately come to regret this.

Take, for example, the recent case in Dover, Pennsylvania, where a group of parents sued the local school board over its requirement that a statement be read to biology students encouraging them to keep an open mind about alternatives to Darwinism. The plaintiffs regarded this requirement as "stealth creationism" — an unanswerable criticism if you think about it — and, backed by the ACLU, they sought relief in the federal courts. There were few heroes to be found in the spectacle that followed. The only bright spot was when a larger group of grownups, the Dover electorate, put a stop to the circus by voting out the school board that had put the offending policy in place. Unfortunately, this happy outcome did not keep the judge from ruling for the plaintiffs, decreeing that teaching about ID is constitutionally proscribed.

Many of my scientific colleagues were involved in this case. One would hope that they would have taken a stance of principled neutrality, offering a robust defense of academic freedom tempered with the sober recognition that freedom means that sometimes people will think, speak, and even teach things one disagrees with. Instead, my colleagues took sides; many were actively involved as advocates for the plaintiffs, and they were cheered on by many more from the sidelines. Although there was general jubilation at the ruling, I think the joy will be short-lived, for we have affirmed the principle that a federal judge, not scientists or teachers, can dictate what is and what is not science, and what may or may not be taught in a classroom. Forgive me if I do not feel more free.

JOHN UPDIKE

Madurai

FROM *The Atlantic Monthly*

From our terrace at the Taj Garden Retreat,
the city below belies its snarl of commerce —
men pushing postcards on the teeming street,
and doe-eyed children begging with their words
so soft the language can't be understood
even were we to try and were not fleeing
the nudge of stirred pity. Can life be good,
awakening us to hunger? What point has being?

Vishnu, sleeping, hatched the cosmic lotus
from his navel. The god-filled polychrome
great temple towers — glaring, mountainous —
assume from here a distant ghostly tone,
smoke shadows in the sleeping cityscape
that dreams a universe devoid of shape.

CHRISTIAN WIMAN

Love Bade Me Welcome

FROM *The American Scholar*

THOUGH I WAS RAISED in a very religious household, until
about a year ago I hadn't been to church in any serious way in more
than twenty years. It would be inaccurate to say that I have been in-
different to God in all that time. If I look back on the things I have
written in the past two decades, it's clear to me not only how thoroughly the forms and language of Christianity have shaped my
imagination, but also how deep and persistent my existential anxiety has been. I don't know whether this is all attributable to the
century into which I was born, some genetic glitch, or a late rever-
beration of the Fall of Man. What I do know is that I have not been
at ease in this world.

Poetry, for me, has always been bound up with this unease, fueled by contingency toward forms that will transcend it, as involved
with silence as it is with sound. I don't have much sympathy for the
Arnoldian notion of poetry replacing religion. It seems not simply
quaint but dangerous to make that assumption, even implicitly,
perhaps *especially* implicitly. I do think, though, that poetry is how
religious feeling has survived in me. Partly this is because I have at
times experienced in the writing of a poem some access to a power
that feels greater than I am, and it seems reductive, even somehow
a deep betrayal, to attribute that power merely to the unconscious
or to the dynamism of language itself. But also, if I look back on the
poems I've written in the past two decades, it almost seems as if the
one constant is God. Or, rather, his absence.

There is a passage in the writings of Simone Weil that has long
been important to me. In the passage, Weil describes two prisoners

who are in solitary confinement next to each other. Between them is a stone wall. Over a period of time — and I think we have to imagine it as a very long time — they find a way to communicate using taps and scratches. The wall is what separates them, but it is also the only means they have of communicating. "It is the same with us and God," she says. "Every separation is a link."

It's probably obvious why this metaphor would appeal to me. If you never quite feel at home in your life, if being conscious means primarily being conscious of your own separation from the world and from divinity (and perhaps any sentient person after modernism *has* to feel these things), then any idea or image that can translate that depletion into energy, those absences into presences, is going to be powerful. And then there are those taps and scratches: what are they but language, and if language is the way we communicate with the divine, well, what kind of language is more refined and transcendent than poetry? You could almost embrace this vision of life — if, that is, there were any actual life to embrace: Weil's image for the human condition is a person in solitary confinement. There is real hope in the image, but still, in human terms, it is a bare and lonely hope.

It has taken three events, each shattering in its way, for me to recognize both the full beauty, and the final insufficiency, of Weil's image. The events are radically different, but so closely linked in time, and so inextricable from one another in their consequences, that there is an uncanny feeling of unity to them. There is definitely some wisdom in learning to see our moments of necessity and glory and tragedy not as disparate experiences but as facets of the single experience that is a life. The pity, at least for some of us, is that we cannot truly have this knowledge of life, can only feel it as some sort of abstract "wisdom," until we come very close to death.

First, necessity: four years ago, after making poetry the central purpose of my life for almost two decades, I stopped writing. Partly this was a conscious decision. I told myself that I had exhausted one way of writing, and I do think there was truth in that. The deeper truth, though, is that I myself was exhausted. To believe that being conscious means primarily being conscious of loss, to find life authentic only in the apprehension of death, is to pitch your tent at the edge of an abyss, "and when you gaze long into the abyss," Nietzsche says, "the abyss also gazes into you." I blinked.

On another level, though, the decision to stop writing wasn't mine. Whatever connection I had long experienced between word and world, whatever charge in the former I had relied on to let me feel the latter, went dead. Did I give up poetry, or was it taken from me? I'm not sure, and in any event the effect was the same: I stumbled through the months, even thrived in some ways. Indeed — and there is something almost diabolical about this common phenomenon — it sometimes seemed like my career in poetry began to flourish just as poetry died in me. I finally found a reliable publisher for my work (the work I'd written earlier, I mean), moved into a good teaching job, and then quickly left that for the editorship of *Poetry*. But there wasn't a scrap of excitement in any of this for me. It felt like I was watching a movie of my life rather than living it, an old silent movie, no color, no sound, no one in the audience but me.

Then I fell in love. I say it suddenly, and there was certainly an element of radical intrusion and transformation to it, but the sense I have is of color slowly aching into things, the world coming brilliantly, abradingly alive. I remember tiny Albert's Café on Elm Street in Chicago where we first met, a pastry case like a Pollock in the corner of my eye, sunlight suddenly more itself on an empty plate, a piece of silver. I think of walking together along Lake Michigan a couple of months later talking about a particular poem of Dickinson's ("A loss of something ever felt I"), clouds finding and failing to keep one form after another, the lake booming its blue into everything; of lying in bed in my high-rise apartment downtown watching the little blazes in the distance that were the planes at Midway, so numerous and endless that all those safe departures and homecomings seemed a kind of secular miracle. We usually think of falling in love as being possessed by another person, and like anyone else I was completely consumed and did some daffy things. But it also felt, for the first time in my life, like I was being fully possessed by being itself. "Joy is the overflowing consciousness of reality," Weil writes, and that's what I had, a joy that was at once so overflowing that it enlarged existence, and yet so rooted in actual things that, again for the first time, that's what I began to feel: rootedness.

I don't mean to suggest that all my old anxieties were gone. There were still no poems, and this ate at me constantly. There was still no God, and the closer I came to reality, the more I longed for divinity — or, more accurately perhaps, the more divinity seemed so obviously a *part* of reality. I wasn't alone in this: we began to say a kind of prayer before our evening meals — jokingly at first, awkwardly, but then with intensifying seriousness and deliberation, trying to name each thing that we were thankful for, and in so doing, praise the thing we could not name. On most Sundays we would even briefly entertain — again, half-jokingly — the idea of going to church. The very morning after we got engaged, in fact, we paused for a long time outside a church on Michigan Avenue. The service was just about to start, organ music pouring out of the wide-open doors into the late May sun, and we stood there holding each other and debating whether or not to walk inside. In the end it was I who resisted.

I wish I could slow things down at this point, could linger a bit in those months after our marriage. I wish I could feel again that blissful sense of immediacy and expansiveness at once, when every moment implied another, and the future suddenly seemed to offer some counterbalance to the solitary fever I had lived in for so long. I think most writers live at some strange adjacency to experience, that they feel life most intensely in their re-creation of it. For once, for me, this wasn't the case. I could not possibly have been paying closer attention to those days. Which is why I was caught so off-guard.

I got the news that I was sick on the afternoon of my thirty-ninth birthday. It took a bit of time, travel, and a series of wretched tests to get the specific diagnosis, but by then the main blow had been delivered, and that main blow is what matters. I have an incurable cancer in my blood. The disease is as rare as it is mysterious, killing some people quickly and sparing others for decades, afflicting some with all manner of miseries and disabilities and leaving others relatively healthy until the end. Of all the doctors I have seen, not one has been willing to venture even a vague prognosis.

Conventional wisdom says that tragedy will cause either extreme closeness or estrangement in a couple. We'd been married less than a year when we got the news of the cancer. It stands to reason we should have been especially vulnerable to such a blow, and in some ways love did make things much worse. If I had gotten the diagnosis some years earlier — and it seems weirdly providential that I didn't, since I had symptoms and went to several doctors about them — I'm not sure I would have reacted very strongly. It would have seemed a fatalistic confirmation of everything I had always thought about existence, and my response, I think, would have been equally fatalistic. It would have been the bearable oblivion of despair, not the unbearable, and therefore galvanizing, pain of particular grief. In those early days after the diagnosis, when we mostly just sat on the couch and cried, I alone was dying, but we were mourning very much together. And what we were mourning was not my death, exactly, but the death of the life we had imagined with each other.

Then one morning we found ourselves going to church. *Found ourselves.* That's exactly what it felt like, in both senses of the phrase, as if some impulse in each of us had finally been catalyzed into action, so that we were casting aside the Sunday paper and moving toward the door with barely a word between us; and as if, once inside the church, we were discovering exactly where and who we were meant to be. That first service was excruciating, in that it seemed to tear all wounds wide open, and it was profoundly comforting, in that it seemed to offer the only possible balm. What I remember of that Sunday, though, and of the Sundays that immediately followed, is less the services themselves than the walks we took afterward, and less the specifics of the conversations we had about God, always about God, than the moments of silent, and what felt like sacred, attentiveness those conversations led to: an iron sky and the lake so calm it seemed thickened; the El blasting past with its rain of sparks and brief, lost faces; the broad leaves and white blooms of a catalpa on our street, Grace Street, and under the tree a seethe of something that was just barely still a bird, quick with life beyond its own.

I was brought up with the poisonous notion that you had to renounce love of the earth in order to receive the love of God. My experience has been just the opposite: a love of the earth and existence so overflowing that it implied, or included, or even absolutely demanded, God. Love did not deliver me from the earth, but into it. And by some miracle I do not find that this experience is crushed or even lessened by the knowledge that, in all likelihood, I will be leaving the earth sooner than I had thought. Quite the contrary, I find life thriving in me, and not in an aestheticizing Death-is-the-mother-of-beauty sort of way either, for what extreme grief has given me is the very thing it seemed at first to obliterate: a sense of life beyond the moment, a sense of hope. This is not simply hope for my own life, though I do have that. It is not a hope for heaven or any sort of explainable afterlife, unless by those things one means simply the ghost of wholeness that our inborn sense of brokenness creates and sustains, some ultimate love that our truest temporal ones goad us toward. This I do believe in, and by this I live, in what the apostle Paul called "hope toward God."

"It is necessary to have had a revelation of reality through joy," Weil writes, "in order to find reality through suffering." This is certainly true to my own experience. I was not wrong all those years to believe that suffering is at the very center of our existence, and that there can be no untranquillized life that does not fully confront this fact. The mistake lay in thinking grief the means of confrontation, rather than love. To come to this realization is not to be suddenly "at ease in the world." I don't really think it's possible for humans to be at the same time conscious and comfortable. Though we may be moved by nature to thoughts of grace, though art can tease our minds toward eternity, and love's abundance make us dream a love that does not end, these intuitions come only through the earth, and the earth we know only in passing, and only by passing. I would qualify Weil's statement somewhat, then, by saying that reality, be it of this world or another, is not something one finds and then retains for good. It must be newly discovered daily, and newly lost.

So now I bow my head and try to pray in the mornings, not because I don't doubt the reality of what I have experienced, but because I do, and with an intensity that, because to once feel the presence of God is to feel his absence all the more acutely, is actually more anguishing and difficult than any "existential anxiety" I have ever known. I go to church on Sundays, not to dispel this doubt but to expend its energy, because faith is not a state of mind but an action in the world, a movement *toward* the world. How charged this one hour of the week is for me, and how I cherish it, though not one whit more than the hours I have with my wife, with friends, or in solitude, trying to learn how to inhabit time so completely that there might be no distinction between life and belief, attention and devotion. And out of all these efforts at faith and love, out of my own inevitable failures at both, I have begun to write poems again. But the language I have now to call on God is not only language, and the wall on which I make my taps and scratches is no longer a cell but this whole prodigal and all too perishable world in which I find myself, very much alive, and not at all alone. As I approach the first anniversary of my diagnosis, as I approach whatever pain is ahead of me, I am trying to get as close to this wall as possible. And I am listening with all I am.

CHARLES WRIGHT

Littlefoot, 14

FROM *The New Yorker*

The great mouth of the west hangs open,
                              mountain incisors beginning to bite
Into the pink flesh of the sundown.
The end of another day
                    in this floating dream of a life.
Renown is a mouthful, here and there.

Rivers and mountains glide through my blood.
Cold pillow, bittersweet years.
In the near distance, a plane's drone
                              rattles the windows.
Clear night. Wind like a predator
                    in the sharp grass of the past.

I find it much simpler now to see
                    the other side of my own death.
It wasn't always that way,
When the rivers were rivers and mountains were mountains.
Now, when the mouth closes,
                    the wind goes out of everything.

Fame for a hundred years
                    is merely an afterlife.
And no friend of ours.
Better to watch the rain fall in the branches of winter trees.
Better to have your mail sent
To someone else in another town,
                    where frost is whiter than moonlight.

Horses, black horses:
                    Midnight, Five Minutes to Midnight.
Rider up, the sparks from their hooves like stars, like spiked stars.
This is a metaphor for failure,
This is the Rest of It, the beautiful horse, black horse.
Midnight. Dark horse, dark rider.

I love the lethargy of the single cloud,
                                        the stillness of the sky
On winter afternoons, late on winter afternoons,
A little fan of light on the tips of the white pines.

I love the winter light, so thin, so unbuttery,
Transparent as plastic wrap
Clinging so effortlessly
                    to whatever it skins over.

— The language of nature, we know, is mathematics.
The language of landscape is language,
Metaphor, metaphor, metaphor,
                            all down the line.

The sweet-breath baby light of a winter afternoon,
Boy-light, half covered in blue,
                                almost invisible as breath,
So still in the flower beds, so pale.

Four days till the full moon,
                        light like a new skin on the dark
Quarter, like light unborrowed, hard,
                                black hole with its golden floor.

Who knows the happiness of fish,
                            their wind-raising, ordinary subtleties?
Describing the indescribable,
Image into idea,
                the transmission of the spirit,
It cannot be done.

The Chinese principle, *breath-resonance-life-motion*,
Engenders, it was believed.
As does the bone method of brushwork,

Creating structure
                    in poems as well as pictures.

Plotting in paint, place in poetry,
Completes composition,
                    the bedrock of spiritual values.
Competent, marvellous, and *divine*
Were the three degrees of accomplishment.
                              And still, it cannot be done.

Image resists all transmutation.
All art is meta-art, and has its own satisfactions.
But it's not divine,
                    as image is,
Untouchable, untransmutable,
                              wholly magic.

Midnight Special, turn your ever-loving light on me.

HAMZA YUSUF

Why Holocaust Denial Undermines Islam

FROM *Tikkun*

EPISTEMOLOGY IS A BRANCH OF PHILOSOPHY that studies the nature and basis of knowledge. How do we know things? It also studies the veracity of "truth." How do we know the difference between belief, knowledge, opinion, fact, reality, and fantasy? The Greek philosopher Carneades believed that knowledge of reality, of what is true or false, is impossible, that nothing can be known with certainty; his philosophy is known as skepticism. It does not reject belief altogether; Carneades felt that our belief about any given matter should be subjected to intense scrutiny and then, using a scale of probability, we should accept or reject the likelihood of its truth or falsehood. But we must make no absolute claims to it. Another Greek skeptic, Cratylus, however, was more radical in his approach and believed that nothing could be known at all, and thus no statements could convey anything true or meaningful. He finally gave up talking altogether.

Most of us are neither moderate nor extreme skeptics; we believe what our teachers told us. Although some of us learned later that perhaps a little skepticism was indeed warranted, we survived with our grasp of reality reasonably intact. We live in a world where facts are meaningful and opinions can be assessed, at least to the degree that we deem them sound or unsound. When it comes to religion, those of us who are raised in traditions often reject such assessments and simply believe what we were taught. For many religious people, skepticism is anathema, the work of the devil. However, our Abrahamic traditions of Judaism, Christianity, and Islam have always been concerned with and seriously interested in epistemology, because each of these faiths have profound truth claims that need substantiation or "believability."

Islam, at its advent, developed a sophisticated methodology for the validation of truth claims. One of the greatest achievements of the Islamic scholastic tradition is 'ilm ar-rijaal, the science of narrators. It is the study of reports of events in the life of the Prophet, especially of his sayings and deeds. Its formulators established a rigid set of criteria to validate the truth claims of those who asserted they saw or heard the Prophet do or say such-and-such. Reports were grouped into two categories: *ahad,* or solitary reports, in which one or a few people claimed to have heard or seen something, and *mutawatir,* or multiply transmitted reports, narrated in numbers large enough to preclude collusive fabrication. The solitary reports must meet many criteria before being accepted as sound statements that nonetheless contain, depending upon the degree to which the criteria were met, a certain probability of error. On the other hand, firmly established multiply transmitted reports, in numbers that rule out collusion, are taken as uncontestable fact.

The Quran, the seventh-century book narrated by Muhammad, is considered *mutawatir,* and thus epistemologically undeniable. Whether one believes it is from God or not is another matter, but the Quran in its current form is the same Quran the Prophet taught to his companions more than fourteen hundred years ago; untold numbers in each generation of Muslims have transmitted the same recitation, making it infallible in its historicity and accuracy. Islamic scholars accepted multiply transmitted reports from Muslims and people of other faiths. Upon this epistemological foundation rests the Muslim faith. Creedal matters are deemed valid only if they are buttressed by multiply transmitted traditions that can be traced back to the Prophet. Although Islamic jurisprudence is largely based upon solitary evidence (hence the differences of opinion in the various schools), the Quran and the creed of Islam are both founded upon multiple narratives that achieve an undeniable status. Early Muslim scholars would certainly consider much of our current knowledge of history to have achieved such status. For instance, there is consensus among historians that the Normans invaded England in 1066; too many accounts of this momentous event exist and have been recounted in each generation through multiple sources. In the case of any solitary original source, healthy skepticism is warranted. When Lee Harvey Oswald claimed to be a patsy, it led to an entire field of conspiracy studies among Kennedy assassination buffs. Did he act alone or didn't he? That aspect of the event is debatable. But was John F. Kennedy shot on November 22, 1963, in a motorcade at Dealey Plaza in Dallas? Far too many accounts of that tragic event exist; to deny it is simply to deny reality and have one's sanity questioned.

Much of what we know about the world and what we accept as truth comes from multiply transmitted accounts. Let's say I claim that Australia doesn't exist and is merely a figment of our imagination, that its origins lie in a whimsical cartographer in the Middle Ages who decided that such a large ocean needed a landmass. And, when confronted with people who claim to be from Australia and can prove it, I dismiss them as part of a conspiracy of cartographers who wish to perpetuate the myth of their forebear. I would be laughed at, or ignored, or deemed "certifiable." While this example seems absurd, many people actually believe things just as fatuous and far-fetched.

Holocaust denial is one such example. As one who has read some Holocaust-denial literature, with the poorly reproduced pictures and claims of the orchestration of these scenes in collusion with the U.S. government, I can attest to the tragic gullibility of people who take such literature as historical truth. To return to the Kennedy assassination, if one reads Mark Lane's version that a rogue element within the CIA killed Kennedy, the "facts" seem overwhelming. But if one reads another version that the Mafia killed Kennedy because of his failure to return Cuba to the gambling lords of Italian America, the "facts" also seem overwhelming. Finally, one can read the version that Mossad killed Kennedy because he wanted to force nuclear inspections in Israel, and again the "facts" seem conclusive. Each of these accounts is presented with utter certainty by the "researchers." In the end, reality is manipulated to meet the needs of the mythologist. Indeed, we are all entitled to our own opinions, but not to our own facts. And those who present alternative versions of "reality" tend to reject everything that does not suit their theory, and cherry-pick and interpret everything — facts, innuendoes, or "coincidences" — that does.

In the case of the Holocaust, the facts are clear and transmitted from multiple sources. Tens of thousands of Jewish and other individuals who survived the death camps and other horrors of Nazi

Germany lived to tell of it. Nazis were brought to trial, evidence was presented in court, and they were convicted. Mass graves were found, and gas chambers were discovered, which were clearly not delousing rooms as some callously claimed. The ovens exist and cannot be reduced to an efficient way of preventing cholera outbreaks or disposing of victims of starvation. I have personally met many Holocaust survivors and their children. I have seen tattoos. I have also heard firsthand accounts of the horrific events. The numbers and details of such events may be legitimate areas of research and inquiry for scholars, but questioning whether the events took place at all undermines the epistemological basis of our collective knowledge. Muslims, of all people, should be conscious of this as their religion is predicated on the same epistemological premises as many major events in history, such as the Holocaust. To deny such things is to undermine Islam as an historical event. That a "conference" examining the historicity of the Holocaust should take place in a Muslim country hosted by a Muslim head of state is particularly tragic and, in my estimation, undermines the historicity of the faith of the people of that state.

In our inherent contradictions as humans, and in order to validate our own pain, we deny the pain of others. But it is in acknowledging the pain of others that we achieve fully our humanity. A close friend of mine, a professor of religion in a Muslim country for many years, recently told me that his wife, an English teacher in that country, had wanted to use *Anne Frank: The Diary of a Young Girl* as a text for her Muslim pupils. But the school administrators repeatedly denied her request because they deemed it inappropriate reading for young Muslims. It is sad that the current political morass in the Middle East has led to this intolerable refusal to confront a people's collective suffering. Perhaps in acknowledging that immense past of Jewish suffering, in which the Holocaust is only the most heinous chapter, Muslims can better help the Jewish community to understand the current Muslim pain in Palestine, Iraq, and other places. In finding out about others, we encourage others to find about us. It would greatly help our Jewish brethren to know the historical facts of Jewish experience in the Muslim world, which are often heartening and humanizing and very different from their European experience. In our mutual edification, we grow together.

Contributors' Notes
Other Notable Spiritual Writing
of 2007

Contributors' Notes

Stephen M. Barr is a professor at the University of Delaware. He does research in theoretical particle physics and cosmology and writes frequently on science and religion for *First Things*, *National Review*, the *Weekly Standard*, the *Public Interest*, *Academic Questions*, and *Commonweal*. He is the author of *Modern Physics and Ancient Faith* and *A Student's Guide to Natural Science*.

Wendell Berry is the author of many books, including *The Way of Ignorance: And Other Essays; Blessed Are the Peacemakers: Christ's Teachings of Love, Compassion, and Forgiveness;* and *Given: Poems*.

Ben Birnbaum is the editor of *Boston College* magazine and special assistant to the president of Boston College. His essays have been anthologized in *Best American Essays*, *Best American Spiritual Writing*, and *Best Catholic Writing*. He is the editor of *Take Heart: Catholic Writers on Hope in Our Time*.

Joseph Bottum is the editor of *First Things*. His books include *The Fall and Other Poems* and *The Pius War*.

Jimmy Carter was born in Plains, Georgia, and served as thirty-ninth president of the United States. He and his wife, Rosalynn, founded the Carter Center, a nonprofit organization that prevents and resolves conflicts, enhances freedom and democracy, and improves health around the world. He is the author of twenty-five books, including the acclaimed spiritual biography *Living Faith* and its companion, *Sources of Strength*.

John Coats is a graduate of Virginia Theological Seminary (Episcopal) and the Bennington Writing Seminars. After eight years as a parish priest in

Texas and California, he traveled in the United States, England, and South Africa for the More to Life program. His first book, *Original Sins,* is forthcoming. He lives with his wife in Houston.

David James Duncan is the author of the novels *The River Why* and *The Brothers K* and the nonfiction books *River Teeth, My Story as Told by Water,* and *God Laughs & Plays.* He was won four Pacific Northwest Literary Awards, two Pushcarts, a Lannan, the 2001 Western States Book Award for Nonfiction, inclusion in four volumes of *Best American Spiritual Writing,* a National Book Award nomination, and many other honors.

Paul Elie is a senior editor at Farrar, Straus and Giroux and the author of *The Life You Save May Be Your Own: An American Pilgrimage,* a group portrait of Dorothy Day, Thomas Merton, Walker Percy, and Flannery O'Connor. He is writing a book about the music of Bach and the great Bach performers of the age of recordings.

Peter Everwine is the author of numerous books of poetry, including *From the Meadow: Selected and New Poems.*

Kate Farrell's books include *Sleeping on the Wing: An Anthology of Modern Poetry with Essays on Reading and Writing* (with Kenneth Koch) and *Art and Wonder: An Illustrated Anthology of Visionary Poetry.* Her essay "Faithful to Mystery" appeared in *The Best American Spiritual Writing 2007.*

Noah Feldman is professor of law at Harvard Law School and the author of *Fall and Rise of the Islamic State; Divided by God: America's Church-State Problem;* and other books.

Natalie Goldberg is the author of eleven books, including *Writing Down the Bones* and *The Great Failure.* Her newest book is the recently published *Old Friend from Far Away: The Practice of Writing Memoir.* She is a teacher, poet, painter, and writer, and teaches writing workshops and retreats nationally. She has studied Zen for thirty years.

David Brendan Hopes is a poet, playwright, and painter living in Asheville, North Carolina. His most recent book of poetry is *A Dream of Adonis.* He is the director of Black Swan Theater.

Walter Isaacson is the president and CEO of the Aspen Institute and has been the chairman and CEO of CNN and the editor of *Time* magazine. He is the author of *Einstein: His Life and Universe; Benjamin Franklin: An American Life;* and other books.

Pico Iyer is the author of seven works of nonfiction and two novels, and writes regularly for the Buddhist magazines *Shambhala Sun* and *Tricycle* as well as the Christian magazine *Portland*. His most recent book is *The Open Road,* describing thirty-four years of talking and traveling across the globe with the fourteenth Dalai Lama.

Heather King is a commentator for NPR's *All Things Considered* and the author of the memoirs *Parched* and *Redeemed: A Spiritual Misfit Stumbles Toward God, Marginal Sanity and the Peace That Passes All Understanding.*

Maxine Kumin has published numerous poetry collections, most recently *Still to Mow.* Her many other books include *Mites to Mastodons; Inside the Halo and Beyond: Anatomy of a Recovery;* and *Always Beginning: Essays on a Life in Poetry.* Her awards include the Pulitzer Prize, the Ruth Lilly Poetry Prize, the Poets' Prize, the Aiken Taylor Award, the 2005 Harvard Arts Medal, and in 2006 the Robert Frost Medal.

Ursula K. Le Guin is the author of many books, including the Earthsea Cycle series and *The Left Hand of Darkness.* Her recent works include *The Mind in the Wave: Talks and Essays on the Reader, the Writer, and the Imagination* and *Incredible Good Fortune: New Poems.* Her awards include the National Book Award, five Hugos, and five Nebulas.

James Loney has been a member of Christian Peacemaker Teams since 2000. He has served on CPT projects in Iraq, Palestine, and Canada.

Nancy Lord is the author of, among other books, *The Man Who Swam with Beavers* (short stories) and *Beluga Days* (nonfiction). She lives in Homer, Alaska.

Thomas Lynch, a funeral director, is the author of *Booking Passage: We Irish and Americans; The Undertaking* (American Book Award for 1998); and other works.

Adam Minter is an American writer in Shanghai, China. He has written and reported on a range of topics in contemporary China, including religion, the environment, and cross-cultural issues between Asia and the West. His work has been published in the *Atlantic Monthly, Slate,* the *Wall Street Journal,* the *Los Angeles Times,* and other publications. He blogs at www.shanghaiscrap.com.

Richard John Neuhaus is editor in chief of *First Things.* His many books include *Catholic Matters: Confusion, Controversy, and the Splendor of Truth; As I*

Lay Dying: Meditations Upon Returning; and *Death on a Friday Afternoon: Meditations on the Last Words of Jesus from the Cross.*

Robert Pinsky served as Poet Laureate of the United States from 1997 to 2000. He is the author of *Gulf Music: Poems; Democracy, Culture, and the Voice of Poetry; The Inferno of Dante: A New Verse Translation;* and other books.

Richard Rodriguez is a journalist for New America Media in San Francisco. He is the author of *Hunger of Memory, Days of Obligation,* and *Brown,* memoirs that form a trilogy concerned respectively with class, ethnicity, and race in America. He is now at work on a book, *The Ecology of Monotheism,* concerned with the influence of desert ecology on the religious experience of the Jew, the Christian, and the Muslim.

Oliver Sacks is the author of *Musicophilia: Tales of Music and the Brain; Oaxaca Journal; Uncle Tungsten: Memories of a Chemical Boyhood;* and other books.

Nick Samaras's first book, *Hands of the Saddlemaker,* appeared through the Yale Series of Younger Poets Award. His next manuscript is nearly completed. Greek Orthodox, he frequently visits the Holy Mountain of Athos.

Mathew N. Schmalz is the director of the college honors program and associate professor of religious studies at the College of the Holy Cross in Worcester, Massachusetts. His scholarly writings include articles and essays on global Catholicism, religion in South Asia, Mormonism, and Jehovah's Witnesses. He is writing a book on the Audrey Santo phenomenon.

Kurt Shaw is the founder and executive director of Shine a Light (www.shinealight.org), a network of some three hundred organizations serving homeless and working children. Films that he has helped street children make have been featured in festivals around Latin America.

Jason Shinder's collections of poetry include *Among Women* and *Every Room We Ever Slept In.* He is also the editor of *The Poem that Changed America: "Howl" Fifty Years Later* and other books.

Sally Thomas is a poet and homeschooling mother in Tennessee.

J. Scott Turner is associate professor of biology at the SUNY College of Environmental Science and Forestry in Syracuse, New York. His latest book is *The Tinkerer's Accomplice: How Design Emerges from Life Itself.*

John Updike's books have won the Pulitzer Prize, the National Book Award, and the National Book Critics Circle Award. Recent publications include *Due Considerations: Essays and Criticism; Terrorist;* and *Americana and Other Poems.*

Christian Wiman is the editor of *Poetry* magazine. His most recent book is *Ambition and Survival: Becoming a Poet.*

Charles Wright's many books include *Littlefoot: A Poem; Scar Tissue: Poems;* and *Black Zodiac,* which won the Pulitzer Prize for Poetry in 1998.

Hamza Yusuf is a Muslim scholar, lecturer, and author, and the cofounder of the Zaytuna Institute in California, which is dedicated to reviving the traditions of classical Islamic scholarship.

Philip Zaleski is the editor of the Best American Spiritual Writing series and the author of many books, most recently *Prayer: A History* (with Carol Zaleski).

Other Notable Spiritual Writing of 2007

KRISTA BREMER
"My Accidental Jihad," *The Sun,* October

STEPHANIE CASSIDEY
"Call of the Sirens," *Fourth Genre,* Fall

ROBERTA CONNER
"We Have Always Been Here," *Portland,* Summer

ADAM G. COOPER
"Redeeming Flesh," *First Things,* May

LAWRENCE CUNNINGHAM
"The Man Who's Become Benedict," *Notre Dame,* Autumn

DAVE DEVINE
"Messy & Defiant & Necessary," *Portland,* Summer

ANTHONY ESOLEN
"Esther's Guarded Condition," *Touchstone,* July/August

NEIL GILLMAN
"How Will It All End?" *Crosscurrents,* Spring

PAUL J. GRIFFITHS
"Student Teachers," *Christian Century,* March 20

HILLEL HALKIN
"Rooting for the Indians — a Memoir," *Commentary,* October

LISA OLEN HARRIS
"Torn Veil," *Relief,* Volume 1, Issue 4

MICHELLE HERMAN
"Seeing Things," *The Southern Review,* Spring

LINDA JOHNSON
"Why Bad Things Happen to Good People," *Yoga Plus,* March/April

LEON KASS
"Defending Human Dignity," *Commentary,* December

JOHN KOESSLER
"Eat, Drink, and Be Hungry," *Christianity Today,* August

PATRICK MADDEN
  "A Sudden Pull Behind the Heart," *Portland,* Autumn
RUSSELL D. MOORE
  "The Brotherhood of Sons," *Touchstone,* May
JACOB NEEDLEMAN
  "Is America Necessary," *Parabola,* Winter
MICHAEL NOVAK
  "Remembering the Secular Age," *First Things,* June/July
EDWARD T. OAKES
  "Eyes of Faith," *Christian Century,* June 26
MARK OPPENHEIMER
  "The First Dance," *The New York Times Magazine,* January 28
ROBERT ORSI
  "When 2 + 2 = 5," *The American Scholar,* Spring
STEPHANIE PAULSELL
  "Where We Come From," *Christian Century,* November 13
ROBERT POLLACK
  "'Intelligent Design,' Natural Design, and the Problem of Meaning in the
    Natural World," *Crosscurrents,* Spring
WILLIAM H. WILLIMON
  "Charms of an Ideologue," *Christian Century,* June 12

THE BEST AMERICAN SERIES®

THE BEST AMERICAN SHORT STORIES® 2008
Salman Rushdie, editor, Heidi Pitlor, series editor
> ISBN: 978-0-618-78876-7 $28.00 CL
> ISBN: 978-0-618-78877-4 $14.00 PA

THE BEST AMERICAN NONREQUIRED READING™ 2008
Edited by Dave Eggers, introduction by Judy Blume
> ISBN: 978-0-618-90282-8 $28.00 CL
> ISBN: 978-0-618-90283-5 $14.00 PA

THE BEST AMERICAN COMICS™ 2008
Lynda Barry, editor, Jessica Abel and Matt Madden, series editors
> ISBN: 978-0-618-98976-8 $22.00 POB

THE BEST AMERICAN ESSAYS® 2008
Adam Gopnik, editor, Robert Atwan, series editor
> ISBN: 978-0-618-98331-5 $28.00 CL
> ISBN: 978-0-618-98322-3 $14.00 PA

THE BEST AMERICAN MYSTERY STORIES™ 2008
George Pelecanos, editor, Otto Penzler, series editor
> ISBN: 978-0-618-81266-0 $28.00 CL
> ISBN: 978-0-618-81267-7 $14.00 PA

THE BEST AMERICAN SPORTS WRITING™ 2008
William Nack, editor, Glenn Stout, series editor
> ISBN: 978-0-618-75117-4 $28.00 CL
> ISBN: 978-0-618-75118-1 $14.00 PA

THE BEST AMERICAN TRAVEL WRITING™ 2008
Anthony Bourdain, editor, Jason Wilson, series editor
> ISBN: 978-0-618-85863-7 $28.00 CL
> ISBN: 978-0-618-85864-4 $14.00 PA

THE BEST AMERICAN SCIENCE AND NATURE WRITING™ 2008
Jerome Groopman, editor, Tim Folger, series editor
> ISBN: 978-0-618-83446-4 $28.00 CL
> ISBN: 978-0-618-83447-1 $14.00 PA

THE BEST AMERICAN SPIRITUAL WRITING™ 2008
Edited by Philip Zaleski, introduction by Jimmy Carter
> ISBN: 978-0-618-83374-0 $28.00 CL
> ISBN: 978-0-618-83375-7 $14.00 PA